The Political Economy of the American West

The Political Economy Forum

Terry L. Anderson and Peter J. Hill, Editors

Rowman & Littlefield Publishers, Inc.

ROWMAN & LITTLEFIELD PUBLISHERS, INC.

Published in the United States of America
by Rowman & Littlefield Publishers, Inc.
4720 Boston Way, Lanham, Maryland 20706

3 Henrietta Street, London WC2E 8LU, England

British Cataloging in Publication Information Available

Library of Congress Cataloging-in-Publication Data

The Political economy of the American West / Terry L.
Anderson and Peter J. Hill, editors.
p.   cm. — (The Political economy forum)
Includes bibliographical references and index.
1. West (U.S.)—Economic policy.   2. West (U.S.)—Economic
conditions.   3. Right of property—West (U.S.)   I. Anderson,
Terry Lee.   II. Hill, Peter Jensen.   III. Series.
HC107.A17P65   1994   338.978—dc20   93–45480 CIP

ISBN 0–8476–7911–X (cloth : alk. paper)

Printed in the United States of America

♾ TM The paper used in this publication meets the minimum requirements of
American National Standard for Information Sciences—Permanence of
Paper for Printed Library Materials, ANSI Z39.48–1984.

Contents

Contents

Tables and Figure

Acknowledgments

With this volume from the Political Economy Research Center's (PERC) annual forum, we are beginning to get production down to somewhat of a routine. But this by no means diminishes the amount of work it takes to complete an edited volume. First, we must thank the authors who have put up with our editing, knowing that some of our idiosyncratic comments must have seemed just that. Second, we thank the participants in the forum who gave useful comments when the papers were first presented. We believe that the academic debate that occurs at the Political Economy Forum is of the highest quality found in any setting.

As with the previous volumes, production of this one would not have been possible without the staff at PERC. Dianna Rienhart is a master of the style used in the volume and of the desktop publishing system. She does more to make the volume readable than any of the rest of us. After Monica Lane Guenther finishes the proofreading, we wonder if we were blind in our editing.

Finally we wish to thank the M. J. Murdock Charitable Trust, the Bennett Chair at Wheaton College, and the Scaife Foundation for the financial support that has made this volume possible. Their dedication to the intellectual underpinnings of modern political economy reflect the private sector foresight that fosters healthy debate.

Terry L. Anderson
Peter J. Hill

Introduction

Traditionalist, Revisionist, and Political Economist: Alternative Approaches to Western History

Terry L. Anderson and Peter J. Hill

The history of the American West is being revisited by historians whose interpretations take on a modern tone. According to this new perspective, the history of the West is one of natural resource waste, minority exploitation, and political manipulation by a power elite. These historical revisionists claim that many of the problems we face today are nothing new and indeed find their roots on the western frontier. Instead of romanticizing the West's heroes, the revisionists burst the bubble of every fan of Lewis and Clark, Wyatt Earp, or Shane by depicting the heroes as exploitive, opportunistic, macho males not representative of the down trodden individuals (especially Indians, women, and other minorities) who form the real foundation of the West.

This revisionist western history is in sharp contrast to traditional historical accounts by scholars such as Frederick Jackson Turner, Walter Prescott Webb, and Ray Allen Billington, who describe the West as a place where people of heroic dimensions triumphed over adversity and hardship to create civilized society. For these historians, the frontiersmen were entrepreneurs who hammered out new institutions in an arid environment where traditional Anglo-American approaches were inappropriate. Hostile Indians were subdued, land was cultivated, minerals were mined, and timber was harvested as part of the economic transformation from wild to civilized. According to this interpretation, were it not for the hardy pioneers, the United States would not have fulfilled its manifest destiny.

Thus the new and the old versions of the American West clash. Were the new settlers heroes or villains? Did the pioneers actually tame a wild frontier or were they a violent lot whose justice was strapped to the hip? Does the West embody America's noblest qualities and represent some of her greatest achievements, or was the West symptomatic of the racism, inequality, and injustice that many believe typify our modern society?

This volume offers a third approach to understanding and interpreting western history that relies on neither triumphant frontiersmen nor villainous exploiters. Rather it concentrates on institutional constraints and the incentives they created to explain why settlers behaved as they did. In this context people do make a difference, but the rules of the game are also important. Instead of classifying participants as heroes or villains, political economy treats human action as a response to benefits and costs determined by both natural and manmade environments. Because the West was settled in an institutional vacuum where the rules governing the use of land, water, minerals, and other resources had to be produced, the political economy of the American West offers the ideal test tube for learning more about how institutions evolve.

The general theme of this volume is that much of western history can be understood in the context of competition for ownership of resources. In the vernacular of economists when the rents (or returns above all other input costs) from a resource are up-for-grabs, potential owners will seek to define and enforce property rights that allow them to capture the fruits of nature.

This process of competing for rents is illustrated in the current debates over use of the federal lands that make up one-third of the nation. Traditionally, the federal estate has been opened to resource users who have captured the returns from mining, logging, irrigating, and grazing. While these users generally have paid some fees, environmentalists question whether the fees reflect the real costs associated with resource use. They counter that fees should be raised and/or that these activities should be eliminated in favor of "nonextractive" uses. But even the "nonextractive" users impose a drain on the fisc as they seek their share of resource rents. Generally hunters, picnickers, and hikers pay little or nothing for the use of federal lands. Yet the costs of managing wildlife, providing picnic areas, and maintaining hiking trails are substantial. With federal policy over land use always up-for-grabs, the various interest groups continually vie for political control of the resources.

Just as the battle rages today, it has been a common theme throughout western history. Who should own the land, who should own the water, who should own the minerals were all questions confronted by frontier settlers. In some cases, these questions were resolved in favor of private ownership and removed from the political fray, but in others the rent-seeking continues every time Congress or its bureaucratic agents attempt to change policy.

This "Political Economy Forum" volume applies the property rights paradigm to a variety of western resource issues. The first three chapters develop the story of "the race for property rights" in the context of land. Anderson and Hill (Chapter 1) contend that various federal policies to distribute land among private owners had different implications for the amount of effort that would go into the rent-seeking process. In particular, they argue that homesteading led to a hard life on the frontier and often resulted in failure because it encouraged would-be property owners to settle too soon. Allen (Chapter 2), on the other hand, argues that homesteading was a least-cost method of defining the property rights to the West vis-a-vis other nations, including American Indians. Of course, whatever the federal policy, the settlers themselves had an incentive to seek efficient ownership institutions. Sanchez and Nugent (Chapter 3) argue that common property arrangements among stockgrowers in the West were a part of these efficient responses.

If land ownership attracted the biggest race for property rights, water development on the arid plains west of the 100th meridian surely ran a close second. Initially the miners and irrigators hammered out the prior appropriation water doctrine for allocating scarce water, but with the Reclamation Act of 1902, the federal government began its efforts to make the "desert bloom like a rose." This started a stampede to obtain water through the political process. Mayhew and Gardner (Chapter 4) examine the political economy of federal reclamation and conclude that the political market place responded by providing substantial subsidies to western irrigation interests. Simmons' consideration of the Columbia Basin Project (Chapter 5) describes how even the most complete planning efforts by the federal bureaucracies ran amuck. The adage that water runs uphill to money but gushes uphill to politics aptly describes federal intervention in water storage and delivery, the legacy of which lives on today.

The process of establishing property rights was not confined to traditional commodities, and in fact Anderson and Hill (Chapter 6) show that amenity values were recognized at an early date. The national park system is often put forward as an example of governmental conservation foresight, but it is better understood in the context of the property rights paradigm. The Northern Pacific Railroad had much to gain from preserving the wonders of Yellowstone and therefore led the charge for its establishment. Anderson and Hill explain why the Northern Pacific Railroad opted for public instead of private ownership and show how the breakdown of the railroad transportation monopoly created a Yellowstone commons with the inevitable overexploitation.

Though the West witnessed a unique opportunity to hammer out new institutions, the evolution of property took place in a legal structure set by government, and the final two chapters consider how this structure encouraged or discouraged rent-seeking activities. Haddock (Chapter 7) applies an innovative model of political economy to Indian tribes, arguing that governments, especially new ones, must be cautious not to exercise their sovereign power to redistribute wealth lest they discourage potential investors. In his analysis, it is rent-seeking by opportunistic governmental officials that can discourage economic development. Brady and Noll (Chapter 8) take up the issue of western exceptionalism, describing the circumstances surrounding the admission of the Western states to the Union and evaluating the impact of the voting power of those states on federal policy. They conclude that most Western states were admitted during periods of Republican control to strengthen the party's position, but that the senators from the Western states did not vote significantly different from their colleagues.

The political economy of the American West described in this volume has a distinct advantage over either the revisionist or the traditionalist approaches: it is based on a rational actor model that emphasizes causal relationships and testable implications. Hence, explanations of land settlement patterns, water development, and political events are driven by rational individuals reacting to their natural and manmade environments. We hope that these essays stimulate other studies of western history guided by the tools of political economists.

1

The Race for Property Rights[†]

Terry L. Anderson and Peter J. Hill

Economics literature on the evolution of property rights has increasingly emphasized the optimal timing for establishing those rights. Yoram Barzel (1968), Dale Mortensen (1982), and Partha Dasgupta and Joseph Stiglitz (1980), for example, have shown that competition among firms for the rents associated with innovative devices and ideas can lead to the dissipation of those rents in the process. When property rights and the rents therefrom are "up-for-grabs," it is possible for expenditures to establish rights to fully dissipate the rents, leaving the efficiency gains from privatization in question (Anderson and Hill 1983). Before any conclusions about the welfare gains from establishing property rights can be reached, attention must be paid to the evolutionary process.

The process whereby property rights are established also determines when resources will be brought into production. Just as the common pool for rights to innovative ideas may lead to "excessively fast research" (Dasgupta and Stiglitz 1980, 1), there can be excessively fast utilization of existing resources if use is necessary to capture future rents.[1] When resource utilization is a necessary condition for establishing private ownership to future rents, competition among would-be owners can induce production before resource rents become positive.

This chapter develops a model that examines the potential for premature production from land, induced by the process of establishing private ownership. The model focuses on three alternative policies, speculating, squatting, and homesteading, each of which has a historical analog. The optimal time for an individual to establish property rights and bring resources into production depends on which of these policies is operative. The model is applied to one of the most important policy questions of our nation's first one hundred years: how to dispose of the public domain. The "first privatization movement" occurred from 1790 to 1920, when over one billion acres of public land were made private. In its early stages, this movement pitted Alexander Hamilton, who favored selling the public lands to enhance the treasury and pay off the Revolutionary War debt, against Thomas Jefferson, who wanted to promote an agrarian ethic by making the land free to those willing to settle the frontier. In 1830, the South Carolina statesman Robert F. Hayne noted the importance of this debate:

> More than half our time has been taken up with the discussion of propositions connected with the public lands. . . . Day after day the charges are rung on this topic, from the grave inquiry into the rights of the new States to the absolute sovereignty and property in the soil, down to the grant of a preemption to a few quarter sections to actual settlers. (quoted in Gates 1973, 10)

From this debate emerged three general land disposal policies:

1. sale to the highest bidder, usually at a minimum price but without any requirement of residence on the land;
2. preemption, which gave squatters the first right to purchase the land at a minimum price; and
3. homesteading, which provided free land to settlers provided they met certain residency and improvement requirements.

In the following section, we model nineteenth century land policy in a manner similar to the optimal timing of innovations and analyze how the different land disposal policies influenced decisions to settle and bring the frontier into production. The third section applies the model to nineteenth century land policy in the United States. The conclusion is that "there ain't no such thing as free land."

No Free Land

Consider the Ricardian notion of the margin of cultivation with respect to time.[2] For example, if the annual value of output from a privately owned parcel of Ohio

Valley land in 1750 was less than costs of production, the land rent for that year would be negative, and the parcel would be beyond the margin of cultivation. If the value of output increased or costs of production decreased over time, however, we would expect the net annual rent, $v(t)$, as shown in Figure 1.1, to be negative for some time (origin to t_f), to rise until it becomes zero (t_f), and to be positive thereafter (t_f to the right). The net annual rent is the difference between the value of output (pecuniary and nonpecuniary) and the production costs. For reasons that will become clear below, it is important to note that the time path of net annual rents takes the property rights as given and does not allow for the costs of defining and enforcing those rights.

Figure 1.1

Time Path of Land Rents

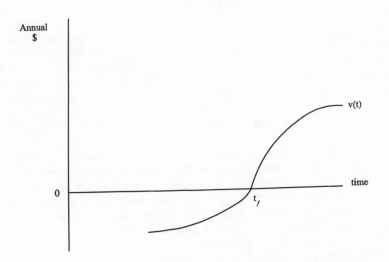

This time path of annual land rents is important for examining the question, when is the optimal time, from society's perspective, for bringing land into production? The net present value of land use would be maximized by bringing land into production at t_f. If the land were brought into production before t_f, the negative rents for the earlier period would have been subtracted from the positive rents that follow t_f, and, of course, the value of the resource would be lower. If, on the other hand, land were brought into production after t_f, some positive rents would be foregone, again reducing the potential total value of land.

This analysis, however, ignores one of the most important costs of settling the frontier, the costs of defining and enforcing property rights.[3] With competition to obtain property rights, the settler may be forced to purchase the land or to expend resources on definition and enforcement activity before the annual rents actually become positive.

In the context of individual rent maximization, given competition among would-be landowners, we can analyze the timing of settlement under (a) speculating, where land is sold by the government to the highest bidder, usually at a minimum price with no residency requirement; (b) squatting, where individuals must first invest some amount by being on the land before purchasing the land at a minimum price; and (c) homesteading, where land has no explicit price but where there are residency and improvement requirements. In each case we assume that people have the same expectations regarding the path of rents and that they face the same relative prices, including interest rates. For all three alternatives, the returns to privatization will be normalized by competition, but the mechanism for normalization will have very different allocative implications.

First consider the outright sale of land by the federal government to land speculators at a minimum price.[4] Offers from speculators would be forthcoming as soon as the discounted net value of production beginning at t_f is equal to the minimum price. If the minimum price is greater than this discounted value at the time that land is put on the market, no sales will be made; if the minimum price is less, there would be above-normal returns, which would encourage bids above the minimum and normalize speculative returns. Regardless of when the land is purchased, farming will be delayed until t_f. Moreover, as long as the dollars of speculators are *exchanged* for land titles, valuable resources will not be consumed in the privatization process.[5]

The timing of establishing property rights and commencing farming under squatting and homesteading can also be analyzed in the context of this model. In the case of squatting, individuals must compete with other claimants by being the first to define and enforce property rights to the land. This competition requires an investment which includes both the opportunity cost of his time and any other expenditures required by his efforts to establish a preemption right by squatting. Under homesteading, an individual must compete for ownership claims by being the first to make this investment *and* must bring the land into production at the time of the expenditure. Timing and allocative implications are quite different.

Maximization of individual rents by squatters generates timing identical to speculating *if* the expenditure on squatting equals the minimum price.[6] Squatters cannot postpone expenditures on property rights because net positive rents would invite earlier definition and enforcement activity by other squatters. Furthermore, once this investment is made, it becomes a sunk cost so that maximization of rents can be treated as if there were no property-rights costs. In this case, competition to be first to define and enforce property rights by expending resources in squatting rather than dollar bids will normalize returns to squatting.[7] In contrast to speculation, however, resources put into squatting will be *expended*, as opposed to *exchanged*, in the process.

With homesteading, the timing differs because competition for land rents is composed of expenditures on definition and enforcement activity *and* expenditures on "premature development." To understand the latter, return to Figure 1.1, and consider production from the land prior to t_f. If farming begins prior to t_f, net rents will be reduced by the amount of negative rents for each period. Individuals would be willing to make this sacrifice only if it were necessary to establish rights to future positive rents. Competition among homesteaders would cause farming to begin sooner than t_f because any delay would leave some net positive rents. Rents will be normalized by the combined expenditure on definition and enforcement activity and premature production. In contrast to squatting, even more resources will be *expended* as homesteaders dissipate the entire discounted value of positive future rents.

Hypotheses and Implications

From this analysis come several implications that can be tested in the context of nineteenth century United States land policy.

1. Since the model predicts that the present value of competitive bids will be determined by the discounted value of rents, the discounted value of governmental receipts from land sales will be independent of the price that is set as long as the land is sold prior to t_f. For example, if at the time land is offered for sale the minimum price is above the discounted value land will not be sold, and governmental revenues will be delayed until the discounted value of production beginning at t_f is equal to the minimum price. On the other hand, if lands are auctioned at any time to the highest bidder, the competitive price will be the discounted value. Thus the first implication of the model is that the *present value* of governmental revenues from land sales will be independent of the timing of sales.

2. The second implication is that competition among would-be landowners will normalize returns on their efforts. Competition among speculators would tend to bid the price up or delay the purchases until the price equals the discounted value of production. Of course, given the uncertainty associated with frontier settlement, we might expect the rate of return to include a risk premium. A corollary to this second implication is that competition among squatters will normalize returns to squatters who pay a "price" in terms of definition and enforcement expenditures.

3. The third prediction from the model is that timing of settlement and farming will vary systematically among speculating, squatting, and homesteading.

Some form of settlement will occur first with squatting when definition and enforcement activity is undertaken, but intensive farming will be delayed until t_f. Settlement and farming will occur simultaneously with homesteading. Finally, settlement and farming will commence last at t_f with speculating, although the land would be purchased earlier. According to this hypothesis, it will appear that speculators are "holding land out of production."

4. The fourth prediction is that squatters will not be able to compete successfully with speculators in land auctions. Assume that the government has the right to exclude nonpayers, that the land is put up for auction, and that squatters and speculators have the same expectations regarding land rents. The bid for the speculator at the time land is made available for purchase would be the value of future production commencing at t_f discounted back to the time of sale.

If the squatter knew before moving to the frontier that he would have to compete in the auction *and* have to expend resources on definition and enforcement activity, his maximum anticipated money bid at any point in time prior to t_f would be the discounted value of future production commencing at t_f *less* the squatting expenditure.[8] Obviously, for the same expectations, the speculator's bid will be greater than the squatter's. This suggests that squatters will find their squatting investment worthwhile only if competition from speculators can be prevented in the auction process.

5. The final implication from the model comes from relaxing the assumption that all participants in the land market face the same relative prices. Suppose that one person has relatively higher opportunity costs of time measured by wages and/or relatively lower costs of borrowing. Since the timing of land acquisition and production is sensitive to discount rates and the level of squatting expenditures required, relaxing this assumption of identical relative prices yields different results.

In the absence of indentured servitude, the transaction costs for borrowing against physical capital will be lower than for borrowing against labor services. Therefore, individuals borrowing against physical capital to finance their purchase of land will face a lower discount rate and will always be able to outbid those with higher discount rates. We predict that individuals endowed with relatively larger amounts of physical capital (and lower discount rates) would support governmental policies that favored the sale of public land and that those with relatively smaller amounts of physical capital (and higher discount rates) would favor governmental policies lenient toward squatters and homesteaders.

This tendency will be reinforced by the fact that individuals with relatively lower opportunity costs of time can afford to move to the frontier sooner. Of course, those with higher opportunity costs could buy the land from squatters or homesteaders after they obtained title, but tax obligations would be reduced and/or public services increased if the land payments went directly to the treasury rather than to compensate squatters or homesteaders for a nonproductive use of time.[9]

Nineteenth Century Land Policy

Historical research on nineteenth century land policy by historians such as Paul Gates, Robert Swierenga, and Benjamin Hibbard provides a fertile testing ground for this model. After considering data on speculative rates of return, settlement patterns, and methods of defining and enforcing property rights, this research generally abhors speculation, advocates free-land policies, and criticizes the timing of disposal. The model presented above, however, casts a different light on each of these conclusions.

Before turning to the specific implications, it is useful to summarize the main trends in early land policy. A major issue following the revolution was whether the state or federal government would dispose of the public domain. This was resolved rather quickly when the states agreed to cede their western lands to the federal government, which took control of disposal. The Ordinances of 1785 and 1787 required the rectangular survey system, limited frontier migration until Indian claims had been settled, and granted fee-simple ownership once the land had been purchased from the government.[10]

Hamilton's position that public lands be sold to generate federal revenue dominated the first fifty years of land policy as large tracts of land were sold to individuals and companies who acted as brokers for smaller owners. These speculators often negotiated special prices and terms with the Congress. Squatting was discouraged by using troops to evict settlers from land that was not open for sale or that had been sold to speculators.

Even during these early years, however, there was strong sentiment favoring special consideration for squatters. The retirement of the national debt in 1835 and growing population in the western states added pressure to allow squatters the first opportunity to buy newly open lands. In 1830, this pressure culminated in the first of a series of preemption acts that granted this privilege.

Preemption was only the first step toward attempting to make the land available at a zero price; politicians rallied around the free-land position and eventually passed the Homestead Act of 1862. With this legislation and subsequent laws, including the Timber Culture Act in 1873, the Desert Land Act in 1877, the Timber and Stone Act in 1878, the Enlarged Homestead Act in 1909, and the Stock-Raising Homestead Act in 1916, land was to be given to anyone willing to endure the hardships of frontier life. Generally these acts required residing on the land, usually for five years; developing irrigation systems; constructing buildings; planting trees; and plowing a specified portion of the claim. The passage of these acts essentially signaled the end of disposal by sale. In light of this brief history, let us turn to the economic analysis of nineteenth century land policy.

Timing of Sales and Governmental Revenues

Once it was decided that land would be sold, the question became: when and at what price? Easterners were concerned that opening the frontier too rapidly would drive down land values and raise wages as labor was siphoned off by the lure of land ownership. Furthermore, until the land was surveyed, it was difficult to define what property was being sold, and since the Ordinance of 1785 required the rectangular survey, this limited how fast land could be placed on the market.

The argument for a minimum price always centered around maximization of revenues from land sales. Indeed, when land was placed on the market at a minimum price of approximately $2 per acre, it often was not sold immediately. And when it was purchased, often payments could not be made and special dispensations for buyers had to be allowed. Whenever it was suggested that prices be lowered, those favoring maximizing revenue from land sales balked. Of course, speculators wanted a lower price and argued that $2 was too high, given that land in western New York, Pennsylvania, and Massachusetts was selling for less than $1 per acre. On the other side, supporters of the $2 price contended that land was selling in Ohio for $4–$6 per acre so that "two dollars was really low, a mere nominal price, yet a safeguard against selling too far below real value" (Hibbard 1939, 64). Even modern economic historians have contended that letting the land go too soon would not maximize revenues: "It would have been to the federal government's advantage to have followed a slow, or restrictive, land policy insofar as it would have probably led to a large increase in its revenues."[11]

The contention that land sales should be delayed to maximize revenues is contrary to the model implication that the present value of government revenues is independent of timing of sales. If those formulating land policy had the same expectations about future land values as the general public and if discount rates were the same in the public and private sectors, the timing of sales would have had no effect on the discounted value of revenue as long as land was sold prior to t_f. Holding land off the market only makes sense if the government has better information about future rents or has a lower discount rate than private speculators.

Returns to Speculation, Squatting, and Homesteading

Controversy always has surrounded the question of how profitable speculation in western land dealing really was. For example, in 1850 the Madison, Wisconsin, *Argus* concluded:

Lands have been entered in this country at one dollar and twenty-five cents per acre, and after paying taxes on them for years their owners have sold them for one dollar per acre to avoid further taxation. Show us a non-resident who has made much money speculating in western land, and we will show you a rare bird, more rare by far than a successful gold hunter. . . . The only way in which anything can be made by buying western lands is to locate in small tracts remote from each other so as not to interfere in the general settlement, and even then the settlers skin the speculator out of his profits by taxation. (quoted in Hibbard 1939, 221)

On the other hand, Robert Swierenga's research led to the opposite conclusion:

Since the average rates of return per dollar invested in frontier land in central Iowa in the mid-nineteenth century were superior to many other forms of investment, it is regrettable that most previous scholars have, after only cursory examination of the land records, created such a misleading picture. If the speculator who make [sic] money in frontier land dealings was truly a "rare bird," as has been asserted, then the American menagerie must have been well stocked with odd specimens. More likely, however, the investor who failed to show a profit was truly the rare bird. (Swierenga 1968, 208)

The data from which Swierenga arrived at his conclusion show that the mean returns between land speculation and the other investments are statistically different, but it does not necessarily follow that land investors were earning above-normal returns. First, the Swierenga (1968, 199) data presented in Table 1.1 are biased upward because he deletes "all tracts selling at the land office minimum or less," arguing that this gives a "more realistic rate of return" because "it is very doubtful if many of these recorded prices were bona fide" (Swierenga 1968, 198). However, this assumes that there were no errors on the part of original purchasers and that any land purchased at the minimum price would never be resold for less than that amount. Including sales recorded at or below the government minimum price in his aggregate data for 1845–1889 reduces the average net return by 14.4 percentage points.

Furthermore, comparing mean rates of return masks the higher risk associated with land speculation. Swierenga (1968, 207) notes that the returns do fluctuate "a great deal more from year to year." The coefficient of variation shown in Table 1.1 measures the extent of these fluctuations. Indeed, the coefficient of variation for land investments is more than four times greater than the same measure for commercial paper. Given such riskiness, it is hardly surprising that the mean return for land speculation is also higher.

Also reported in Table 1.1 are rates of return for Illinois land speculation that, on average, are more than one-third less than the Swierenga mean but still above returns on commercial paper. Recognizing that the coefficient of variation for land speculation remains nearly four times greater than for commercial paper, Allan Bogue and Margaret Bogue's (1957, 24) conclusion is consistent with our prediction of normal returns to speculation:

> Their [speculators'] experience does not prove either that frontier land speculation in the United States during the nineteenth century was generally well rewarded or generally unremunerative. Despite the assumptions of a number of historians, perhaps neither alternative is correct, and the speculative losses of some real-estate plungers were canceled by the speculative gains of others.

Table 1.1

Rate of Return for Land Speculation and Commercial Paper
1846 – 1884

Year	Iowa Land Speculation	Illinois Land Speculation	Commercial Paper
1846	70.2	7.0	8.33
1847	16.3	—	9.59
1848	2.7	7.0	15.1
1849	52.9	—	10.25
1850	58.2	6.0	8.04
1851	19.1	6.4	9.66
1852	27.1	9.1	6.33
1853	21.2	10.3	10.25
1854	156.6	7.1	10.37
1855	60.1	7.4	8.92
1856	72.5	17.5	8.83
1857	66.3	11.56	—
1858	73.2	—	4.81
1859	155.9	46.0	6.14
1860	45.0	17.1	7.31
1861	6.9	15.0	6.7
1862	32.2	30.6	5.32
1863	107.1	19.2	5.65
1864	31.4	16.7	7.36
1865	10.8	18.1	7.77
1866	4.1	20.5	6.33
1867	9.8	21.5	7.32

(more)

Table 1.1
(continued)
Rate of Return for Land Speculation and Commercial Paper
1846 – 1884

Year	Iowa Land Speculation	Illinois Land Speculation	Commercial Paper
1868	12.1	125.3	7.28
1869	12.3	41.5	9.66
1870	8.3	19.1	7.23
1871	4.5	24.1	6.98
1872	6.3	17.9	8.63
1873	5.7	12.0	10.27
1874	10.1	12.1	5.98
1875	10.8	14.0	5.44
1876	−4.5	—	5.13
1877	5.9	4.0	5.01
1878	—	—	4.82
1879	6.4	—	5.14
1880	6.5	—	5.23
1881	6.9	—	5.36
1882	−.7	8.0	5.64
1883	—	7.4	5.62
1884	6.2	—	5.21
Mean	31.14	19.58	7.45
Standard deviation	39.94	22.28	2.26
N	39.0	29.0	39.0
Coefficient of variance	1.28	1.14	.30

Sources: Iowa land speculation: Swierenga (1968, 202); Illinois land speculation: Bogue and Bogue (1957); commercial paper: Homer (1963, 319–20).

In addition to variance of returns, it is important to realize that normalization of returns required some time to adapt expectations based on new information. Therefore, we would expect rates of return in land speculation to move closer to other assets as information about land quality, weather, and other physical characteristics improved. Table 1.2 reports rate of return for speculation in Nebraska for 1877–1904. As expected, the variance and the mean rate of return to speculation declined dramatically.

Our model also suggests that competition to claim free land via squatting or homesteading would dissipate above-normal returns in a variety of ways. Premature settlement forces production prior to the time when net annual rents are positive. In addition, the homestead acts generally limited land holdings to a size that was economically inefficient, with the result that too many people inhabited the land. Moreover, the acts required unnecessary investments, such as irrigation ditches, that would not otherwise have been built; trees planted where they would not grow; and soil plowed for farming that was better suited for grazing.

Table 1.2

**Rate of Return for Land Speculation and Commercial Paper
1877 – 1904**

Year	Nebraska Land Speculation	Commercial Paper
1877	12.00	5.01
1878	11.00	4.82
1879	8.90	5.14
1880	9.20	5.23
1881	16.00	5.36
1882	19.20	5.64
1883	11.90	5.62
1884	14.00	5.21
1885	11.30	4.05
1886	16.00	4.77
1887	13.00	5.73
1888	10.00	4.91
1889	11.90	4.85
1890	9.60	5.62
1891	10.20	5.46
1892	12.20	4.10
1893	8.30	6.78
1894	7.30	3.04
1895	7.20	2.83
1896	7.70	5.82
1897	6.90	3.50
1898	8.60	3.83
1899	8.00	3.83
1900	7.10	4.15

(more)

Table 1.2
(continued)
Rate of Return for Land Speculation and Commercial Paper
1877 – 1904

Year	Nebraska Land Speculation	Commercial Paper
1901	5.70	4.28
1902	6.90	4.09
1903	6.00	5.44
1904	12.00	4.21
Mean	10.29	4.76
Standard deviation	3.25	.90
N	28.0	28.0
Coefficient of variance	.32	.19

Sources: Nebraska land speculation: Bogue and Bogue (1957); commercial paper: Homer (1963, 319–20).

Though it is difficult to get sufficient, detailed data to show the exact amount of rent dissipation, Libecap and Johnson (1979, 137) conclude that "expenditures attributable to Federal restrictions and which involved real resources: agent payment, development costs, and miscellaneous expenditures," amounted to between 60 percent for the Timber and Stone Act and 80 percent for the Preemption Act of the total land value. Dissipation was made worse by the fact that many of these 285 million acres were taken up more than once and that, on approximately another 140 million acres, entries were made but not completed (Clawson 1951, 69).

Therefore, the standard interpretation of land disposal policy that suggests it provided free land must be corrected on two counts: first, land was not free since competition for rents encouraged premature settlement; and, second, the resulting premature development of the frontier created a drain on national income. The problem is that homesteading and squatting required the *expenditure* of resources that had alternative uses in contrast to the outright sale of public land, which resulted in the *exchange* of resources.

The Timing of Settlement

Our model predicts that speculators, who purchased rights to the land directly from the government, would hold it out of production until t_f with no apparent settlement activity, while squatters and homesteaders would engage in premature development of the land. It was the speculators who undertook socially efficient action by not doing anything on the land until t_f.[12]

This conclusion is quite the opposite of most historians who contend that "the dead hand of the speculator created many problems which were to stunt the growth and waste the resources" (Gates 1973, 110). It was the intention of speculators "to hold the land until rising prices . . . should enable them to sell at a profit. They had no intention of improving their land or in any other way aiding in the development of the prairies" (Gates 1973, 130).

> One of the worst effects of speculation was that it held land out of the market for at least a time and so compelled settlement to pass around or across it. Such would be the natural course of events, and testimony that it happened is abundant. Agriculture necessarily remained for an unnecessarily long time in a backward condition under these circumstances. (Hibbard 1939, 219)

Indeed, the data do support the prediction that speculators would hold their land out of production. Table 1.3 shows Iowa farm acreage as a percentage of acreage assessed for taxes for the period 1850–1862. These data show that "by 1862 approximately two-thirds of the privately owned land in Iowa was included in neither the improved nor unimproved portions of the state's farms and could only have been held for speculation" (Swierenga 1968, 45). Gates found that only 6 percent of the land in one county of northern Indiana and 13 percent in two others had been improved by 1860. "It was not until well into the 1860s that these counties began to develop and much of their land was not improved until after 1880" (Gates 1973, 130). As predicted, speculators were holding land out of production.

Table 1.3

Iowa Farm Acreage as a Percentage of Acreage Assessed for Taxes 1850 – 1862

Area	1850	1856	1859	1862
Eastern	58.1	55.3	55.3	57.8
Central	53.3	34.7	33.0	29.3
Western and Northern	15.8	22.8	34.1	17.3
Entire state	55.9	36.8	38.8	31.5

Source: Swierenga (1968, 44).

Testing the hypotheses that squatters would enter the land prior to homesteaders and refrain from farming until t_f and that homesteaders would enter after squatters and would begin farming immediately is more difficult. One problem is the difficulty of distinguishing between resident (squatters) and nonresident speculators. Gates' (1973, 50) description of the frontiersmen highlights this difficulty:

> Although frontiersmen, as a rule, possessed little or no capital, they were anxious to own as much land as possible. The first wave of settlers who followed the fur trader squatted upon choice locations, made rude improvements, and, when new arrivals came in, sold their claims and moved on to a new frontier before the government auction took place. These squatters were in a sense speculators.

Swierenga (1968, 211) also notes that farmer-speculators were criticized along with nonresidents for holding land out of production.

Whenever possible, squatters did try to minimize their expenditures on land improvement until t_f. Arthur Bentley (1893, 11) draws attention to the fact that even before Nebraska land was open to settlement, "a few of the more impatient ventured across the river and laid out for themselves squatters' claims, but they rarely remained longer than the day or two required to blaze the boundaries of their chosen pieces of land."

A mechanism used by residents to establish property rights in land and to delay intensive farming was the land claims club or association. These clubs were established for the purpose of registering a settler's claim prior to the actual opening of land by the government and insuring that it would be honored. The associations often drafted elaborate constitutions that specified how claims could be registered and perfected. Because members of the association were residual claimants, they minimized expenditures on definition and enforcement,[13] but they still had to expend some amount. For example, the Webster County (Iowa) club *required* members to expend labor worth $10 for each month after the first, and the Poweshiek County club *required* $30 during the first six months and $30 for each succeeding six months. While there were some land improvements made, land claims clubs offered a way to keep definition and enforcement expenditures to a minimum until t_f, while still establishing property rights earlier. The activities of Fort Dodge and Johnson County associations led one resident to write to his relatives, saying, "Everybody speculating, nobody raising" (Swierenga 1968, 17).

Testing the implications of the model regarding homesteading appears impossible since homesteading did not occur simultaneously with squatting or outright sales. In fact, if homesteading had been allowed simultaneously, the homesteaders always would have been too late. It is perhaps for this reason that, once introduced, the homestead acts precluded other forms of property-rights establishment.

Squatters versus Speculators

If squatters were to compete with speculators for property rights to land, they would have had to restrict competition in the bidding process. Preemption allowed squatters a right of first refusal at the minimum price on the land they had settled, but settlement required some expenditure of resources in the definition and enforcement process. If the minimum sale price when the land was placed on the auction block was less than the actual discounted present value of the land at t_f, competition among bidders would force the price up. But since squatters had already made an investment in competing for preemption rights, they could not afford to bid as much as speculators who had not.[14] Hence, squatters could obtain land at auction only if they could restrict competition in the bidding process.

Again, the land claims association provided the mechanism for the squatter to do this. An observer in 1830 described the associations as follows:

> The citizens occupying this land, together with a few others, have held a meeting or convention, and entered into written and solemn resolutions to prevent all, and every person, whatsoever, from viewing or exploring the land previous to the day of sale. They have pledged themselves to do this by force of arms. They have further resolved for one individual in each township to bid off the whole of the land that they or any of their body may wish to buy, and the balance of the company to be armed with their rifles and muskets before the land office door, and shoot, instantly, any man that may bid for any land that they want. . . . In consequence of the large body that is united, and their determined violence, they have, and will keep every individual from examining or buying the land. (Hibbard 1939, 199)

One resident of Fort Dodge, Iowa, recalled that the local association advertised "that any one attempting to Settle on any Lands Claimed by any Member of the Club Would be dealt With by the Club and his life Would not be Safe in that Community" (Swierenga 1968, 17). In light of these descriptions, it is not surprising that Gates (1973, 148) found that "capitalists rarely clashed with squatters over the selection lands. They early acquired a respect for the law of the claim association."[15]

Political Support for Preemption and Speculation

The final prediction of the model is that individuals facing lower discount rates or higher wage rates would support public sale of lands, while those with higher discount rates and lower wage rates would favor preemption and homesteading. The political alignments for and against preemption and homesteading legislation provide evidence on this issue.

The fact that laborers who likely faced higher interest rates and lower wage rates backed preemption legislation supports this proposition. "The National Labor Union Convention in 1867 passed a series of drastic resolutions on the subject of the public domain, denouncing Congress for having allowed speculators to buy land, and demanding that it be made free to settlers" (Hibbard 1939, 140).

The debates on homestead legislation also suggest that there was concern for the frontiersmen who "possessed little or no capital" (Gates 1973, 50). Mr. Galusha A. Grow argued vociferously for homesteading by emphasizing the struggle between labor and capital:

> The struggle between capital and labor is an unequal one at best. It is a struggle between the bones and sinews of men and dollars and cents; and in that struggle, it needs no prophet's ken to foretell the issue. And in that struggle, is it for this Government to stretch forth its arm to aid the strong against the weak? Shall it continue, by its legislation, to elevate and enrich idleness on the wail and woe of industry? (quoted in Hibbard 1939, 369–70)

Commenting on President Buchanan's veto of an early homestead bill, Horace Greeley argued that the public domain should be distributed through homesteading because the poverty of the settler makes payment for new land impossible and speculation easy (*New York Tribune*, August 25, 1860).

Conclusion

Economic analysis allows us to consider the efficiency of processes by which property rights are established, and United States land policy offers an interesting test case of theories about the optimal timing of establishing rights. Three substantially different policies were followed, each of which led to different rates of establishment. Our analysis questions the conclusion that returns to speculation were above normal. It explains why speculators held land out of production, and why squatters had to restrict competition from speculators. Above all, the analysis suggests that rents were dissipated through resource expenditures under squatting and homesteading and therefore questions whether disposal of the public domain unambiguously increased national output (Fogel and Rutner 1972, 390). Efforts to give away the public domain created a commons into which squatters and homesteaders rushed to compete for the rents. In the process, pioneers paid for the land in terms of foregone wealth, privations, and hardships, demonstrating that "there ain't no such thing as free land."

Notes

1. For additional discussions of this point, see Dennen (1977); Haddock (1986); and Southey (1978). Also, see Gordon (1954) for early discussion of rent dissipation in the commons.
2. The model presented here follows that of Southey (1978), which was brought

to our attention by Donald Gordon. In the "academic homesteading race," we independently developed a similar model used in North, Anderson, and Hill (1983). Also, see Stroup (1988).

3. For a similar analysis of establishing property rights, see Dennen (1977); and Libecap and Johnson (1979).

4. This case, of course, assumes the government has exclusive ownership of the resource and can exclude nonpayers.

5. Of course, there may be rent-seeking for the government revenues, but this is beyond our analysis. See Lee and Kreutzer (1986).

6. Note that this assumes that, once the expenditure is made, the property rights are secure and there are no other costs. Southey (1978, 556) points out that this analysis ignores the important complication introduced by the "costs of returning to the otherwise more profitable activity." In other words, there is an opportunity cost of remaining on the frontier because labor could be employed in other activities. Given the transportation costs of returning to these activities, individuals may have to remain on the frontier, thus adding to the cost of established property rights prior to t_f.

7. Note that this result is the same as that described by Anderson and Hill (1983).

8. Again note that once the squatting expenditure has been made, it is a sunk cost, but before squatting takes place, the expenditure is a marginal cost that must be covered by rational investors. Therefore, in the long run the squatter's bid must account for the squatting expenditure.

9. We thank an anonymous referee for bringing this point to our attention. For a further discussion, see Anderson and Martin (1987).

10. For a further discussion of these ordinances, see Anderson (1987).

11. See note 11 in Gunderson (1976, 236). It should be noted that Gunderson may be arguing that releasing large blocks of land would have supply-side effects on prices, which is different from the argument that holding a specific tract of land for later sale would increase the discounted value of revenue.

12. If possible, squatters would not have engaged in intensive farming until t_f also. However, if one way of establishing property rights was to farm, some activity would have been necessary. Also, if establishing rights required the full-time presence of the squatter, the opportunity cost of farming (to the farmer) might have been quite low. The farming that occurred prior to t_f should still be seen as unnecessary from the viewpoint of society, however, since outright sale of the land by the government provided a more efficient method of establishing rights.

13. See Anderson and Hill (1983, 443–6), for a more complete discussion of the activities of claims associations.

14. Of course, the squatting expenditure was a sunk cost that would have been ignored by squatters who found themselves competing with speculators. But if they anticipated that they would find themselves in this position, they would not have squatted in the first place because their total expenditure was not sunk before going to the frontier.

15. For additional discussion of the role of force in the establishment of property rights, see Umbeck (1981, 9).

References

Anderson, Gary M., and Delores T. Martin. 1987. The public domain and nineteenth century transfer policy. *Cato Journal* 6: 905–23.

Anderson, Terry L. 1987. The first privatization movement. In *Essays on the economy of the old Northwest*, edited by David C. Klingaman and Richard K. Vedder. Athens: Ohio University Press, 59–75.

Anderson, Terry L., and Peter J. Hill. 1983. Privatizing the commons: An improvement? *Southern Economic Journal* 50(2): 438–50.

Barzel, Yoram. 1968. Optimal timing of innovation. *Review of Economics and Statistics* 50(3): 348–55.

Bentley, Arthur F. 1893. The condition of the western farmer: The economic history of a Nebraska township. Vol. 7–8. *Johns Hopkins University Studies in Historical and Political Science*, edited by Herbert B. Adams, 11th series. (July–August): 7–92.

Bogue, Allan G., and Margaret B. Bogue. 1957. "Profits" and the frontier land speculator. *Journal of Economic History* 17 (March).

Clawson, Marion. 1951. *Uncle Sam's acres.* New York: Dodd, Mead.

Dasgupta, Partha, and Joseph Stiglitz. 1980. Uncertainty, industrial structure, and the speed of R & D. *Bell Journal of Economics* 11(1): 1–28.

Dennen, Taylor A. 1977. Some efficiency effects of nineteenth-century federal land policy. *Agricultural History* 51 (October).

Fogel, Robert W., and Jack L. Rutner. 1972. The efficiency effects of federal land policy, 1850–1900: A report of some provisional findings. In *The dimensions of quantitative research in history*, edited by William O. Aydelotte, Allen G. Bogue, and Robert William Fogel. Princeton, NJ: Princeton University Press.

Gates, Paul W. 1973. *Landlords and tenants on the prairie frontier.* New York: Cornell University Press.

Gordon, H. Scott. 1954. The economic theory of a common property resource. *Journal of Political Economy* 62 (April): 124–42.

Gunderson, Gerald. 1976. *A new economic history of America.* New York: McGraw-Hill.

Haddock, David. 1986. First possession versus optimal timing: Limiting the dissipation of economic value. *Washington University Law Quarterly* 64: 775–92.

Hibbard, Benjamin H. 1939. *A history of the public land policies.* New York: P. Smith.

Homer, Sidney. 1963. *A history of interest rates.* New Brunswick, NJ: Rutgers University Press.

Lee, Dwight, and David Kreutzer. 1986. Privatizing the commons: A comment. *Southern Economic Journal* 52(4): 1162–4.

Libecap, Gary D., and Ronald N. Johnson. 1979. Property rights, nineteenth-century federal timber policy and the conservation movement. *Journal of Economic History* 39(1): 129–42.

Mortensen, Dale T. 1982. Property rights and efficiency in mating, racing, and related games. *American Economic Review* 72(5): 968–79.

North, Douglass C., Terry L. Anderson, and Peter J. Hill. 1983. *Growth and welfare in the American past: A new economic history.* Englewood Cliffs, NJ: Prentice-Hall, Inc.

Southey, Clive. 1978. The staple thesis, common property, and homesteading. *Canadian Journal of Economics* 11(3): 547–59.

Stroup, Richard L. 1988. Buying misery with federal land. *Public Choice* 57: 69–77.

Swierenga, Robert P. 1968. *Pioneers and profits: Land speculation on the Iowa frontier.* Ames: Iowa State University Press.

Umbeck, John R. 1981. Might makes rights: A theory of the formation and initial distribution of property rights. *Economic Inquiry* 19(1): 38–59.

2

Homesteading and Property Rights:
Or, "How the West Was Really Won"[†]

Douglas W. Allen

Homesteading gets no respect. Both historians and economists alike find only bad things to say about it, and on the surface it is easy to see why. Homesteading creates incentives to establish property rights too early. Competition to acquire farmland, when in the form "first come, first served," causes farmers to rush to the land in an effort to preempt other potential farmers and, in the process, dissipate the value of the land.[1] In the past, homesteading also imposed costs and hardships on settlers. Homesteaders settled land that was initially beyond feasible markets for their goods and had to support themselves while waiting for markets to reach them. Further, many settlers bore the brunt of Indian attacks and raids from interloping desperadoes. But to argue, as many economists have, that the United States homestead policy was a mistake because land values were dissipated and settlers suffered is premature.[2]

Homesteading officially began in the United States with the Homestead Act of 1862 and officially ended in 1934. Federally administered homesteading in

[†] Reprinted with permission from the *Journal of Law & Economics*, vol. 34 (April 1991). © 1991 by the University of Chicago. All rights reserved.

Canada lasted from 1872 to 1930. Other countries, including Israel, the Philippines, and South Africa, either had, or have, homesteading policies. Could a policy like homesteading, lasting over seventy years in the United States, and existing across different countries, be inefficient? Could there be an economic rationale for homesteading, and could such a justification explain the differences in homesteading across time and jurisdictions? This chapter answers "yes" and provides a positive theory of homesteading that focuses on the state's role as contract enforcer.[3]

The emphasis here is on the United States experience with homesteading, although some attention is given to Canada and Australia. On the surface, the United States experience is puzzling because the federal government *began* disposing public land through auctions and other price mechanisms *before* it established the practice of homesteading. Further, the federal and state governments continued to dispose public land through land grants, preemption, and private sales during the heyday of homesteading. If an auction or price mechanism always allocates resources best, then why did the United States government move from a pure price to a mixed price and nonprice allocation method for some lands?[4]

The hypothesis of this chapter is that the United States' public land policies of the nineteenth century were appropriate in light of the costs of enforcing property rights.[5] Due to the Indian's simultaneous claim on public lands and the costs imposed by this dispute over property rights, the land policies were efforts to "hire" settlers to reduce the costs of enforcement. The state may have a comparative advantage in enforcing property rights through violence; however, when disputes occur, the state will use a least-cost strategy to secure ownership. In this light, homesteading is a substitute for direct military force and acts to mitigate the costs of violence. Where disputes over land claims are greatest, more state intervention is expected, and, hence, more homesteading is predicted. This hypothesis explains much of the rise in nonprice land allocation and the various differences in applications of these laws across states.

The next two sections present a simple argument for state involvement in homesteading. These are followed by an examination of the historical record of the United States homestead era and by a test of the hypothesis that when the sovereignty of a region is threatened, settlement is promoted to help establish property rights and mitigate the enforcement costs by violence.

The Cost of State Enforcement

Every exchange requires some method of securing property rights—for without property rights there can be no exchange. Most economic studies on the formation and protection of property rights focus on private individuals or small "states" such as Indian tribes, fishermen, farmers, and miners.[6] In most cases, the endogenous property rights structure is chosen to maximize wealth subject to the constraint of violence or theft. Thus, Umbeck found that California miners divided mining claims equally among themselves to avoid claim jumping, and Johnsen argues that the Pacific Coast Indian custom of potlatch was used to enforce private rights over salmon streams. Although contract theories of the state are not new, and the modern government is casually referred to as an institution to preserve and protect property rights, economists are generally more comfortable applying the model to small levels of government organization. This chapter extends the contract theory of the state and argues that, at least for the American frontier, the federal government acted to maximize the net value of the territory.

Recent studies on the creation and protection of property rights demonstrate the aversion of wealth maximizers to engage continuously in violence as a method of enforcing their claims over the goods in question. Violence dissipates wealth. Since both parties who lay claim to a good are willing to spend up to its expected value to obtain it, and since past losses due to violence are sunk, the costs of enforcing property rights through violence tend to exceed the total value of the good being fought over. Even the credible *threat* of violence is costly when the articles of war provide no other service. When disputes over valuable resources span long periods of time, the high cost of violence encourages the use of other methods to secure property rights over the resource.

On the American frontier, land ownership was indeed tenuous. Settlers not only had to compete with wild animals, harsh conditions, and other settlers for much of what they owned, they also had to compete with hostile Indians who, for the most part, did not recognize the claims of white settlers. In an effort to increase their wealth, settlers employed a host of protection methods: some simple, like owning a firearm; others more complex, like forming local claiming associations. Along with private methods of protection, the federal government acted as a third-party enforcer of some rights. Frontier settlers used the U.S. Postal Service, federal marshals and other law enforcement officers, federal land offices, federal and state surveyors, the federal court system, the Bureau of Indian Affairs (BIA), and, perhaps most important in the early days, the U.S. Army. At the same time, however, all of the above institutions used the frontier settler. By adjusting land policies and applying them with different intensities in different areas, the U.S. government used settlers to lower the cost of enforcing state ownership over the western frontier.

The Benefit of Homesteading

When only one individual, or one group, lays claim to an area of land, there will be no physical disputes with other groups over it. When two groups lay claim to an area of land, but one group is expected to be a clear victor in a dispute, there will also be an absence of violence. Physical violence only occurs when the outcome is uncertain and the parties differ in their expectation of who will win. On the American frontier, disputes did not arise until settlement began, even though the federal government had always asserted jurisdiction over the entire public lands. Once disputes occurred, military expenditures were made by both sides. I assume that the per capita enforcement costs (including military, policy, and administrative costs) as a function of the relative population of the disputing groups rise over some range and then decline to a very low level because the outcome is unclear. Homesteading is a method of "skipping" over this low population level. By allowing homesteading, the federal government was able to avoid military expenditures that could exceed the value of the land being fought over.

An important aspect of military intervention is that the services of the state are used at zero (or almost zero) marginal cost to the settler—no cavalry ever presented a settler a bill for "Indian services rendered." Since public expenditures on protection are ignored by private settlers, too much protection is demanded. When individual settlers were not required to pay for state protection services, they settled on property that may have had positive private gains but negative social ones. Settlements will be more scattered and less dense under a system of complete private decisions.

By instigating homesteading, the U.S. government restricted the choices of settlers by providing an incentive to rush *one area*. The sudden arrival of tens of thousands of people into a given territory destroyed much of the Indian way of life and forced the Indian tribes to accept reservation life or to join the union. The selective and intensive settlement caused by homesteading also reduced the cost of defending any given settlement. Further, due to the remoteness of homesteads, settlers tended to have low marginal projects, which lowered the cost of protecting their land with violence.[7] Because homesteading itself dissipates the value of the land settled, not all land within a territory is expected to be homesteaded.

Homesteading, then, was a method of helping to establish the United States and Canadian claims in the western territories, and, as I will show, its rise and fall as the staple in North American public land policy is positively related to the threat of simultaneous land claims made by others. This hypothesis also explains the *form* of land policy intervention since the state not only used homesteading to mitigate military costs but also designed the homesteading laws to maximize the value of western settlement.

A Brief History of U.S. Public Lands

The State of the Frontier, 1800–1890

The bulk of public lands required by the United States came by purchase from European powers rather than conquests.[8] The Louisiana Purchase (1803) added over 500 million acres, the Florida Purchase (1819) added 43 million acres, Texas (though the 200 million acres were never part of the public lands) was annexed in 1845, the Gadsden Purchase (1853) added another 19 million acres. The Oregon

Territory was settled diplomatically with Britain in 1846, and, although a war with Mexico was fought over the Pacific Southwest, its 334 million acres were eventually purchased in 1848. This peaceful process of acquisition, along with our knowledge of the final securing of the forty-eight continental states, lends the impression that a complete set of property rights was transferred with each treaty. This was hardly the case, and for most of the early nineteenth century the future ownership of many western public lands was unclear.

The greatest threat in the West came from Mexicans and Indians. In 1851, at a treaty-making council at Fort Laramie, Wyoming, agents of the BIA were struck by the size of Indian forces. As Richard Dillon (1984, 7) reports, "10,000 Indians camped around the post. The entire [U.S.] Army, stretched from Maine to California, totaled only 10,000 men, and that was on paper. Its actual strength was probably closer to 8000." In the decade following the Civil War there were over 200 Army clashes with western Indians. By 1876, the year of Custer's (and the Army's) greatest defeat, over 50,000 Indians were in rebellion, and by the end of the century over 1,000 battles had been fought (Dillon 1984, 120). Aside from the loss of life and property, the financial costs of the Indian wars were great. After a heavy expedition in 1865, "The Army hurriedly cut back on large-scale operation. The Quartermaster General himself went west to investigate the expenditure in the District of ten millions of rations and forage and an equal sum for other supplies. The Indians were bankrupting the Army!" (Dillon 1984, 46).

In retrospect, it is easy to downplay the significance of the Indian wars, but the federal grasp of the entire public lands was tenuous at best, and early Indian negotiations reflect this. Throughout the early nineteenth century, so great was the Indian presence that it was generally assumed they would be given their own land that would be relatively independent of the United States. The federal government negotiated treaties with Indian chiefs assuming they were dealing with individuals with authority similar to European monarchs. If, as the BIA assumed at the time, tribal Indians were bound by the promises of their leaders, it is quite possible that independent Indian nations might exist today.[9] Regardless of what might have happened, United States officials did not have, nor did they believe they had, control over the West. The Indian rebellion, along with the strain of the Civil War and wars with Mexico, left much of the West outside federal control.

Disposing the Public Lands

By 1850, the United States claimed over 1.2 billion acres of public lands, a land mass approximately one-half of its present-day size. Just as the timing and method of acquisition changed throughout the late eighteenth and first half of the nineteenth centuries, so too the release of these public lands took on various forms.

The initial goal of releasing public lands was to generate revenue (Gates 1968). The Land Act of 1796 established the rectangular system of survey whereby a township would consist of 6 square miles and would be subdivided into 36 sections of 640 acres each. The land was to sell for $2 per acre, with credit extended over a year after purchase. Initial sales were slow, but reductions in the size of tract and longer periods of credit generated large sales in Ohio, Mississippi, and Alabama (although delinquencies were also high).

In 1820, credit for the purchase of public land was terminated and replaced by a cash sales system that required full payment at the time of purchase. The public auction was retained, the minimum price per acre was lowered to $1.25, and the minimum plot size was reduced to 80 acres. Public lands could be purchased only after they had been publicly surveyed and could be bought in larger tracts only after each section had been placed in public auction. In one form or another, cash sales were available throughout the entire nineteenth century.

A major change in United States land policy came in 1830 when squatters were given limited preemptive rights. The 1841 Preemptive Act fully established the right of a squatter on *surveyed* public land to have the first opportunity to purchase his land at $1.25 per acre. From 1853 to 1862 squatters were allowed to preempt on unsurveyed land first in California, then in Oregon, Washington, Kansas, Nebraska, and Minnesota. Finally, in 1862 they were given the right to preempt on all unsurveyed public lands.

The 1862 Homestead Act lowered the price of surveyed tracts of 160 acres or less to zero, contingent on a $10 entry fee, and five years of continuous residence on the property. The homestead could be preempted at $1.25 per acre after residing on the homestead for six months. The Homestead Act was followed by the Timber Culture Act (1873) which again transferred title to the settler at a zero price, provided 40 acres (later reduced to 10) of the quarter section were cultivated in trees. The Desert Land Act (1877) gave preferential treatment to settlers on the condition that the land be irrigated within three years. Two other homestead acts, in 1909 and 1916, raised the size of homesteads to 320 and then to 640 acres.

Perhaps the most interesting aspect of United States public land disposal was the progression of an allocation scheme based on price, to one based on "first come, first served." Anyone willing to argue that the homestead laws were misdirected or inefficient must contend with the fact that public lands were initially sold exclusively and that the homestead laws were extended over time, not repealed. It seems unlikely that, if land sales were the efficient allocation mechanism, that the federal government would have changed the law, and having changed it not repealed the law once it learned how "wasteful" it was.[10]

Testing the Theory of Homesteading

The Structure of Homesteading

By offering land on a first-come, first-served basis, the U.S. government effectively made the public lands a public domain. It appears that, in an effort to acquire the land, the land was cultivated too early, and its rents were dissipated.[11] Yet despite the appearance, the entire frontier was not cast into the realm of common property, and the policy of homesteading was not indiscriminately used. Not only did homesteading not have free rein, but the restrictions placed on it are consistent with the state *avoiding* large rent losses while at the same time trying to populate the West in the face of aggressors.

Not all land was available for homesteading. In the eight years after the passage of the Homestead Act, 127 million acres were granted to railroads and another 2 million for wagon roads and canals (Gates 1936). Aside from the land granted to the railroads, all land next to such grants could not be homesteaded and had to be purchased with cash. Further, homesteads that were within the limits of a railroad were restricted to 80 rather than 160 acres. A further 140 million acres of public land were granted to state governments to produce revenues or endowments for state institutions. Many of these lands were sold at public auction. Moreover, the cash sale system did not end entirely with the enactment of the Homestead Act, with 84 million acres available for sale in 1862 alone. After 1862, between 100–125 million acres of Indian reservation land were sold to white settlers. Marion Clawson (1970) claims that of the 1,031 billion acres of public land disposed of, 285 million acres went to homesteads, the rest went to states, railroads, and private claims. Thus even if homesteading totally dissipated the value of a given farm, since it was applied to only one-quarter of the available land, it could not have dissipated the entire value of the public land.

Of the land that was set aside for homesteading, there seems ample historical evidence to suggest that it was the least valued of the frontier land. By disallowing homesteads near railroads or on state land, the value of homesteads would have been lower than privately sold land.[12] As an Iowa pamphlet for private land sales pointed out: "Under the homestead law the settler must, in order to get a good location, go far out into the wild and unsettled districts, and for many years be deprived of school privileges, churches, mills, bridges, and in fact of all the advantages of society" (Gates 1936, 663). Thus, to the extent land rents were dissipated, the dissipation was limited to the lands with lower rents.[13] And to the extent the lands were located in hostile territory where the future ownership of the land was uncertain, the notion of dissipation is quite meaningless.[14]

Aside from the low price, the other distinctive feature of homesteading was the restrictions placed on the settlers. Homesteads were available only on surveyed lands of no more than 160 acres, and in order to obtain unconstrained ownership farmers were required to be in residence for five years and had to make improvements on the land. All of these requirements are consistent with the government using the settler to control hostile Indians. By using only surveyed land, territory was opened up on sections. Postponing entry would tend to increase the ultimate rush by raising the average value of the land. Surveying further increased the value by reducing the chance of border disputes with other settlers. In raising the value of the land, the government better assured that the bulk of allotments would be taken.[15] Restricting homesteads to surveyed lands also provided the state with the discretion over where to locate settlers. If the Northern Plains Indians were particularly hostile, then settlers could be directed there.[16] Further, restricting the plot size to 160 acres created a more dense population than under private sale since it is generally agreed that 160 acres was below the optimal size for a western farm. Finally, requiring residence maintains the initial population on the farm. In the face of threats by Indians, the army would have an easier time defending a contained, dense population compared to one sparsely distributed.[17]

The proposition that homesteading was used to populate the West in the face of simultaneous land claims further explains subsequent changes in land policy law. After the Homestead Act, a similar law, the Timber Culture Act of 1873, was passed. This act granted 160 acres to a farmer willing to cultivate 40 acres (later reduced in 1878 to 10 acres) of trees. There were 290,278 entries for over 43 million acres made under this act, and almost all were in Kansas, Nebraska, and the Dakota Territory (Gates 1968, 400). In 1877, Congress passed the Desert Land Act, which gave a settler the option to buy 640 acres if proof could be shown that irrigation had reclaimed the land. There were 159,704 claims made on over 32 million acres of desert land, most of which was in Nevada, Arizona, New Mexico, and California (Gates 1968, 402).

Both the Timber Culture Act and the Desert Land Act are generally criticized because only 25 to 30 percent of the entries were successful. Growing trees on the bad prairie and bringing water to parched lands was a costly affair, and no doubt an unconstrained farmer would use resources differently (Anderson and Hill 1975). Further, these acts were subject to a great deal of fraud (Libecap and Johnson 1979). Under the Timber Act, a settler could control his claim for thirteen years before it lapsed into nonfulfillment, at which time he could preempt or homestead, and all the while avoiding tax. The Desert Act was mostly used by cattlemen to acquire valuable water rights. In this context, Gates (1968, 401) states "that many could not have taken the obligations of the law seriously."

Despite the diversion of resources, the fraud, and the lack of completion, these acts did provide further incentives to occupy what was then enemy territory. During the latter half of the nineteenth century there were three major Indian wars: the Modoc wars (1872–1873) along the Nevada-California border; the Sioux wars (1854–1890) in the Dakota, Nebraska, Montana, and Wyoming territories; and the Apache wars (1881–1900) in Arizona and New Mexico. These wars saw such battles as the Little Bighorn and Wounded Knee, with leaders like Sitting Bull, Crazy Horse, and Geronimo. That their legend lives on is some evidence to the intensity of the times, and that the federal government applied special grants to these areas is evidence that homesteading was a method of enforcing white property rights in disputed territory.[18]

The final homestead acts of the early twentieth century raised the allowable homestead from 160 to 320 and then to 640 acres. Most historians agree with Clawson (1983, 23) when he says "[t]hese acreages were too small and came too late to meet the needs of ranchers trying to acquire native rangeland." They came too late because much of the land had been settled under the previous homestead law. As mentioned above, the 160-acre requirement was a binding constraint in the arid Midwest, but necessary to increase population density. With the easing of the Indian threat in the 1890s, it is consistent with the hypothesis here that the minimal homestead farm size be increased to accommodate more technically efficient farming practices.[19]

Five State Cases

Florida and Texas. From 1842 to 1862, the federal government passed several special donation acts whereby settlers of various areas were given tracts of land for free. It is clear that these grants were given where the Indian menace was greatest. The Armed Occupation Act of 1842 is the most obvious case of homesteading to induce settlement in the face of Indian problems. Spain had tried several times to place settlements in Florida, but failed for the most part because of the hostile Indians. The act of 1842 gave 160 acres to any man capable of bearing arms who was willing to move south of Gainesville and improve the land for five years. The policy was a success. Of the 200,000 acres allotted, 1,048 permits for 167,680 acres were taken up within two years (Gates 1968, 388).

Texas provides an even better example of a state using aggressive homesteading policies to help establish property rights over disputed territory.[20] Texas was originally a Spanish territory and became part of Mexico with that country's independence from Spain. Mexico, worried over the quick expansion by its northern neighbor, developed an *empresario* system whereby large grants were given to foreign citizens on the condition a given number of families be recruited to settle the area, make improvements, become Mexican citizens, and convert to Catholicism. For every family brought to the colony, the *empresario* was given title to various amounts of land within the colony. Steven Austin was greatly responsible for this system and was the first to act on it.[21] Others quickly followed, and soon the Anglo-American population outnumbered the Mexicans four-to-one, and they successfully ousted the Mexican authority in 1836 to form the Republic of Texas.

Texas now faced hostile Indians to the west, Mexicans to the south, and an expanding United States to the north. With a population less than 100,000, constant threats of Indian and Mexican raids, and a debt-ridden treasury, the republic's future was hardly secure. Historian Bobby D. Weaver (1985, 5) reports: "The Republic of Texas faced a major credit problem because it used its public lands and the integrity of the new nation for collateral. Yet, the value of the public lands remained limited because the republic seemed unable to protect itself." In the end, efforts to strengthen the new nation were insufficient, but it is worth examining land settlement methods when its future ownership had yet to be defined.

The Texas republic first passed three "headright" laws to attract new settlers. These laws granted free lots ranging from 640 to over 4,000 acres to any family head settling in Texas before several specified dates between 1837 and 1841. The settler, once certified, was free to stake out and settle anywhere in Texas, and quite naturally, given the threat of Comanche and Mexican raids in the West, most chose the eastern portions of the republic. The failure to occupy western and southern Texas, where the bulk of public lands existed, further tarnished the credibility of the young nation and exacerbated the problem of raising capital.[22]

In 1842 the Texas Congress granted President Houston the authority to enter *empresario* contracts. The first of these granted over 10 million acres along the northern Red River border to the Peters Colony, a consortium led by W. S. Peters. Under this contract, 200 colonists were to be settled within the region each year for three years. Each colonist would receive 640 acres from the *empresario*, although a charge of up to 320 acres could be levied for *empresario* expenses. Finally, the *empresario* received ten sections of land for every hundred heads of households and five sections for every hundred single men.

Like the U.S. Homestead Act, colonists were required to make improvements of the land, cultivate fifteen acres, and live on the property for three years before obtaining title (Weaver 1985, 21). In all, twelve land grants were issued. Seven of the smaller grants (600,000 to 3 million acres) were issued along the Rio Grande. The other five (including the 9 million acre Fisher-Miller grant) were issued along the western frontier. Together they formed a buffer against Texan enemies, and, although the president was required to grant land only in unsettled regions, their formation into a "front" is consistent with the hypothesis of this chapter.[23] Although more successful than the headright acts, the colonial efforts were viewed as largely unsuccessful.[24]

Perhaps the most interesting aspect of Texan land policy occurred after statehood in 1846. Because Texas entered the Union as a republic and not a territory, it has always maintained control over its public lands and their disposal and the federal government could never use Texan public lands the way it could in the other states. Therefore, it could not use them to complement military enforcement efforts, even though the responsibility for the sovereignty and defense of Texas against Mexicans and Indians resided solely with the federal government after 1846—not with Texas. No *empresario* grants were made after statehood, and no more free lands were given to settlers. The state made land grants to railroads and attempted minor efforts to sell public land, but certainly there was an absence of aggressive land disposal until 1873, and then only in the form of land sales (Connor 1971, 258). This sudden alteration in land policy is consistent with the theory of homesteading as a method of establishing property rights. Once the U.S. government took responsibility for protection, public lands in Texas ceased to be used for the purpose of mitigating military expenditures.[25, 26]

California, Utah, and Alaska. In populated states, the threat of raids by Indians was reduced. California and Utah, because of the gold rush and the establishment of the Mormon colony, needed no bounty to induce settlers. According to Paul Wallace Gates (1978, 8), "[T]he government's slowness in establishing [Californian] land offices, making appointments and surveying the public lands delayed for a decade the first opening of public lands to purchase and generally those first opened were remote, distant from settled areas, and, for the time, less attractive."

In 1857, President Buchanan ordered almost 44 million acres of public lands to the auction block, of which over 25 percent was in California. California was also given special advantages under the Morrill Land Grant Act of 1862 to convert 150,000 acres of agricultural land grants to private sales (Gates 1978, 14). In 1853, California became the first state where preemption was authorized on unsurveyed lands. In addition, individuals were allowed to preempt two claims in California rather than just one, as elsewhere. All of these measures increased the concentration of California land holdings and "marked a further reversal of the homestead principal with its generally understood corollary that public lands were to be reserved for settlers" (Gates 1978, 15).

Although the Mormon colony arrived in the Salt Lake Basin in 1847, it was offered no bounty or donation grants for future settlement and was without the benefit of a public land system or survey until 1869 (Gates 1978, 389). As a result, Utah ranged twenty-fourth out of thirty-one states in terms of the number of final homestead entries. There were 16,798 entries made in Utah compared with 107,618 in Colorado; 97,197 in South Dakota; 87,312 in New Mexico; and 67,315 in Wyoming (Gates 1978, 797). The fact that the federal government generally ignored the Utah Territory is often attributed to religious bigotry, but the hypothesis here suggests another explanation. The Mormons believed that the Indians were God's chosen people and part of a lost tribe of Israel called the Lamanites. The early Mormon settlers, although they appropriated land without payment, made it a practice to feed and clothe local Indians.[27] Conflicts over water rights and land claims arose and Mormons did kill Indians, but their behavior was a long way from the frontier creed that "the only good Indian is a dead Indian."

The Mormons may have respected Indians, but they took precautions against them as well. The homogeneity of the white settlers in Utah allowed them protective measures that would have been too costly for other individuals on the frontier.[28] First, Mormon communities were settled in fort-like arrangements with a wall around each village and with all males over eighteen members of the territorial militia. Second, only selected members of a village were allowed to trade with Indians. Third, each settlement had a tithing house, to which each member brought one-tenth of all production. From this community storehouse, "gifts" were given to local and visiting Indians. And finally, the Mormon women formed the Indian Relief Society, which made and helped distribute clothes and bedding to the natives (Arrington and Bitton 1979, 149). Brigham Young summarized his policy in an 1854 address to the Utah legislature:

I have uniformly pursued a friendly course of policy towards them [the Indians], feeling convinced that independent of the question of exercising humanity towards so degraded and ignorant a race of people, it was manifestly more economical and less expensive, to feed and clothe, than to fight them. (Arrington and Bitton 1979, 148)

The density of Mormon settlement may also have eased the establishment of property rights over Indian land. Although Utah contains 84,916 square miles, less than 3 percent of it is useful for settlement, and, of course, settlement took place in only a few key valleys. When the Mormons first arrived in the Salt Lake region, there were 148 families, but by 1877 their ranks swelled to 147,000 in 357 settlements. Despite their early small numbers, the practice of Mormon settlement increased the density of their settlements.

Some unique problems arose in Utah in connection with the government method of distribution of the land. . . . When the Mormons first arrived, the church fathers parceled out to each settler a small irrigable plot . . . later, when U.S. surveys were run . . . several of these early settlers were found living on one 160 acre tract. (Dick 1970, 152)

Alaska provides one final example of the federal government's reluctance to give away public lands when its jurisdiction is not threatened. Alaska was purchased from Russia in 1867. Initially, there were only 450 military personnel, and by 1900 there were still fewer than 30,000 white settlers—most of whom were involved in mining or the military. Settlers, compared to their southern counterparts, faced no Indian threat, not because there were no Indians, but because the small white population and the lack of land-intensive farming led to few simultaneous land claims. Consistent with the hypothesis of this chapter, there was no homesteading policy. In fact, in 1884 Congress passed a law stating that the land laws should *not* apply to Alaska (Gruening 1968, 325).

The story of land in Alaska is one of contrast between natural plenty and man-made restriction. . . . To start there was not in Alaska . . . a general pre-emptive law . . . an individual 'first come–first served' right to claim land. . . . In Alaska there was not merely *lack* of such law, but a definite prohibition. (Gruening 1968, 323)

The Effect of Population and Railroads

Simultaneous land claims by the federal government and Indian tribes led to no violence when there was no white settlement. Confrontations only arose when whites moved into an area and began to compete for the land with Indians. The more direct and intense this competition for land, the more violence that occurred, the more homesteading would be expected to be used relative to other methods of settlement to help establish the white settlers' claims to the land. Similarly, the introduction of railroads into new territory made patchwork of Indian lands and increased the level of violence. Again, homesteading would be expected to be positively correlated with railroad activity to counter the Indian reaction.

In order to test this hypothesis, I collected data on population, acres sold and homesteaded, the ratio of rural to urban settlers in a territory, and the ratio of public land sales to railroads, by state for the year 1880.[29] The sample consists of twenty-seven states and territories where homesteading was taking place. The chapter appendix presents the variable definitions. The ratio of acres homesteaded to acres sold to private interests is the dependent variable.[30]

Table 2.1

Ordinary Least Squares Regression Results*

Variable	Coefficient	*t*-Statistic	Predicted Sign
Population density	.082	2.07	+
Population squared	−.0013	−2.22	−
Rural/urban	.05	1.58	+
Rail/size	.15	4.54	+
Constant	.57	1.02	
$\overline{R}^2$	.55		
Sample size	27		

* Dependent variable is acres homesteaded/acres sold, 1880.
Sources: U.S. Bureau of the Census (1878–1900) and (1975); Donaldson (1884).

As settlers move into a region, conflicts arise, and, therefore, more homesteading relative to land sales are expected. As the population continues to increase, however, the sheer volume of people helps to enforce white claims to the land and the amount of homesteading relative to land sales should fall. Hence the coefficient for population density is predicted positive, but the coefficient for population density squared is predicted negative. The more rural a community, the more likely land disputes will occur. Since rural settlement is more sprawled and less dense than urban settlement, the chance of interfering with Indian claims is greater, and the ability to defend successfully lower for rural areas. Thus the chance of a confrontation is higher, and, therefore, more homesteading relative to land sales are predicted in the more rural western states. And finally, the more active railway development, the more interference Indians experience in their way of life, and the more likely disputes and, therefore, homesteading. Table 2.1

presents the results of an ordinary least squares regression where all signs are as predicted and all variables but rural/urban are significant at the 5 percent level.

The Role of Preemption

On the surface, one institutional feature appears inconsistent with the hypothesis presented here—preemption. Preemption allowed the first squatter the right of first refusal when federal lands were offered for sale. By allowing preemption, the United States federal government relaxed the restrictions on squatting. Moreover, throughout the first half of the nineteenth century the rights of squatters increased and, perhaps, culminated in 1862 with the right to settle on all unsurveyed land. If the state was interested in mitigating policing costs on the frontier, it seems inconsistent to allow squatters to forge ahead and settle on the locations of their choice. These scattered farmers caused frictions with Indians that interfered with the treaty process and would appear to have forced the troops to spread too thinly in their patrols.[31]

The first preemption act was passed in 1830 and required continual renewal by Congress. The most notable feature was that squatters only had preemptive rights on surveyed land. Even the Preemptive Act of 1841 required that the land be surveyed. As long as the land required a survey, preemption is consistent with the hypothesis of settlement used to mitigate state enforcement costs. Surveys restricted the areas that were open to settlement, and, if anyone settled on unsurveyed land, then the state had no obligation to protect them. The rise of preemption, then, was simply a precursor to the homestead movement. The state was encouraging settlement in areas where it wanted a better definition of property rights over land.

The problem with preemption is its applicability to unsurveyed lands. Once the federal government allowed squatting, it became obliged to protect the squatter, and, although squatters had private incentives to avoid clashes with Indians, since they used the government's threat of violence free of charge, the probability of disputes was higher than had they made completely private decisions. I conjecture that preemption was allowed because of the rising cost of surveys in Indian territory. Surveys were most useful when done ahead of settlement, and the first surveyors must have experienced countless natural dangers. However, surveying in a war zone would be next to impossible. Clawson (1970, 55–6) quotes the following from some 1854 surveyor field reports:

> On arriving in the field we found our work was immediately in the vicinity of headquarters of the hostile Indians and after skirmishing with us 2 days, they fired the prairies, completely demolishing everything for our cattle to subsist on for many miles, in fact the whole country lying between the Solomon and Republic Rivers, and we were forced to abandon our work.
>
> It is my duty to inform you that Messrs. Armstrong and McClure, deputy

surveyors, have arrived at Leavenworth bearing the information that while they were running the line of surveys their camp was attacked by a band of hostile Indians. They report that one of their assistants, A. H. Morgan by name, was instantly killed and that the Indians destroyed their wagons, tents, provisions, etc.

At this place a party of Indians fired on me and my men. Their design was to kill us; they had previously threatened to shoot me and my men if I did not quit surveying there. A shell struck a tree against which I was leaning at the time, while my compass needle was sitting not 6 inches from me.

Dick (1970, 26) states that, "[o]n August 19, 1871, E. C. Cunningham, the surveyor general for the Nebraska area, wrote to a member of Congress that except for the summer of 1870 there had not been a single season since 1863 during which the government surveyor had been allowed to do his work unmolested." The problems of harassment were, not so much in the loss of surveyors, but the fraud it encouraged. Dick (1970, 27–36) reports massive amounts of graft and poor quality work done by surveyors on the edge of the frontier.[32] Some lines were later found to be over five miles off, spans of up to thirty miles showed no signs of survey, and many settlers found themselves with homesteads of less than 100 acres. Preemption on unsurveyed lands, then, could be explained by the rise in the cost of survey. With no reliable survey, homesteading in very hostile areas could not be carried out, and preemption may have been a viable alternative to military action. Certainly consistent with this is the fact that the Preemption Act of 1841 was repealed in 1891 after the battle of Wounded Knee, which ended the Sioux wars, and after survey inspections became more common.[33, 34]

Canada and Australia

Unlike the United States, there were no Indian wars in Canadian history.[35] The establishment of the mounted police, the incentives of the Hudson's Bay Company to peacefully trade with Indians, and the British recognition of Indian rights all led to a relatively peaceful settlement of the Canadian prairies. There were also few squatters on public lands, which may also have reduced the likelihood of conflicts. And since the Canadian Pacific Railroad went ahead of most pioneers,[36] virtually all of the West was surveyed before settlement. The threat of sovereignty over the western provinces came, not from hostile natives, but the rapid expansion of United States settlement to the south. The Canadian government was not so much concerned with military clashes with American settlers as with simply losing jurisdiction by American occupation, as had happened with the Oregon territory. Thus on the Canadian frontier, homesteading as a method of mitigating military costs was never an issue. The major concern was simply to establish a Canadian presence in the West.[37] Although the Canadian system of homestead is almost identical to the American one, the minor differences reflect this difference in emphasis.

The Dominion Lands Act of 1872 established free homesteading on western public lands with exactly the same conditions found in the United States. Lots were 160 acres, there was a $10 registration fee, and a five-year residence requirement. Unlike the American law, however, settlers could reserve an adjoining quarter to be paid for by cash. In addition, all even-numbered quarters were subject to homesteading, and this included even-numbered quarters close to the railway. Finally, the entire Canadian frontier was opened at once, rather than in sections. All of these differences increased the value of a given quarter and, therefore, increased the incentive to rush the land. They also encouraged settlements that were less densely populated. This is also consistent with the Canadian need to simply establish settlers without regard to defending the settlements by force.[38]

Australia faced a much different set of constraints in its development when compared to the United States or Canada. Australia faced no threat from external powers and no serious internal threat from natives for the crown land. Australia to this day remains one of the least densely populated nations and one of the most urbanized, with 90 percent of its population living on 12 percent of its land mass. Settlement in Australia was never needed to quell internal struggles nor repel aggressive neighbors. Australia's land policies have reflected this. To begin with, since 1829, land policies related to disposal were under provincial discretion—there was no national public land policy. Second, although land grants were given to the first settlers for services rendered, Australia has never had a homestead policy and since 1825 has either sold or leased its public lands (Heathcote 1972).

Conclusion

Other things held constant, the better the defined property rights, the greater the gains from trade. In making this statement operational, however, one needs to know what the actual alternatives are facing decision makers. On the western frontier, the alternative was *not* to use public lands as a source of revenue but, rather, to forgo those lands to Mexicans, Indians, possibly Texans, or even the British, Spanish, or Russians.[39]

In this chapter, I have argued that homesteading was used to "rush" settlers to land where federal ownership (in an economic sense) was uncertain. Consistent with this hypothesis is the general structure of homesteading policies, their application in hostile parts of the country, their absence in Alaska, Maine, and Texas after annexation, their low profile in California and Utah, and their use and nonuse in Canada and Australia. The slow, but eventual, removing of homesteading and other costly disposal devices was not, as is often stated, the result of a change in attitude toward the public domain. Rather the more "economical" policies of public land management are possible because of the removal of simultaneous claims made on these lands. Conservation of public lands is only meaningful when access is closed. Given this, the policy of rushing settlers to limited parts of the territory to *establish* rights over the land cannot be viewed as inefficient. That it was costly there can be no doubt, but that it was not a perfect solution is irrelevant.

Notes

1. For formal models on the effect of homesteading, see Southey (1978); Anderson and Hill (1983); Stroup (1988); and Anderson and Hill (1990).
2. For example, Stroup (1988, 76) states: "The lessons for any future privatizing of land should be obvious. It is difficult to give away value systematically, since nonprice competition for the value, unlike competition in exchange (bidding, for example), will tend to waste resources up to, or even past the point where the waste is equivalent in value to the rents being sought."
3. To my knowledge, Yoram Barzel (1989) is the first person to suggest that homesteading was efficient and that the source of efficiency is savings in state enforcement costs. In what follows, I treat the U.S. government as a single decision-making agent. I do this in order to focus on why homesteading policies were successful, rather than examine why or how they came about.
4. Also interesting is that the price of homesteading was more intensive in some states than in others.
5. Property rights are defined as one's ability to exercise one's choice over the use of a good. In this case, they refer to the U.S. federal government's ability to exercise its authority over the public lands.
6. For examples of private incentives to form "governments" to enforce property rights, see Demsetz (1967); Johnsen (1986); Cheung (1970); Anderson and Hill (1975); and Umbeck (1981).
7. Expectations of high future returns on land generated incentives to defend it.
8. Throughout, "public lands" will refer to land legally owned by the federal government. "Public domain" will refer to the situation where the state is unable to control access to the public lands.
9. Under Indian customs, the tribe was not bound by any treaty signed by its chief, and the chief had little authority in stopping his warriors from breaking the contract. If the Indian chiefs could have controlled their tribes, and if the federal government had upheld their commitments, Indian land claims would be at least three times their current size.
10. One might argue that the practice of land sales was different from the policy itself and that homesteading laws were simply legalizing what was already happening, but this begs the question of why land sales were not better enforced.
11. One of the most dramatic examples of a "sooner" occurred at the "Oklahoma Opening." In 1889, a large area of what is now Oklahoma that had been reserved for Indians was opened up for white settlement. Thirty-six thousand potential settlers arrived days before the official opening, positioned themselves at a starting

line, and, at the sound of a gun, raced off to stake their claim, only to find that many "sooners" had beat them to it (Clawson 1970).

12. Gates (1936, 664) reports the average price per acre of privately sold land in Kansas was between $4.49 and $5.94 during the 1870s. Given that homestead land was available at this time, and could be commuted at $1.25, it seems reasonable to assume that the homestead land, at least at the margin, was of lower quality.

13. A point that is seldom mentioned is that the land is only dissipated by the marginal settler. To the extent the marginal and average settler are different, the entire value of homesteaded land is not dissipated.

14. Barzel (1989) makes this point; you cannot dissipate wealth that is not there to begin with.

15. With no restrictions on entry, settlers would arrive on the land at different intervals since settlers would have different expectations over the value of the land and the land was not of uniform quality.

16. This counters the exact opposite incentive of settlers to avoid hostile areas.

17. Settlers were required to make improvements to the land, which, since they would be sunk costs, gave each settler a disincentive to run when confronted by Indians.

18. Note that, if the government restricted homesteading just to these areas, homesteading gains elsewhere would have been lost. The Timber Culture Act and Desert Land Act created additional incentives to homestead hostile Indian country, without eliminating the incentive to populate the West in general.

19. In personal correspondence, professors Terry Anderson and David Friedman have asked why homesteading started in 1862 when Indian problems existed earlier and why it continued until 1934 when most of the threat was over by 1900. Of course, the model here is too general to suggest an exact starting and ending date, but at the risk of being ad hoc I offer the following speculations. Compared with later settlements in the West, Indian skirmishes east of the Mississippi were relatively minor. This is likely because Indians initially moved West as their former territory was settled. Only when settlers began crowding the Indians did war break out. An explanation of the ending date seems more troublesome. Perhaps, as Friedman has pointed out, by the time the Indian threat was gone, homesteading had developed a political constituency that was able to maintain it for another few decades.

20. The major reference for this section is Connor (1971).

21. Ironically, most grants were given to Americans, which likely explains the Mexican failure to establish property rights over Texas. Had the U.S. government granted most homesteads to Indians or Mexicans, a United States map might look very different today.

22. Unlike the United States, the Texan government never took the initiative to survey the land. Even the large *empresario* grants were poorly laid out, and this resulted in several costly border disputes. The inability to raise capital is the likely cause for the lack of public surveying, and, as a result, homestead policies failed.

23. For example, the land grants could have been issued in one major clump, which would have lowered the costs of servicing the colonies.

24. Although most of the grants completed their quotas, none did so on time. Further, Connor (1971) estimates that perhaps as many as two-thirds of the colonists abandoned their homesteads and headed to safer territory in eastern Texas. Both homesteading attempts seemed to have failed because they did not encourage a dense settlement rush to one area. The headright acts allowed relatively large settlements anywhere in Texas, while the colonial efforts inhibited rushing since settlers were required to go through the *empresario*.

25. One cannot make the claim that disputes over Texan land ceased with annexation. Texas sold over 76 million acres to the U.S. government that later became parts of Kansas, New Mexico, Colorado, Wyoming, and Oklahoma. Of course, the U.S. government maintained homesteading policies on these lands (Martin 1938).

26. Maine purchased its land from Massachusetts and so, like Texas, was responsible for public land disposal. Maine faced no threat of losing its land to an enemy, and although its land was cheap (selling for an average of $.35 per acre), credit was accepted, and one could even pay for the land in "road service." Maine never had a homesteading policy. See Smith (1969).

27. To the extent Mormon life raised a settler's marginal product in domestic production, it also raised the cost of violence, hence the tribute.

28. At the time of Utah's entrance into the union, there were over 200,000 white settlers, of which close to 99 percent were Mormon.

29. The year 1880 was the earliest I could find data on *all* of the variables needed.

30. This ratio is used rather than the level in order to measure the intensity of homesteading and also to avoid the problem of different-sized states.

31. The evidence is mixed on the government's record of defending squatters. Squatters were assisted by the army, but it appears the army did not go out of its way to do so.

32. Surveyors simply took an oath that the work would be completed properly. Inspections were usually done well after the work was finished and were instigated more by complaints rather than as a matter of routine.

33. There are no data on the amount of preemption that actually took place since all grants were recorded as cash sales.

34. Canada never had preemptive rights for squatters. There was no Indian threat, and surveys were done along with construction of the Canadian Pacific Railroad, thus the incentive and ability to cheat for Canadian surveyors was reduced.

35. This section is based mostly on Martin (1938).

36. The rugged Canadian shield of northern Ontario was all but impenetrable for settlers to manage on their own.

37. The Philippine experience was similar to the Canadian one in this respect. To stave off the settlement of American and Japanese sugar farmers, the Philippine colonial government passed a homestead act in 1903. Between 1903 and 1935 over 212,000 homestead applications were made. See Pelzer (1945).

38. It might appear that a better plan would have entailed homesteading only along the border. Border areas were settled first, however, because of climate and terrain conditions. Restricting homesteading to the border would also have allowed for the possibility of American squatters north of Canadian settlements. Once surrounded by Americans, Canadian control of the prairies might have been jeopardized.

39. The Russians, of course, owned Alaska but also had settlements in northern California until 1840.

Appendix

Definition of Variables

Dependent variable	=	Number of acres homesteaded in a state in 1880 divided by the number of acres sold to private individuals in that state in 1880.
Population density	=	1880 population of the state or territory per square mile.
Population squared	=	Population density squared.
Rural/urban	=	Ratio of rural settlers to urban ones.
Rail/size	=	Ratio of acres sold to railroads in 1880 to size of the state or territory in acres.

References

Anderson, Terry L., and Peter J. Hill. 1975. The evolution of property rights: A study of the American West. *Journal of Law and Economics* 18(1): 163–79.

———. 1983. Privatizing the commons: An improvement? *Southern Economic Journal* 50(2): 438–50.

———. 1990. The race for property rights. *Journal of Law and Economics* 33 (April): 177–97. Reprinted this volume.

Arrington, Leonard, and Davis Bitton. 1979. *The Mormon experience: A history of the Latter-Day Saints.* New York: Random House.

Barzel, Yoram. 1989. *Economic analysis of property rights.* Cambridge: Cambridge University Press.

Cheung, Steven N. S. 1970. The structure of a contract and the theory of a non-exclusive resource. *Journal of Law and Economics* 13 (April): 49–70.

Clawson, Marion. 1970. *Uncle Sam's acres.* Westport, CT: Greenwood Press.

———. 1983. *The federal lands revisited.* Washington, DC: Resources for the Future.

Connor, Seymour. 1971. *Texas: A history.* New York: Macmillan Publishing Co.

Demsetz, Harold. 1967. Toward a theory of property rights. *American Economic Review* 57 (May): 347–59.

Dick, Everett. 1970. *The lure of the land.* Lincoln: University of Nebraska Press.

Dillon, Richard H. 1984. *Indian wars: 1850-1890.* New York: Park South Books.

Donaldson, Thomas. 1884. *The public domain, its history, with statistics.* Johnson Reprint Corp.

Gates, Paul Wallace. 1936. The homestead law in an incongruous land system. *The American Historical Review* 41(4): 652–81.

———. 1968. *History of public land law development.* Washington, DC: U.S. Public Land Law Review Commission.

———. 1978. California land policy and its historical context: The Henry George Era. In *Four persistent issues,* edited by Paul W. Gates. Berkeley: Institute of Governmental Studies, University of California.

Gruening, Earnest. 1968. *The state of Alaska.* New York: Random House.

Heathcote, R. L. 1972. The evaluation of Australian pastoral land tenures: An example of challenge and response in resource development. In *Frontier settlement,* edited by R. Ironside, V. Proudfoot, E. Shannon, and C. Tracie. Alberta: Dept. of Geography, University of Alberta.

Johnsen, D. Bruce. 1986. The formation and protection of property rights among the Southern Kwakiutl Indians. *The Journal of Legal Studies* 15(1): 41–68.

Libecap, Gary D., and Ronald N. Johnson. 1979. Property rights, nineteenth-century federal timber policy and the conservation movement. *Journal of Economic History* 39(1): 129–42.

Martin, Chester B. 1938. Dominion lands policy. In *Canadian frontiers of settlement,* edited by W. Mackintosh and W. George. New York: Macmillan Publishing Co.

Pelzer, Karl. 1945. *Pioneer settlement in the Asiatic Tropics.* New York: American Geographical Society.

Smith, David C. 1969. Maine and its public domain. In *The frontier in American development,* edited by David Ellis. New York: Cornell University Press.

Southey, Clive. 1978. The staple thesis, common property, and homesteading. *Canadian Journal of Economics* 11(3): 547–59.

Stroup, Richard L. 1988. Buying misery with federal land. *Public Choice* 57: 69–77.

Umbeck, John R. 1981. Might makes rights: A theory of the formation and initial distribution of property rights. *Economic Inquiry* 19(1): 38–59.

U.S. Bureau of the Census. 1878–1900. *Statistical abstract of the United States.* Various issues. Washington, DC.

———. 1975. *Historical statistics of the United States: Colonial times to 1970.* Part 1. New York: Basic Books.

Weaver, Bobby D. 1985. *Castro's colony: Empresario development in Texas, 1842-1865.* College Station: Texas A&M University Press.

3

When Common Property Rights Can Be Optimal: Nineteenth Century Cattle Grazing in the Semiarid American West

Nicolas Sanchez and Jeffrey B. Nugent

Existing analyses of the American West have given due attention to externality problems arising in the use of land and other natural resources of the region. They have, however, focused almost exclusively on a single form and source of externality, namely that arising in open access to such resources. In such a context, each resource user disregards the negative externality of his (her) use on other users, thereby inducing overuse of the resource and leading to the well-known tragedy of the commons.

Natural resource theorists (e.g., Dasgupta and Heal 1979) and property rights theorists (Furubotn 1985; Barzel 1989) alike make it quite clear that, in principle, the externality problem can be overcome by the creation and enforcement of either private or common property rights.[1] They also point out that the practical choice between these alternative property rights regimes should depend on both equity and transaction cost considerations.

Economic historians of the American West, however, have generally attributed the very considerable problems and inefficiencies observed in the use of the natural resources of the region to the failure to establish private property rights.[2] While this begs the question of why common property rights typically emerged prior to private property in much of the region, it has generally been argued (Dennen 1975 and 1976; Anderson and Hill 1975 and 1983; Libecap 1981b) that this was due to the then prevailing constraints on the creation and enforcement of private property rights there, such as the artificially high price and low maximum size limitations imposed by the government on the sale of public land.[3] Common property rights were but a second-best solution. This argument seems to have been accepted in the latest reviews of this literature (Barzel 1989; Eggertsson 1990).

The purpose of the present paper is to argue that common property rights need not have been only a second-best property rights arrangement in the context of animal husbandry activities in the arid and semiarid regions (ASARs) of the American West in much of the nineteenth century. This is because, in such a context and with the technology available, other externalities were present which gave rise to very substantial transaction costs. The use of common property rights allowed these externalities to be internalized more easily, thereby saving on these transaction costs. As evidence in support of our argument, we show that common property rights were chosen with considerable success even when and where the aforementioned constraints on the emergence of private property rights were absent.

The presentation of the paper is as follows: A simple theoretical demonstration of the optimality of common property rights in ASARs is presented first. Then, we identify the specific technology used in cattle raising, and the way in which common property rights were established and enforced in the American West of the 19th century. The third section presents evidence on property rights regime choices in Texas, California, and other regions where, because of the earlier distribution of very large private land grants by Spanish and Mexican rulers and nonapplicability of American law, the artificially low maximum acreage limitations and artificially high minimum price on land sales were not operative. If common property rights were only second-best to private property, one would not have expected them to be as prominent there as elsewhere. Yet, in fact, they were at least as common in these regions as in the other Western states. The last section provides a summary and the main conclusions.

Theory

In this section we present a stylized model that explains the economic logic of communal institutions in ASARs.[4] Consider the case of an ASAR like much of the American West characterized by:

   a. significant local variability in rainfall,
   b. poor and arid soils generally well-suited only to husbandry (primarily grazing by cattle), with agricultural production (crops and hay) being limited to a few of the more well-watered parts of the region,
   c. the resulting lack of trees and other vegetation making fencing costs extremely high,

d. low population density and the absence of human settlement,
e. the virtual absence of formal law and order and hence vulnerability to animal theft,[5]
f. many dangers to the life and health of cattle (ranging from disease and collision with railroad trains[6] to prairie fires, drought, and winter blizzards),
g. difficulties in gaining access to markets for their animals,[7]
h. potentially high capital and transaction costs of having both to traverse, and to gain access to, land that is far from home, and
i. because of the high cost of fencing, the high cost of keeping the animals of different breeds and/or owners apart, and away from the reach of predatory animals and poisonous plants.

Suppose that the first settlers to the region encounter no regulations or restrictions on resource use. As a result, they would begin to treat the region as an open access area amenable to both grazing and agricultural activities. Eventually, as more settlers are attracted to the region, the absence of regulations and well defined rights would give rise to severe conflicts among the settlers. On the one hand, animals would trespass and destroy the areas devoted to agriculture. On the other, settled stock owners, unable to prevent outsiders from using their pastures, would have the incentive to make excessive use of the land. In short, the region would begin to experience overcrowding, overuse, and reduced yields.

Assume that most settlers to the region had come from the eastern part of the U.S. where private property rights were not only the rule but also had proved to be both allocatively and dynamically efficient (North and Rutten 1987; Anderson 1987; North 1990). Suppose also that, being inculcated by both the Jeffersonian ideal of the wide dispersal of small, private farms, and the frontiersman's desire for rugged independence, the settlers would agree to subdivide the open access area into lots, the stock owners receiving larger lots of lower quality and the farmers smaller ones of higher quality.

Nevertheless, because of conditions (c), (e), (f), (h), and (i) above, the transaction costs of separating the animals of the different owners, and of keeping the animals off the crops and the intruders out would be extremely high. These problems would be compounded by the high variability of rain and temperature and by the generally poor quality of the soils,[8] implying that all settlers would be vulnerable to substantial risks of drought-induced production failure.

Farmers among the settlers might be able to reduce their risks by subdividing their land holdings and then mutually exchanging the parcels so as to achieve diversification of their land holdings.[9] Although subdivision and diversification would introduce higher transport costs, for want of better ways of reducing risks, the farmers might be willing to accept them.

In the case of animal herds, however, not only can the herds be decimated by prolonged droughts but, once decimated, the time required for returning to pre-drought levels is generally much longer than for crops. As a result, the production risks in animal husbandry are even greater than those in agriculture.[10] Since stock raising is more land-intensive and subject to economies of scale in animal supervision, the use of the agriculturalists' strategy of reducing production risks through parcel diversification would be prohibitively costly. Moreover, since the need to move the animals from one nonadjacent parcel to another would almost inevitably damage the pastures or crops of other parcel owners, when applied to animal husbandry, parcel diversification would likely exacerbate the conflicts among the various settlers (Nugent and Sanchez 1989).

Suppose instead that there is an alternative production technology based on letting the animals (cattle) roam and then periodically collecting them (in a roundup), separating them into the herds of different owners, and then either selling them or letting them grow more. Suppose also that there are substantial economies of scale not only in these operations but also in the provision of security against animal theft, and that these are largely external to the individual herdsman.[11] Because of the local variability of rainfall, it is beneficial for the cattle to roam rather far so as to be able to find the pasture and water needed for survival.[12] As a result, roundups and security operations undertaken by a single herdsman-rancher would be less effective than ones undertaken jointly by a group of ranchers. For all of these reasons, the total costs of production and transactions in husbandry could be reduced significantly by engaging in some husbandry activities collectively in large scale.

Faced with this situation, the owners or controllers of various individual lots could increase the total value of their productive activities and in the process lower their production risks by pooling their land in such a way that each member of the pool would have the right to take his or her animals anywhere within the pool.[13] Such an arrangement would not only allow for economies of scale in production to be reaped but also reduce the transaction costs of security, monitoring, insurance, and other services.

An agreement to pool their grazing land and to engage in some joint production activities like roundups would by no means imply open access (the absence of property rights).[14] Moreover, it need not even imply that all members of the pool always have the right to take their animals everywhere in the pooled area. For example, rights of access to some parts of the pooled area during certain periods of time could be prohibited for conservation purposes. In any case, common property rights might be easier to monitor and enforce, and therefore be better monitored and enforced, than individual property rights. As a result, a move from individual to common property rights could be expected to lower the transaction costs of property rights enforcement, internalize technological and other externalities, and increase the carrying capacity of the range (less pasture being wasted on animals who would subsequently die prematurely).

Admittedly, not all husbandry activities would be subject to such external economies of scale. For example, breeding, caring for calves, and milking activities are ones in which individual ownership of land on a relatively small scale can be transaction cost-reducing. Likewise, large scale of operations, cooperation, and common ownership would not be required for raising cattle either outside of ASARs or in ASARs where it would pay to bring feed and water to the animals (as in modern feedlots) or for raising sheep, other animals, and even certain breeds of cattle which need more guidance by herders to get to pasture and water.

The model would predict, therefore, that some husbandry activities in ASARs under the technological and environmental conditions of the nineteenth century American West would benefit from the use of common property rights in land but private property rights in animals. But other husbandry activities, such as dairying (in which animal movement has a harmful effect on milk production), intensive cattle feeding, and sheep raising would not benefit from the economies of scale and the use of common property rights. By virtue of the private ownership of animals, each owner would have both the right and incentive to make his or her individually optimal microeconomic decisions on when, where, and how much to sell, and on reinvestment, animal care, etc.

Eventually, however, even those ASARs characterized by the aforementioned conditions in which cattle pools and common property were optimal might be expected to change. For example, there might occur technological developments, such as the invention of barbed wire (greatly reducing the costs of fencing) and new higher valued breeds of cattle (which would benefit from more sedentary conditions and more supervision than the hardy cattle mixed with Texan longhorns for which the free-roaming technology was well suited). Indeed, the settlements might be expected to reach a higher stage of development in which capital would become more available, land more crowded, underground water more accessible (thus making agriculture more competitive with husbandry), and state-supplied security and other services more reliable. Quite naturally, such changes would tend to undermine the advantages of both husbandry over agricultural activities and the scale economy externalities associated with husbandry activities undertaken with common property rights. In other words, with conditions (a)–(i) fulfilled, common property rights in some of the grazing land would likely be optimal but, when not fulfilled, private property rights would generally be optimal.

Cattle Pools in the American West

The purpose of this and the following sections is to demonstrate that the generally thin settlements of the ASARs of the American West and the technology of cattle raising prior to the late 1880s conformed to the conditions identified in the previous section as ones in which common property rights would be optimal. After the 1880s, however, these conditions were no longer generally fulfilled and hence private property rights became optimal.[15]

In this section the focus is on those parts of the West in which the aforementioned restrictions on the transfer of land from the U.S. government to private hands applied. The applicability to the West of the various conditions identified above for common property rights and collective action via cattle pools to be advantageous has already been demonstrated in the notes to the text of the previous section. While the existing literature has acknowledged some (but not all) of the advantages of such pools and their existence, it has attributed them to the inappropriate (for western conditions) restrictions on land transfer in the Land Act of 1796 and the Homestead Act of 1862.[16] In other words, according to conventional wisdom, common property arrangements existed only because the optimal private property rights were ruled out by legal restrictions. We deny neither the inappropriateness nor the existence of these restrictions for western conditions but contend that their importance has been greatly exaggerated. This is because from rather early times there existed, even in those parts of the West where these restrictions were in force, alternative means of obtaining private ownership of land in larger parcels and at more realistic prices than from the government under the aforementioned regulations.

One such means of obtaining land (via rental or purchase) in large blocs was from the huge grants of land that had been made to the states and their school districts upon statehood by the federal government. Another was from the huge grants of land the railroads had received from the government as an incentive for railroad construction (Gates 1968). Notably, land from such sources was generally available for rental or sale without artificial price floors or size ceilings.[17] Also, some of the land on large Indian reservations was available for lease by ranchers, at least prior to their being declared illegal by President Harrison in 1889.[18] Finally, large land parcels could be put together by large cattle owners by encouraging each of their several hired hands to file for homestead parcels, and then subsequently taking them back under their ownership in return for an appreciable reward.[19]

Despite the ability to obtain large parcels of land under private ownership in any of these ways, it is generally acknowledged that, at least prior to the 1890s,[20] the most common arrangement was common property rights largely on the public domain. While these rights were never officially recognized by the federal government, they were so recognized by the cattle owners and even state governments. Typically, these common property arrangements were accomplished by several individual ranchers homesteading on small parcels with water and then claiming in the name of their cattle pool vast amounts of drier, but nevertheless usable, land on adjoining public domain.

Regardless of the means of creating the common property rights, in order to avoid degeneration into open access and hence the tragedy of the commons, two conditions had to be satisfied. These were: (1) the exclusion of nonmembers of the cattle pool from the range claimed by the pool, and (2) "stinting" on, or regulating, the use of the range by members of the pool. How were these conditions satisfied?

The exclusion of nonmembers from common property land was accomplished in a variety of ways. In the early period with much empty (unclaimed) range, one only needed to circulate the claim that range was already fully stocked and that additional entrants would not be welcomed. Given access to low cost alternative pastures, few cattle owners would be interested in challenging such claims, especially since failure to respect such claims would undermine the validity of their own range claims. A second (though illegal) method was to post "no trespassing" signs, if necessary threatening also the use of firearms (Pelzer 1936, 213; Osgood 1929; Goff and McCaffree 1967).

A more common and effective means of limiting access was by excluding nonpool members from roundups. Given the prevailing technology in which the cattle were allowed to roam freely with virtually no supervision, roundups were the means of locating one's cattle. Given the large size and openness of the utilized range, exclusion from the roundup effectively meant that one's own stock could be confiscated by others or that one would have to engage in costly activities by oneself. Hence, the simple exclusion of nonmembers from the roundup was indeed a powerful sanction on the encroachment of pooled land by nonmembers.[21] Since (as mentioned above) in many cases pool members had private property rights over the small but valuable land parcels controlling access to permanent water sources, such as rivers, streams, and lakes, within the common range, the cattle of nonmembers of the pool could legally be denied access to such sources. Without access to water, a necessary complement to pasture, there would be little reason for nonmembers to seek access (even if it were their right) to the (generally waterless) adjacent range.[22]

Stinting was also carried out relatively easily. In this case, it was done by linking (a) the share of each member's maximum herd size in the overall carrying capacity of the range (itself varying with the weather and other conditions) to (b) the proportion of the permanent water sources in the pooled range owned by the individual member (Frink, Jackson, and Spring 1956, 88; Dennen 1975 and 1976; Dary 1981, 141; Libecap 1981b, 16). Naturally, this rule would be vulnerable to some free riding. But, since there were generally but few participants in the pool, the number of cattle belonging to each was observable, and any excess numbers were always marketable, neither the ability nor the incentive to free ride on the restrictions was very substantial.

Frequently, because of seasonal changes in temperature, rainfall, and wind conditions, the cattle used different ranges during different seasons. Naturally, this would provide opportunistic members and nonmembers with an incentive to put their cattle on a seasonal range ahead of that of others. In order to control this form of opportunistic behavior, the members of different pools would cooperate (often through their regional and state cattle associations) in designating the starting date for grazing in a particular seasonal grazing area, requiring all members to participate in large-scale general roundups held immediately prior to the change of grazing areas and imposing severe penalties on any member or nonmember caught using the area prior to the designated date (Briggs 1934).

Naturally, if the pools and associations were unsuccessful in limiting use by others, the present value of the rent streams derived from the customary range rights would be zero (Bromley 1989 and 1991). Evidence of the success of the cattle pools and associations in this respect is thus reflected in the generally quite remunerative values of such range rights (Dennen 1975).[23] The accepted practice of such transfers was to sell the private property of waterfront land along with the customary rights over the associated range (even though the latter was still legally in the public domain). The marketability of such rights demonstrated their widespread recognition.[24] Moreover, it was also the common practice of the stockholding companies formed in the 1880s to include the value of customary range rights among their assets in their reports to stockholders (Dennen 1975).[25]

Quite obviously, the protection of their common property rights in land would be neither feasible nor necessary if the private property rights in animals could not be protected. As noted above, in the absence of both law and order and a more dense population, this was in general no easy task. Although the threat of cattle theft was ever-present, due to economies of scale in the provision of security and its collective provision by the cattle pools and associations, for the most part this type of opportunistic behavior was controlled to a degree sufficient to make investments in cattle highly profitable.

The creation and maintenance of private property rights in animals required the ability to distinguish the animals of different owners. This was done by (1) requiring all animals to be branded and the brands registered,[26] (2) exercising control over the animals' reproductive rights,[27] (3) tightly regulating the time and manner of branding,[28] and (4) engaging in various activities designed to minimize the incidence of theft.[29]

Still other collective activities complementary to the maintenance of common property rights were: (prior to the railroads) organizing cattle drives (and cattle trails) for getting the cattle to markets, (after railroads) reducing railroad freight rates, penalizing countries for imposing import duties on U.S. meat (Burmeister 1956, 144), establishing a means of compensating herd owners for cattle killed by passing trains in unfenced lands (Peake 1937), introducing quarantine areas and veterinary services to limit the spread of cattle disease from migrating cattle (Fletcher 1960),[30] and offering bounties encouraging the control of beasts of prey (especially wolves), poisonous plants, cattle thieves, and arsonists (Fletcher 1960).[31]

To enforce common property rights and expedite these other collective activities, it was important to keep the internal transaction (governance) costs of the pools and associations to a minimum. One important means of doing so was by inculcating certain social norms among pool members. Studies of cattlemen emphasize the importance of conforming to a code of behavior in order to command the respect of one's fellow members and to attain positions of leadership. The code of behavior was multifaceted and applied even to dress; outsiders like Easterners were open to public ridicule and socially ostracized for their nonconformity. Norm maintenance was facilitated by the fact that memberships in these associations were generally for life (Cox 1895; Webb 1931; Pelzer 1936; Peake 1937; Texas State Historical Association 1991).

Quite naturally, the extent of the external economies of scale in husbandry varied with environmental conditions, such as the proximity and frequency of areas well-suited to agriculture, local variability of rainfall, and the relative importance of threats to law and order. As a result, the optimal size of the cattle pools and associations would vary. It is important to realize, however, that the optimal and actual sizes of the cattle pools could be extremely large. For example, throughout most of the 1880s the roundups, security functions, and other functions of the cattle pools of Wyoming were operated jointly by a single association covering virtually all the two million cattle in Wyoming and even several hundred thousand head of cattle in neighboring states. Moreover, the winter of 1886–87 was sufficiently severe to prompt the cattlemen of that region to extend their collective activities to an even larger scale. In particular, in 1887 they formed a national pool known as the American Cattle Trust with headquarters in New York. Although overly ambitious and hence short-lived, this trust (among other things) was designed to take advantage of economies of scale in handling, feeding, and selling and to assure that not all ranges would suffer from the ravages of bad weather during the same season (the whole state of Wyoming having been devastated by the winter of 1886–87). Moreover, the diaries of the key leaders of this scheme make clear that the (external) economies of scale emphasized in this paper were well recognized by them and a major motive for their actions (Larson 1942; Gressley 1961).

The importance of the cattle pools and associations and state regulations over roundup districts cannot be overestimated. For instance, besides the cases of Wyoming (discussed above) and Texas (discussed below), in Colorado as late as 1883, nine-tenths of the cattle in the state grazed on the public domain via such arrangements (Frink, Jackson, and Spring 1956, 79) rather than on private farms, and cattle raising was the leading industry. Thus, this institutional framework contributed to the success not only of the cattle industry itself but also to economic development throughout the Great Plains and western prairies. The cattle pools and associations came into being to produce certain public goods and to solve the various externalities problems faced by cattle owners. These problems would have existed even if the bulk of the land had been privately owned. Indeed, as suggested above, in many respects, private ownership with no trespassing rules would have made matters worse rather than better.

Consistent with the speculations presented at the end of the previous section, beginning in the middle and late 1880s various environmental conditions changed in such a way as to undermine the incentives supporting the cooperative activities among cattlemen in general and common property rights in particular. The fact that these changes all occurred at more or less the same time in the late 1880s no doubt contributed greatly to the eclipse of common property rights, cattle pools, and their various collective activities at that time. Indeed, since there was no appreciable change in the legal restrictions on private property during these years but the environmental conditions did change, this experience strongly favors our thesis that the property rights were chosen so as to fit the relevant environmental conditions over its more popular rival, the legal restrictions (second-best) explanation.

Among the more important of these changes were:

1. The very success of cattle pools in husbandry activities, especially with the high meat prices of the early 1880s which attracted so many to the industry as to render no longer feasible the aforementioned low cost means of excluding nonmembers from the generally accepted, though extra-legal, shared ranges.

2. The expansion of railroads reduced the need for long distance cattle drives and improved the marketability of agricultural products, thereby making agriculture more competitive with husbandry.

3. The development and spread of barbed wire for fencing (McCallum 1965) reduced the transaction costs of exclusion, hence decreasing the transaction cost advantage of common over private property rights (Field 1989). This change also reduced the cost of separating animals of different breeds, thereby encouraging investments in breed improvement and the substitution of the higher valued but more fragile Eastern breeds for the lower valued but more physically robust Texas or Spanish cattle.

4. The development and spread of windmills on the Great Plains greatly increased the returns to creating private rights in land, thereby undermining the advantage of cattle raising via cattle pools and common property (Baker 1989).

5. The penetration of sheep into "cattle kingdom" had a profound effect on the viability of the cattle pools and their collective activities in that existing cattle pools found themselves unable to enforce their rules over the sheepmen (Osgood 1929, 189).[32] Sheep required constant supervision and thus joint roundups were not used. Neither were sheep belonging to several owners trailed to market together. Thus several of the activities of cooperative production which served as enforcement mechanisms in cattle production were lost when sheep entered the picture.

It should also be considered that in relatively isolated areas not seriously affected by the aforementioned environmental changes, cattle pools and associations continued to survive. For example, Peake (1937, 86) reported that in the 1930s cattle were run in the national forests of Colorado in pools large enough that "not infrequently one or two riders were able to care for the stock of as many as fifty members."

Evidence of Cattle Pools and Common Property Arrangements

In this section, we turn to the property rights and cattle pools in those areas of the American West where the aforementioned price floors and size-of-holding ceilings on land acquisition were not operative, or at least not to the same extent as elsewhere. While there are other cases, our survey concentrates on Texas, California, and a few other states.

Texas

The experience of Texas is probably as important and instructive as all the other states and territories put together. Among the reasons for this are its huge size,[33] its long and varied historical experience,[34] its remarkably diverse climate and natural resource endowment, and that it served as the launching pad for the spread of the industry throughout the West.

With respect to land, many large land grants were made to private individuals by the Spanish, Mexican, Republic of Texas, and finally State of Texas governments. Many of these individual grants were very large. Indeed, the Spanish grants ranged up to 10 million acres apiece and, even during its short existence, the Republic of Texas made private grants amounting to more than 42 million acres (Lang 1932, 243). The State of Texas was also a major grantor of land to private parties, the sizes of those grants ranging up to three million acres. At independence every married resident of Texas was granted 4,605 acres of land and immigrants were sometimes granted more (Lang 1932). Even these more modest grants were over thirty times the size of the parcels that could be obtained under the Homestead Act.

After its annexation to the United States, Texas was allowed to retain its heritage of Spanish custom and law, especially with respect to land. Hence, most of the land remained in large private blocs despite the bias in U.S. law toward homesteading and small family farming. Notably also, despite the existence of large private landholdings, at least since 1574 the cattle industry featured cooperative institutions like the common range and roundups throughout not only Texas but also the rest of the Spanish dependency in North America (Dusenberry 1963).[35]

Although these institutions were originally brought to the New World by the Spanish crown, by the time of the Republic of Texas in the 1830s and 1840s, the number of Spanish-Mexicans in the Republic was relatively small. Since some large land grants in Texas had been to Americans and the inflow of Americans was even greater during the Republic, the continuing pervasiveness of roundups and cattle pools in the region cannot be ascribed simply to their original importation by the Spaniards. Given the leadership exerted by Anglo-Americans (who had not had prior experience with such institutions) after annexation by the United States, it seems likely that the traditional collective practices that they came to adopt in the period 1850–1890 were freely chosen. Judging from Dobie (1943), based as it was on a contemporary account, even as late as 1874 Texan cattle owners who had come from the East were still only gradually gravitating to these arrangements.

The single most important event in the evolution of institutional arrangements in Texas and subsequently throughout the West was the Civil War. In the 1850s there had been a gradual build-up of cattle stock in Texas territory. With the outbreak of the Civil War in 1860, however, Texan males were sent off to defend the Confederacy's eastern front, leaving the region's already sizeable cattle stock almost entirely unattended. The blockade of Texan and other Southern ports including New Orleans, heretofore the major market for Texan cattle, moreover, reduced the prices of such cattle during the war to almost nothing, thereby severely discouraging the industry's development. When the soldiers returned from the war in the mid-1860s (along with many other Southerners desiring to move west), however, they found that the (by that time) rather wild cattle stock had grown at a spectacular rate all by itself. This clearly demonstrated the advantages of the open range system in which cattle would be allowed to roam freely with little supervision.[36]

Several other conditions of post-Civil War Texas gave a tremendous boost to the cattle industry, to the cattle pools and associations, and to the roundups and various other collective activities that they undertook. Among the more important of these were lack of security,[37] instability of weather conditions in the years immediately following the war (Cox 1895; Dobie 1943), and the need to find new outside markets for the greatly expanded herds and to create trails to those markets.[38] Often, these trails passed through territory occupied by yet unsubdued Indian tribes, thus adding significantly to the already severe security problem. At other times, they passed through narrow mountain passes and across not easily fordable rivers, or over barriers imposed at border crossings by local residents opposed to the passage of Texan cattle,[39] thereby posing further challenges to the cowboys steering the excitable cattle.

These challenges were more formidable than elsewhere and could not be successfully met by individual animal owners, implying that collective action in the form of cattle pools and associations was necessary for success. Not surprisingly, therefore, these pools and associations started earlier and developed a more comprehensive set of activities and institutions in Texas than anywhere else in the West (Clarke 1976).

California

Another state in which the land was not subject to the artificial size ceilings of the Homestead Act was California. Like Texas, California had been a Spanish dependency prior to Mexican independence in 1821. Much of the inhabited territory of Spanish California had been granted by the Spanish authorities to a chain of 21 huge missions and at least 300 ranchos, the latter generally about 40,000 acres in size. Mexican independence changed virtually nothing and indeed, under Mexican rule, the governor of the region made some 500 large grants, subject only to a maximum of 50,000 acres (Robinson 1948). Quite a few of the Mexican land grants were made after the Secularization Act of 1833 which ended mission rule and ushered in the golden age of the ranchos. Under mission rule the missions had been given vast lands which, although theoretically held in trust for the indigenous Indian population of the region, were under the exclusive control and use of the mission personnel for a finite but indefinite period. Even before secularization, pressure had been building among ranchers in the dry southern half of the region to strip the missions of their land and convert them into a state-owned commons for use by local ranchers (Cleland 1941).

Nevertheless, perhaps because of the virtual absence of any state bureaucracy for managing and regulating the public domain, when secularization took place, instead of creating a public domain, huge grants of land with full private property rights were made to those petitioning for it and satisfying certain requirements. The requirements were to (a) have an occupation, (b) build a house (no matter how primitive) within one year, and (c) put a hundred or more head of cattle on the granted land. Since fences were not economic and the technology used in cattle raising was again that of cooperative land pooling with periodic roundups, in effect exclusive use of the land was granted to all members of the common pool, despite the fact that much of it was, in fact, privately owned. Apparently, very little attention was given by the authorities to enforcing conditions (a)–(c) above for the legitimacy of the grants (Cleland 1941).

The treaty annexing California to the United States in 1846 required the United States to respect the existing laws with respect to property and hence the legitimacy of the ranchos which ranged in size up to 115,000 acres, several of which might well be owned by the same person (Robinson 1948). Despite the importance of large private landholdings, in 1851 the new state of California passed a law codifying many of the existing institutional features of commons-type cattle ranching, including requirements concerning the registration of brands, numbers of roundups, advance public notice of the time and location of such roundups and the "juez de campo" (or judge of the plains) who must be present to supervise and settle any disagreements at such roundups (Cleland 1941; Robinson 1948; Burcham 1961). The Trespass Law of 1850 made agricultural settlers liable for any damages of cattle to crops unless previously protected on all sides by a strictly defined legal fence. The southern California cattle boom was further accentuated by the growing market for meat in the north brought about by the gold rush. Most of the meat was marched north on the hoof just as it was from Texas to points north and east.

Unfortunately, the boundaries of the private land titles were frequently not clearly defined. Under pressure from newly arriving land seekers (resulting from the gold rush of the late 1840s and early 1850s), by the early 1850s numerous legal challenges to the legitimacy of the Spanish and Mexican land grants were raised. Although eventually the authenticity of the vast majority of these grants was confirmed, by the mid-1860s the formal process (which took place in front of the Land Commission and, on average, took some 17 years to complete!) had forced many of the original landowners into bankruptcy or at least to sell off sizeable portions of their original landholdings to cover their legal expenses.[40] Given the fragmentation of the landholdings and the continuing need to sell off more land, the post-Civil War influx of farmers and miners to southern California resulted in the interspersal of farms among the ranches and increased the demand for fencing. This undermined the rationale for the traditional system of cattle pools. That system was further undermined by the substitution of sheep for cattle on the near-bankrupt smaller ranches encouraged by a substantial rise in the price of wool relative to that of beef during and after the Civil War. Both in California and elsewhere, "the sheepmen, being largely nomadic and continually moving their flocks from area to area seeking the best grazing land available, were generally opposed to any form of control in the use of the domain" (Burmeister 1956, 147).

Two points are notable in the Californian experience. First, even though between 1820 and the mid-1860s the bulk of California's useable ASAR land was privately owned in relatively large parcels of at least 40,000 acres, the same cattle pools and other cooperative institutions as in Texas and the rest of the American West were sufficiently dominant to be codified into law pertaining to the whole state. Second, for a variety of reasons, the forces leading to the downfall of the collective institutions of cattle raising occurred some twenty years earlier in most of California than elsewhere in the American West.[41]

Other Regions

Other Western states in which the aforementioned constraints on large private landholdings were inoperative or at least much less operative were Utah, New Mexico, and Arizona. In New Mexico and Arizona the reason they were inoperative was the same as in Mexico and California. In both these cases, however, the proportion of land possessed by the original recipients of large private land grants declined substantially over time.

In the case of Arizona, only one-eighth of the claims were confirmed after review of the claims by the relevant Land Commission.[42] This did not imply the absence of large parcels of private property inasmuch as cattlemen in Arizona were especially successful in appropriating large amounts of public domain by getting their hired hands to homestead contiguous parcels, and then combining them. As elsewhere, they also claimed substantial territory remaining in the public domain for joint use, operated in cattle pools and formed an association (the Arizona Cattle Growers Association) which exercised considerable leadership in virtually all activities of such associations identified above. Their efforts were rather instrumental in the eventual adoption of the Taylor Grazing Act of 1934 allowing for long term leasing by cattle pools of grazing land on the public domain (Wagoner 1952).

In the case of New Mexico, few of the original grant claims were initially rejected by the Surveyor General of New Mexico. But, a critical fire in the building where the land titles were registered and stored and the subsequent reconstitution of the land claims review process under an easily manipulated Court of Land Claims allowed many of the original Indian and Spanish-Mexican landholdings to be taken over by Americans. There remained, however, many large private landholdings (Gomez 1985) and husbandry activities in the state became dominated by the same institutions as in Texas and other ASARs of the West (Brand 1961; Cox 1895; Peake 1937; Oliphant 1968).

In the case of Utah, the reason why the restrictions of the Homestead and other acts were less operative was because Mormon Utah rather flagrantly disregarded the laws of the United States. Federal law notwithstanding, in 1853 the Mormon spiritual and political leader Brigham Young "advised . . . cattle owners . . . to group into fencing companies and to enclose vast tracts of land—plots of 'about fifty thousand acres'—until 'all the vacant land is substantially enclosed.' He showed the same indifference to the federal government's right to the final disposition of this land in his message as governor to the territorial legislature in 1853. He recommended that legislation be passed for the strict regulation of herding and grazing grounds. . . . For some 20 years, the territorial government legislated control over the public domain. In a series of laws not in strict harmony with federal policy, the Utah Legislature prevented non-resident herders from encroaching upon grazing grounds necessary to settlements and regulated resident stockmen in their use of the surrounding public domain" (Peterson 1964, 200–1).

In particular, between 1855 and 1857 more than 30 acts were passed granting herd grounds on the public domain in Utah to individuals, groups, and the Mormon church. Several of these grants were more than one hundred square miles in size. The Herdsman Act of 1854 authorized county courts to regulate their local grazing grounds (on the public domain). Backed with this kind of legislative, executive, and judicial support at the state level, it is clear that common property range rights were relatively secure in Utah. As elsewhere, things changed in the late 1880s when Utah backed away from its earlier confrontational position with respect to federal laws. Also, at this time conflicts arose between sheepmen and cattlemen, and irrigation agriculture became more competitive with husbandry.

Summary and Conclusion

It may indeed be true that good fences make good neighbors and that private property rights may be generally more suitable for prevailing technological and environmental conditions in animal husbandry. Yet it is our claim that this was not the case for the late nineteenth century American West. The model developed in the first section identified various environmental conditions in which common property rights would be optimal. The following section showed that these conditions were largely realized in the region at that time. It was also shown that the restrictions on the conversion of the public domain into large private parcels were either greatly exaggerated or inapplicable. The fact that, even so, the landowners chose to pool their land in common property provides support for our thesis that such arrangements were optimal, not just second-best. Additional support for the thesis is provided by the fact that the transition to private property occurred at a time in which the environmental conditions identified in our model changed but not the restrictions on private property.

Notes

1. For a recent discussion of the efficacy of common property and several historical applications, see Anderson and Simmons (1993).
2. This is not to say that there have not been some more careful exceptions. Notably, Barzel (1989), Anderson and Hill (1983), and Libecap (1981a and 1981b) have argued that the relative transaction costs of creating and maintaining (enforcing) different forms of property rights could favor common property rights in some circumstances.
3. Under the Land Act of 1796 federal lands were open to purchase by individuals or firms at a fixed minimum price. From 1820 until the end of the 19th century the minimum purchase price was set at $1.25 per acre, which was generally at least two or three times the free market price for land of equal quality. The Homestead Act of 1862 made it possible for an individual (but not a firm) to obtain land at a zero price by residing on the land for five years and making specified improvements. Homesteads, however, were subject to an upper limit of 160 acres (later expanded to 320, then 640 acres), a size which is only a small fraction of the minimum size for a viable cattle ranch.
4. For a more formal and thorough presentation of the model in a different context, see Nugent and Sanchez (1993).
5. Attacks by hostile Indians was a common and serious source of such insecurity, especially after the Indians had managed to master the use of horses and techniques for cattle stealing but prior to their subjugation in the 1890s.
6. The importance of such events should not be underestimated. For example, in Colorado the state association secured legislation that required railroads to compensate the cattlemen for the cattle killed at two-thirds of their market value. As a result, even a single railroad paid cattlemen in that state over $30,000 for cattle killed during the winter season of 1883–84 (Peake 1937, 247).
7. The main markets for animal products were in the East and Midwest, frequently over 1000 miles from the grazing areas. Before the spread of railroads in the 1870s and 1880s, these distances had to be traversed on the hoof, imposing substantial

weight losses on the animals and subjecting them to health, security, and price risks while on route. Not infrequently, too, communities along the way would impose barriers to their passage. Even after the railroads reduced the distances traversed on the hoof, the stock raisers frequently claimed that the railroads imposed excessive (monopolistic) freight charges and deficient service and that the buyers (Chicago packing houses) practiced monopsonistic behavior.

8. See, e.g., Binswanger, McIntire, and Udry (1989); Monteverdi (1978); Huff and Shipp (1968); and Oladipo (1986).

9. This argument has been powerfully made by McCloskey (1972) and Dahlman (1980) in the context of the mixed system of commons and private fields which long characterized medieval England.

10. For evidence, see Nugent and Sanchez (1993).

11. My activities help find your animals, thereby protecting your property rights, whereas yours help find my animals, thereby protecting my property rights.

12. Indeed, cattle are highly regarded for being able to find water in desert areas. Hence, humans in search of water often save themselves from death by dehydration by following the cattle.

13. Pooling the land would be much more transaction cost-efficient than pooling of income since in the latter case the asymmetries of information between the income earner and others in the pool would be greater, making it more difficult to control labor-shirking (Smith and Boyd 1990).

14. This is because typically all those who are not members of the pool are excluded from use of the pooled land and use by members may be tightly regulated. For strong demonstrations of the difference between open access or no rights and common property rights, see Ciriacy-Wantrup and Bishop (1975); Bromley and Chavas (1989); and Bromley (1989 and 1991).

15. There may have been certain areas in the American West, e.g., Indian reservations, where these conditions were satisfied even after the 1880s.

16. The Land Act of 1784 set a minimum price of $2 per acre on large parcels of land, making it difficult for the average frontiersman to purchase public land. While the revised Land Act of 1796 limited the size of the down payment (thereby providing credit on the remaining portion of the purchase which could be paid off over time), when little of this credit was repaid, the revised Land Act of 1820 abolished credit but reduced the minimum plot size to 40 acres and reduced the minimum price to $1.25 per acre (Dennen 1975; North and Rutten 1987). While the Homestead Act of 1862 provided the homesteader with land at a zero price, it also imposed the low ceiling of 160 acres and required that a residence be established and certain costly improvements be made. Later on, the upper bound on free acreage under the Homestead Act was relaxed somewhat (to 640 acres) for desert land (The Desert Land Act of 1877) and then in 1916 for grazing land (under the Stock Raising Homestead Act of that year). Qualification for these exemptions, however, was tightly restricted, at least until 1934 when the Taylor Grazing Act was passed (Libecap 1981b; Mosk 1944). The Taylor Act provided

60   THE POLITICAL ECONOMY OF THE AMERICAN WEST

for long-term lease arrangements on grazing lands in large parcels and legalized the construction of fences on the public domain (Logan 1962).

17. For example, one grazing group managed to buy 500,000 acres of railroad land at only $.50 per acre (Mothershead 1971).

18. Indeed, during the 1880s, one group of non-Indian cattle owners owning a quarter million head of cattle leased a bloc of 6 million acres from one such reservation in Oklahoma belonging to the Cherokee Indians (Savage 1973; Alston and Spiller 1992). Substantial portions of Indian reservations were also sold to cattle ranchers according to the provisions of the Allotment Act (or Dawes Act) of 1887 (Carlson 1981).

19. See especially Nimmo (1897); Osgood (1929); Fletcher (1960); Dennen (1975); and Libecap and Johnson (1979).

20. By this time the cattle ranching industry was overextended and a higher stage of settlement had been reached.

21. The basic procedure of the roundup was to form a large circle over a large territory. All the animals within that circle would then be goaded towards the center of the circle; a smaller circle would then be formed, and again the animals prodded toward the middle of the circle. After successive repetition of this procedure, ultimately the animals would be gathered in a restricted area where representatives of individual pool members would find their branded animals along with their new calves (associated with their branded mothers). At this point, the calves could be branded and an individual member's animals cut from the larger group (Goff and McCaffree 1967). While roundups on a relatively large scale became very common only after the Civil War (Dary 1981, 163), they appear to have been practiced on a smaller scale for some time. The origin of the western roundup is usually thought to be Mexican, having been instituted by local cattle associations known as mestas (Dusenberry 1963).

22. Also, by the 1880s at least, the cattle of nonmembers of the pool were commonly excluded by creating fences on the public domain (even after their being declared illegal by President Cleveland).

23. The prices of range rights were especially high in the early 1880s at which time meat prices were high and the common property rights to the range relatively secure (Holden 1930). Notably, meat prices started to fall only after that (when homesteaders started to claim portions of the nearby public domain).

24. As Youngblood and Cox (1922, 71) noted: "The agreements regarding such matters as the partition of the range and the use of water became property rights and were frequently bought and sold as land is sold today. Once a man's range rights were determined, they were respected by all." Similarly, nonmembers were excluded from the use of all corrals needed for various important activities such as the branding and separating of the animals (Webb 1931; Nordyke 1955).

25. Indeed, there were many examples in which such values amounted to several hundred thousand dollars.

26. Specifically, each owner was required to brand his cattle with a unique brand.

The brand had to be registered at both the local (county) and state levels and brand books containing all the registered brands were widely distributed and brought up to date. Owners attempting to move their cattle long distances were required to use another set of distinguishing characteristics, namely, "road marks." Violations of the brand and road mark conventions were subject to criminal penalties and the cattle associations were active in creating and maintaining such systems.

27. First, since full-grown bulls, whose presence among the cows was necessary for procreation, generally commanded attractive prices in the market, each owner had an incentive to sell his own bulls and to free ride on the bull services of other owners. To overcome this incentive the cattle pools generally required each member to contribute to the pool the services of a number of bulls proportional to the size of her herd.

28. Since young calves born since the time of the last roundup would normally be unbranded, there were strong incentives for both members and nonmembers to put their own brands on any young calves they could round up by themselves. However, since roundups and branding before the cold winter's weather had ended could endanger the health of the animals, for the health of the industry it was important to overcome the incentives for excessively early roundups. Almost universally the cattle pools and associations did so by: (1) making it a criminal offense to be caught with one's own brand on a calf at a date prior to the specified date of the spring roundup; (2) specifying the date of the spring roundup to be neither too early to endanger the health of the calves nor too late so that the calves would not still be close to their mothers (for suckling purposes); (3) requiring that each calf be branded with the brand of its associated mother regardless of the particular range in which it was found; (4) since calves could be separated from their mothers (thereby becoming "mavericks") by artificial means such as cutting the tongue of the calves, imposing severe penalties (including banishment from the pool and the roundup) on anyone caught with tongueless calves. Mavericks were made the common property of the pool or association and then auctioned off to the highest bidder and the proceeds used to finance its detective bureaus and other activities.

29. This was done by (1) requiring the registration of information pertaining to the names of both the buyers and sellers and the brands and road marks of all cattle sold, (2) setting up detective bureaus and inspection stations at strategic locations in the marketing chain and maintaining first-rate teams of inspectors and detectives, (3) maintaining "blacklists" of purchasing agents, ranch hands and so on who had been suspected of participating in cattle theft or of otherwise violating association rules, and (4) offering rewards for information on cattle thieves (Osgood 1929; Dale 1960).

30. The most important diseases were the Texas fever in the 1870s and pneumonia from Eastern cattle in the 1880s and 1890s.

31. In one year alone (1884) the state of Colorado paid out $117,000 in bounties for the poisonous loco weeds dug up and brought in by residents. In 1890 it paid

out a substantial fraction of this amount for bounties on the scalps of wolves (Carman, Heath, and Minto 1892, 798).

32. There were several reasons for this. First, since their sheep required continuous attention, sheepherders had no need for roundups. Second, since sheep can travel considerably farther without water than cattle, at least as long as there is sufficient moisture in the grass, denial of access to the privately owned parcels with water was a much weaker deterrent to free riding on the range claimed by cattle pools for sheep owners than for cattle owners. These important differences would imply that sheep owners would have no incentive to respect the common property rights claims of the cattle owners. Not surprisingly, cattle owners repeatedly complained that the sheepmen failed to respect the territorial claims and association rules of the cattlemen (Briggs 1937, 177; Gilfillan 1929; Lehmann 1962). Sheep owners were seldom reticent in calling attention to the illegitimacy of the cattle owners' claims over the public domain.

33. Modern day Texas has over 260,000 square miles, an area larger than any country in Europe west of Russia. The original territory, moreover, was even larger, consisting of portions of the present states of Colorado, Kansas, New Mexico, and Wyoming.

34. In particular, it was a dependency of Spain until Mexico declared its independence in 1821 after which it became a dependency of Mexico. Between 1835 and 1845 it was a separate republic (the Republic of Texas). It was annexed to the United States and became a state in 1846. Part of the state, however, was ceded to the United States in 1850 and later on used in forming the states of Kansas, New Mexico, Colorado and Wyoming.

35. The institutional arrangements in husbandry activities in Spanish America were borrowed from the Spanish Mesta and described as follows: "The ordinances provided that from San Juan Day in June (the 25th) until the middle of November each year, stockmen should engage in weekly roundups of livestock in places designated by local judges. All stockmen in each vicinity were obligated to assist in the roundup. Each was to cut out animals on which he should recognize his brand and drive them to his (ranch). Roundups were to take place by turn on (ranches) in any given locality until all livestock were worked. . . . Steps were taken to assure adequate supervision of each roundup. It was the custom to summon four to six reputable (ranchers) who were to oversee the rodeo and to make sure that each stockman took only those animals having his brand on them" (Dusenberry 1963, 67).

36. Apparently quoting a contemporary observer, the author of the first comprehensive monograph on the Texan cattle industry stated: "in the semi-wild condition which followed the animals were better able to take care of themselves, and when food was scarce it was found that the less herding was done the better. . . . The animals always had a habit of splitting up into bunches and taking possession of a valley or slope where water was available. . . . As long as water remained, they strayed but little, but when either food or water would run out, they would travel

immense distances in search of pools and brooks, and many a lost traveller has had his life saved by locating a single-file cattle trail and following it to water" (Cox 1895, 1:61).

37. Many of the returnees from the war front brought with them their arms and the inclination to use them.

38. The large price differentials for cattle between Texas and the distant markets of the East and Midwest gave tremendous incentive for long-distance cattle drives.

39. Residents of Kansas, Montana, and other states were worried primarily about Texas fever (thought to be carried by Texan cattle) and the effects of the intrusion of such cattle on local farms and pastures.

40. A major crash in cattle prices in the early 1860s also contributed to bankruptcies among the large ranchers and land fragmentation.

41. This is not to say that the traditional system totally disappeared. Indeed, as noted by Ellickson (1986 and 1991), the traditional system has remained at least partially intact in one California county (Shasta County) until rather recently.

42. This was primarily because the original claims had been abandoned and only much later bought up at extremely low prices by opportunistic California land speculators.

References

Alston, Lee J., and Pablo T. Spiller. 1992. A congressional theory of Indian property rights: The Cherokee Outlet. In *Property rights and Indian economies*, edited by Terry L. Anderson. Lanham, MD: Rowman & Littlefield Publishers, Inc., 85–107.

Anderson, Terry L. 1987. The first privatization movement. In *Essays on the economy of the old Northwest*, edited by David C. Klingaman and Richard K. Vedder. Athens: Ohio University Press, 59–75.

Anderson, Terry L., and Peter J. Hill. 1975. The evolution of property rights: A study of the American West. *Journal of Law and Economics* 18(1): 163–79.

———. 1983. Privatizing the commons: An improvement? *Southern Economic Journal* 50(2): 438–50.

Anderson, Terry L., and Randy T. Simmons. 1993. *The political economy of customs and culture: Informal solutions to the commons problem.* Lanham, MD: Rowman & Littlefield Publishers, Inc.

Baker, T. Lindsay. 1989. Irrigating with windmills on the Great Plains. *Great Plains Quarterly* 9: 216–30.

Barzel, Yoram. 1989. *Economic analysis of property rights.* Cambridge: Cambridge University Press.

Binswanger, Hans, John McIntire, and Chris Udry. 1989. Production relations in semi-arid African agriculture. In *The economic theory of agrarian institutions*, edited by P. Bardhan. Oxford: Clarendon Press, 122–44.

Brand, Donald D. 1961. The early history of the range cattle industry in Northern Mexico. *Agricultural History* 35: 132–9.

Briggs, Harold E. 1934. The development and decline of open range ranching in the Northwest. *Mississippi Valley Historical Review* 20: 521–36.

———. 1937. The early development of sheep ranching in the Northwest. *Agricultural History* 11: 161–80.

Bromley, Daniel W. 1989. Property relations and economic development: The other land reform. *World Development* 17: 867–77.

———. 1991. *Environment and economy.* Oxford: Basil Blackwell.

Bromley, Daniel W., and Jean-Paul Chavas. 1989. On risk, transactions and economic development in the semi-arid tropics. *Economic Development and Cultural Change* 37: 719–36.

Burcham, L. T. 1961. Cattle range and forage in California: 1770–1880. *Agricultural History* 35: 140–9.

Burmeister, Charles A. 1956. Six decades of rugged individualism: The American National Cattlemen's Association. *Agricultural History* 30: 143–50.

Carlson, Leonard A. 1981. *Indians, bureaucrats and the land: The Dawes Act and the decline of Indian farming.* Westport, CT: Greenwood Press.

Carman, Ezra A., H. A. Heath, and John Minto. 1892. *Special report on the history and present condition of the sheep industry of the United States.* Prepared under the direction of Dr. D. E. Salmon, chief of the Bureau of Animal Industry. Washington, DC: Government Printing Office for the U.S. Department of Agriculture.

Ciriacy-Wantrup, Siegfried V., and R. C. Bishop. 1975. Common property as a concept in natural resource policy. *Natural Resources Journal* 15: 49–70.

Clarke, Mary Whatley. 1976. *A century of cow business: A history of the Texas and Southwestern Cattle Raisers Associations.* Fort Worth: Texas and Southwestern Cattle Raisers Associations.

Cleland, Robert Glass. 1941. *The cattle on a thousand hills.* San Marino, CA: The Huntington Library.

Cox, James. 1895. *Historical and biographical record of the cattle industry.* St. Louis: Woodward and Tiernan.

Dahlman, Carl J. 1980. *The open field system and beyond: A property rights analysis of an economic institution.* Cambridge: Cambridge University Press.

Dale, Edward Everett. 1960. *The range cattle industry.* Norman: University of Oklahoma Press.

Dary, David. 1981. *Cowboy culture.* New York: Alfred A. Knopf.

Dasgupta, Partha S., and Geoffrey M. Heal. 1979. *Economic theory and exhaustible resources.* Cambridge: Cambridge University Press.

Dennen, Rodgers Taylor. 1975. *From common to private property: The enclosure of the open range.* Ph.D. dissertation, University of Washington, Seattle.

———. 1976. Cattlemen's associations and property rights in land in the American West. *Explorations in Economic History* 13: 423–33.

Dobie, J. Frank. 1943. *A vaquero of the brush country.* Boston: Little Brown and Co.

Dusenberry, William H. 1963. *The Mexican Mesta: The administration of ranching in colonial Mexico.* Urbana: University of Illinois Press.

Eggertsson, Thráinn. 1990. *Economic behavior and institutions.* Cambridge: Cambridge University Press.

Ellickson, Robert C. 1986. Of Coase and cattle: Dispute resolution in Shasta County. *Stanford Law Review* 38: 623–87.

———. 1991. *Order without law.* Cambridge: Harvard University Press.

Field, Barry C. 1989. The evolution of property rights. *Kyklos* 42(3): 319–45.

Fletcher, Robert H. 1960. *Free grass to fences, the Montana cattle range story.* New York: University Publishers.

Frink, Maure, W. Turrentine Jackson, and Agnes Wright Spring. 1956. *When grass was king.* Boulder: University of Colorado Press.

Furubotn, Eirik G. 1985. The gains from privatization: A general equilibrium perspective. Department of Economics, University of Texas at Arlington.

Gates, Paul. 1968. *History of public land law development.* Washington, DC: U.S. Public Land Law Review Commission.

Gilfillan, Archer B. [1929] 1957. *Sheep: Life on the South Dakota range.* Reprint. Minneapolis: University of Minnesota.

Goff, Richard, and Robert H. McCaffree. 1967. *Century in the saddle.* Denver: Colorado Cattlemen's Centennial Commission.

Gomez, Placido. 1985. The history and adjudication of the common lands of Spanish and Mexican land grants. *Natural Resources Journal* 25: 1039–80.

Gressley, Gene M. 1961. The American Cattle Trust: A study in protest. *Pacific Historical Review* 30: 61–77.

Holden, William C. 1930. *Alkali trails.* Dallas: Southwest Press.

Huff, F. A., and W. L. Shipp. 1968. Mesoscale spatial variability in Midwestern precipitation. *Journal of Applied Meteorology* 7: 886–91.

Lang, Aldon Socrates. 1932. Financial history of the public lands in Texas. *The Baylor Bulletin* 35(3).

Larson, Alfred. 1942. The winter of 1886–87 in Wyoming. *Annals of Wyoming* 14: 5–17.

Lehmann, V. W. 1962. *Forgotten legions: Sheep in the Rio Grande Plain of Texas.* El Paso: Texas Western Press.

Libecap, Gary D. 1981a. Bureaucratic opposition to the assignment of property rights: Overgrazing on the Western range. *Journal of Economic History* 61: 151–8.

———. 1981b. *Locking up the range: Federal land controls and grazing.* Cambridge: Ballinger.

Libecap, Gary D., and Ronald N. Johnson. 1979. Property rights, nineteenth-century federal timber policy and the conservation movement. *Journal of Economic History* 39(1): 129–42.

Logan, Richard F. 1962. Post-Columbian developments in the arid regions of the United States of America. In *Problems of the Arid Zone*, vol. 18 of *Proceedings of the Paris Symposium*. Paris: UNESCO, 277–97.

McCallum, Henry D., and Frances T. McCallum. 1965. *The wire that fenced the West*. Norman: University of Oklahoma Press.

McCloskey, Donald M. 1972. The enclosure of the open fields: Preface to a study of its impact on the efficiency of English agriculture in the eighteenth century. *Journal of Economic History* 32 (March).

Monteverdi, John Paul. 1978. *A meteorological analysis of the variability of precipitation in the Great Plains, U.S.A.* Ph.D. dissertation, Ann Arbor: University Microfilms.

Mosk, Sanford A. 1944. *Land tenure problems in the Santa Fe Railroad grant area*. Berkeley: University of California Press.

Mothershead, Harman Ross. 1971. *The Swan Land and Cattle Company, Ltd.* Norman: University of Oklahoma Press.

Nimmo, Joseph, Jr. 1897. *Report on the internal commerce of the United States*. Washington, DC: House Ex. Doc. 1, part 5.2937. 52nd Congress, 2d session.

Nordyke, Lewis. 1955. *Great roundup: The story of Texas and Southwestern cowmen*. New York: William Morrow.

North, Douglass C. 1990. *Institutions, institutional change and economic performance*. Cambridge: Cambridge University Press.

North, Douglass C., and Andrew R. Rutten. 1987. The Northwest Ordinance in historical perspective. In *Essays on the economy of the old Northwest*, edited by David C. Klingaman and Richard K. Vedder. Athens: Ohio University Press, 19–35.

Nugent, Jeffrey B., and Nicolas Sanchez. 1989. The efficiency of the Mesta: A parable. *Explorations in Economic History* 26: 261–84.

———. 1993. Tribes, chiefs and transhumance: A comparative institutional analysis. *Economic Development and Cultural Change* 42(1): 87–113.

Oladipo, E. Olukayode. 1986. Spatial patterns of drought in the interior plains of North America. *Journal of Climatology* 6: 495–513.

Oliphant, J. Orin. 1968. *On the cattle ranges of the Oregon country*. Seattle: University of Washington Press.

Osgood, Ernest S. 1929. *The day of the cattleman*. Minneapolis: University of Minnesota Press.

Peake, Ora Brooks. 1937. *The Colorado range cattle industry*. Glendale, CA: The Arthur H. Clark Company.

Pelzer, Louis. [1936] 1969. *The cattlemen's frontier*. Reprint. New York: Russell and Russell.

Peterson, Levi S. 1964. The development of the livestock law of Utah, 1848–1896. *Utah Historical Quarterly* 32: 198–216.

Robinson, William Wilcox. 1948. *Land in California*. Berkeley: University of California Press.

Savage, William S. 1973. *The Cherokee Strip Live Stock Association*. Columbia: University of Missouri Press.

Smith, Erik Alden, and Robert Boyd. 1990. Risk and reciprocity: Hunter-gatherer socioecology and the problem of collective action. In *Risk and uncertainty in tribal and peasant economies*, edited by Elizabeth Cashdan. Boulder, CO: Westview Press, 167–92.

Texas State Historical Association. 1991. *History of the Cattlemen of Texas*. Austin.

Wagoner, J. J. 1952. History of the range cattle industry in southern Arizona, 1540–1940. *Social Science Bulletin*, no. 20, vol. 23. Tucson: University of Arizona.

Webb, Walter Prescott. 1931. *The Great Plains*. Boston: Ginn and Company.

Youngbloud, B., and A. B. Cox. 1922. An economic study of a typical ranching area on the Edwards Plateau of Texas. College Station: Texas Agricultural Experiment Station, bulletin 297.

4

The Political Economy of
Early Federal Reclamation in the West

Stewart Mayhew and B. Delworth Gardner[†]

The Reclamation Act of 1902 represents a major turning point for the western region of the United States. It involved the federal government in water planning and development in a significant way and greatly changed the economic and social landscape. This chapter explores and analyzes the power struggle between two political forces that produced western reclamation: the Progressives, who saw government as the savior of the West, and the redistributionists, who saw reclamation as a mechanism for producing wealth, much of it resulting from income transfers to the region from the taxpayers in the remainder of the country. It will be shown that the Reclamation Act necessarily synthesized the interests of these competing groups, and that the subsequent history of federal reclamation saw the gradual abandonment of the act's Progressive underpinnings in favor of regional

[†] The Bureau of Reclamation supplied part of the funding for the research project that produced this paper. Drew Johnson and John Warner, undergraduate students in economics at Brigham Young University, assisted in gathering materials and checking references.

redistribution. Understanding the ultimate triumph of the redistributionists will be aided by utilizing a model of a market for political favors.[1]

The Market for Political Favors

The 1992 Nobel laureate for economics at the University of Chicago, Gary S. Becker (1983, 372) presents the basic assumptions for modeling a political market:

> The economic approach to political behavior assumes that actual political choices are determined by the efforts of individuals and groups to further their own interests. Competition among these pressure groups for political influence determines the equilibrium structure of taxes, subsidies, and other political favors.

In particular, it is assumed that political favors are transacted in a market where interest groups are the demanders of such favors and politicians (who create and regulate income transfers through taxes, subsidies, and other policies) are the suppliers (Peltzman 1976, 212). Both demanders and suppliers of political favors have scarce financial and time resources which can be allocated to the political process or to valuable alternative uses. Transactions are negotiated and terms of trade (prices) are established in these markets.

Demanders and suppliers of political favors are assumed to be rational in that they attempt to maximize the net benefits to themselves from trading with each other. If demanders become more efficient in bringing pressure, i.e., reduce their costs, or if they place themselves in a position to benefit more from political favors, then, *ceteris paribus*, the equilibrium quantity of political pressure will rise. Likewise, if suppliers become more efficient in producing political favors or discover ways of benefiting more from the "payments" from the demanders, the quantity of political pressure will rise.

As in all markets, each demander and supplier desires to exchange one "commodity" for another. At least two tangible "commodities" are desired by typical suppliers of political favors (politicians) as they trade with demanders (interest groups): votes needed to acquire and remain in political office, and the perquisites that come with holding office.[2] The demanders of political favors can provide votes at the polling booth or can make election campaign contributions in cash or services. Such contributions may then become the means of informing and persuading other voters and getting them to the polls.[3] The commodities that the suppliers provide to the demanders include subsidies, tax reductions, and favorable regulations (such as protection against imports), all of which are expected to enhance the profits and wealth positions of demanders. Alternatively, politicians might provide immunity from harm (increased taxes, reduced subsidies, or costly regulations) that could potentially be inflicted by government action.[4]

The costs of government programs that transfer income and wealth among occupational and age classes, and regions of the country, are of two kinds: economic and political. The distinction between the two is crucial because legislators know that the economic costs of subsidies transferred to demanders will be borne by taxpayers or consumers. Therefore, these economic costs may not be much of a factor in determining whether a political favor is transacted. Thus, the model predicts that transfers will diffuse the costs to less well organized groups and concentrate the benefits on better organized groups, thus making the transfers politically expedient (see Gwartney and Stroup 1992). There also will be some political costs in the form of lost political support.[5]

Obviously the equilibrium price of political favors depends on the expected values of the commodities transferred as well as the costs of making those transfers. One of the significant costs of organizing for group political action arises from the "free rider" problem (Olson 1965). Where group membership provides benefits from which nonparticipants in the political action cannot be excluded, an incentive exists for an individual to ride free. Coping with the free-rider problem raises "the total cost of bringing pressure," which is "the sum of the costs of direct political activity and the costs of controlling free riding" (Becker 1983, 377). The conclusion that emerges from this theory is that given the size of the subsidy and the group's success in overcoming the free-rider problem, the degree of pressure brought by any group will be inversely correlated with the size of the group (Olson 1965, 29).

The history of western reclamation, described below, is consistent with this political market theory. Political pressure to transfer income via irrigation subsidies was great when the western region was developing and constituted only a small part of the U.S. economy. Irrigators were able to exert political pressure and congressmen selected themselves to congressional committees that could facilitate the wealth transfers to the western region through irrigation projects. Regulations that would have impeded such redistributions were modified to make the transfers less costly.

The Reclamation Act

By the turn of the twentieth century, supporters of federal irrigation development had kindled enough public interest that Republican, Democrat, and Silver Republican party platforms in the 1900 election advocated western water development by the federal government.[6] Hence, the question was not whether federal activity would occur but when and in what form. Several people played a role in the movement that led to the passage and implementation of the Reclamation Act of 1902.

Major John Wesley Powell's survey of the arid West was instrumental in stimulating national interest in irrigating these vast lands. Although Powell was not directly involved with the Reclamation Act of 1902, his *Report on the Lands of the Arid Region of the United States* (1879) is said to have "started the movement toward Federal reclamation" (Davison 1979, 38–9). Despite claims to the contrary, Powell did not advocate federal construction of water storage facilities (Davison 1979, 114–35). Rather, he argued that the government should conduct extensive surveys to locate feasible reservoir sites and allow local cooperatives to do the actual building.

Even though Powell made a large impact on the early reclamation movement, some of his ideas were inimical to the goals of western irrigationists. Because of limits imposed by the region's precipitation, Powell believed that too much public land had passed into private ownership by 1893 and therefore future irrigation development should deliver water only to those lands already in private hands (National Irrigation Congress 1893, 109; Davison 1979, 153). This view was not popular with those such as William E. Smyth[7] who wanted even greater privatization and irrigation of the public lands. After Powell vigorously expounded his views in a controversial speech to the National Irrigation Congress in Los Angeles in 1893, he was effectively ostracized from the irrigation movement.

Another key figure in western reclamation was Frederick H. Newell, one of Powell's colleagues and disciples in the U.S. Geological Survey (USGS), who clearly shared the views represented by Powell at the 1893 Congress. Newell, however, managed to evade the enthusiastic outpouring of fury aimed at Powell and maintained a position of power in the irrigation community. As chief hydrographer for the USGS, Newell conducted an extensive investigation of potential reservoir sites throughout the West, including the technical and economic feasibility of several potential projects (U.S. Congress 1901).

Other Progressives associated with reclamation included Gifford Pinchot, Roosevelt's "conservation guru" and head of the Bureau of Forestry (later the Forest Service); Elwood Mead, an irrigation expert in the U.S. Department of Agriculture (USDA); President Theodore Roosevelt himself; E. A. Hitchcock, secretary of the interior in the Roosevelt administration; and Charles D. Walcott, an early director of the USGS. Their various roles and contributions will be described below.

In the Congress, federal reclamation was spearheaded by Representative (and later Senator) Frances G. Newlands of Nevada. Newlands was an author of several bills promoting irrigation and represented one of the states that stood to gain most from the Reclamation Act. Although associated with the "special interest" aspects of the legislation, Newlands also provided a critical link between the Progressive idealists and the national legislature.

Alston and Spiller (1992, 86) document some of the important changes that occurred in the composition of congressional committees that generated and promoted western interests. They show that the self-selection of members of Congress to committees can change the prospects for specific legislation. At the turn of the century, the committee in the Senate primarily responsible for water projects was the Committee on Irrigation and Reclamation of Arid Lands. In 1895 only two of the eight members of the committee represented states west of Colorado, the states with the most to gain from federal water projects. However, the committee gradually changed so that by 1902 (the year of the Reclamation Act), nine of thirteen members of the committee represented states west of Colorado.

In 1901, Representative Newlands introduced a bill that would initiate federal activity in irrigation (Congressional Record 1901, 1542). Consistent with Progressive idealism, the purpose of the bill was said to bring about "the largest development and the greatest good to the greatest number, consistent with an economic expenditure" (Golzé 1961, 24).[8] Although it failed to pass in 1901, the bill was re-introduced the following year when committee membership in the Senate was more conducive to its passage. With President Roosevelt's support and pressure on Congress, the Reclamation Act, also known as the Newlands Act, was passed and signed into law on June 17, 1902 (Gates 1968, 654; Reisner 1986, 177).

Eastern and midwestern legislators opposed the Newlands Act on several grounds (U.S. Congress 1901, 89; Wahl 1989, 20), but the principal one was that water development by the government would be primarily redistributive; it was "class legislation benefiting only a small portion of the population with public monies belonging to the whole people" (Golzé 1961, 25). Throughout the congressional debate, Representative Hepburn of Iowa was the bill's most outspoken opponent:

> The proposition involved in this bill is the most insolent and impudent attempt at larceny that I have ever seen embodied in a legislative proposition. These gentlemen simply do what? They ask us . . . to give away an empire in order that their private property may be made valuable. . . . I insist now, as I have before, that this is a thinly veneered and thinly disguised attempt to make the Government, from its general fund, pay for this great work—great in extent, great in expenditure, but not great in results. . . . Certainly there can be no return to the General Government. The lands that are to be affected by it . . . are in private hands . . . they are lands that you own now, and you are trying to compel the General Government to improve your lands. (Congressional Record 1902, 6742, 6762)

In order to pass the act, the Progressive leaders of the "reclamation movement" joined with the irrigation enthusiasts from the western states. This coalition, however, faced a dilemma of how to design redistributive legislation that would benefit the region without compromising the ideological principles of Progressivism or inciting opposition from nonwestern legislators.

The task of drafting the bill was given largely to Newell, whose experience in the USGS enabled him to implement a federal reclamation program. Representatives Newlands and Mondell are on record as advising Newell that, in order to consolidate congressional support for the bill, the legislation should be written so that every state in the arid region should have at least one federal project (U.S. Congress 1901, 61). To make the bill politically viable, Newell also incorporated Progressive tenets against land monopoly and special-interests into the legislation. Under the plan, Newell was to administer the federal reclamation program within the Department of the Interior. Both of Newell's direct superiors, Charles D. Walcott of the USGS and Secretary of the Interior E. A. Hitchcock, were proponents of reclamation, so by nesting the responsibility for reclamation in the Department of the Interior, Newell could depend on the support of his superiors. Once the act had passed, Secretary Hitchcock immediately delegated the task of implementation to Walcott, who, in turn, created the Reclamation Service and appointed Newell as the agency's first head. To ensure projects for each state, Section 9 of the Reclamation Act stipulated that at least 50 percent of the revenues acquired from sales of public lands within each arid state must be spent on projects within that state. Newell set a goal of authorizing at least one project in every state by the end of 1905 (Merrill, Snyder, and Andersen 1982) and completed this task in December, 1905, with the authorization of the Strawberry Valley Project in Utah. Mission accomplished, Section 9 was repealed on June 25, 1910.

The Strawberry Valley Project

The authorization and construction of the Strawberry Valley Project in Utah provides an example of the local initiatives that accompanied political activity at the national level. As early as 1889, the communities of Springville and Mapleton in southern Utah County considered the option of diverting waters from the Strawberry River in the Colorado River drainage into Spanish Fork Creek, which ultimately drains into the Great Basin. This was to be accomplished by means of canals and a 600-foot tunnel through the dividing summit. Although the Reclamation Act was not even on the legislative drawing board, the locals expressed hope "that through Government means something may be done for our relief in the near future" (Merrill, Snyder, and Andersen 1982, 35).

After passage of the Reclamation Act, Frederick Newell toured the western states looking for potential projects and meeting with each state's irrigation leaders. This gave local leaders the opportunity and incentive to fight for their own pet projects. When Newell arrived in Salt Lake City, he was greeted by the Utah State Irrigation Congress and treated like royalty (Merrill, Snyder, and Andersen 1982, 38). At the ensuing conference, Henry Gardner, a local political and religious leader, and Heber C. Jex, Spanish Fork's mayor, presented their plan for the diversion of the Strawberry River. Several other projects also were presented.

Newell suggested that Utah would have a much better chance of securing federal reclamation funds if the Irrigation Congress could select a single project and lobby for it in a unified manner. Accordingly, a special committee was appointed, and the next morning it lobbied for a single, expansive project that contained the Strawberry River Project as one of its several components.

After further investigation, the other components were deemed to be technically infeasible. Moreover, fractious political struggles between various regional leaders and numerous disputations over water rights within the state made Utah the last state to get its project approved on December 15, 1905. Even then, the project was approved subject to conditions outlined by Secretary Hitchcock (Merrill, Snyder, and Andersen 1982, 46):

1. existing water rights would be settled,
2. the project would cost no more than $1.25 million, and
3. the estimate of the amount of money that would be repaid to the fund made by the Board of Engineers was accurate.

The problems associated with state water rights were settled, but the second and third conditions were never satisfied. The nominal cost of the project turned out to be approximately $3.5 million, and due to changes in the repayment obligation described below, much of the original construction cost of the project was forgiven entirely. Even the reimbursable portion of the cost was not fully repaid until 1974 (Merrill, Snyder, and Andersen 1982, 126).

Progressivism vs. Redistribution

Building a coalition to support the Newlands Act required coalescing the western interests, who gained directly, with the Progressives, who believed governmental management could improve efficiency but were skeptical of special interests. Accordingly, the act's authors included several stipulations that de-emphasized redistribution to the special interests. For example, the act required that owners of improved lands reimburse the government for the full construction costs of projects affecting them.

At the hearings, Representative Mondell stated:

> . . . we simply ask that the Government use the proceeds of the sales of the land . . . for the purpose of making the irrigable land fit for cultivation and habitation; and then we propose that the settlers on those lands . . . shall pay to the Government every dollar of its expenditure in bringing water to their land, and in addition to that, the great cost of building laterals, of leveling the land, and preparing it for irrigation. . . . If our lands are pledged to their own reclamation we believe that the arid West will reclaim itself, without the cost of a penny to any American citizen. (Congressional Record 1902, 6742)

The repayment obligation of the irrigators is explicit in the text of the Reclamation Act of 1902:

The secretary of the Interior . . . (shall) give public notice . . . of the charges which shall be made per acre upon the said entries, and upon lands in private ownership which may be irrigated by the waters of the said irrigation project, and the number of annual installments, not exceeding ten, in which such charges shall be paid and the time when which payments shall commence. The said charges shall be determined with a view of returning to the reclamation fund the estimated cost of construction of the project.[9]

If costs had been rigorously defined and if reimbursement had been rigidly enforced, only economically feasible projects would have been undertaken. And, if farmers receiving federal water were required to bear the full costs of reclamation, presumably they and their surrogate politicians would only have supported projects for which expected benefits exceeded expected costs. Thus, the act would have satisfied the Progressive push for "efficiency" without subsidizing special interests.

From the theory developed in the first section, however, we would expect interest groups to use the act for redistributive purposes, and the emergent water repayment rules provided the mechanism. Because the act made no mention of interest charges on the capital construction costs, repayment obligations were assumed to be interest-free. This immediately gave irrigators using federal water a large subsidy,[10] since by far the largest category of costs on long-lived capital-intensive projects was interest charges.[11] Another important subsidy arose when repayment charges were suspended, in many cases long after water actually had been delivered to irrigators. In addition, the stipulation that the beneficiaries should pay the separable costs of their component of a project was systematically removed and replaced with repayment schemes that shifted costs to other sources (Wahl 1989, chap. 2).

Even so, modifications of the original repayment requirement might not have been severely damaging to the Progressive ideal of efficiency if the feasibility requirement of the Reclamation Act had been stringently enforced. The act stipulated that projects must be "feasible" before they could be authorized for construction. Although what was "feasible" remained ill-defined at the turn of the century, the focus of the USGS irrigation studies (especially under Newell) indicates that project feasibility was understood to include both engineering practicability and economic efficiency.[12]

In 1901, Newell stated that feasibility was to be determined by comparing the project's cost with the value of the crops to be grown from the irrigated lands. Newell and the USGS employed primitive methods for conducting feasibility analyses, and, retrospectively, their estimates were optimistic in favor of federal development (Haveman 1972, 96). Nevertheless, the point remains that the Progressive doctrine dictated that economic feasibility should be required for federally constructed water projects. Although its formal methods were not well developed until the last half of the twentieth century, benefit-cost analysis was the economic component of the conservationist (Progressive) paradigm (see Feldman 1991, 160–1).

In principle, therefore, the feasibility clause in the Reclamation Act could have prevented the construction of uneconomic projects, but the early USGS feasibility studies proved to be inaccurate. Unfortunately, this problem persisted after the passage of the Reclamation Act, and the requirement failed to screen out economically infeasible projects. Although Progressive efficiency motivated the feasibility requirement, no standard methodology ensuring feasibility was imposed, so the Reclamation Service was free to adopt its own guidelines for measuring benefits and costs (Holmes 1972, 19). Nothing prevented them from selecting methods that promoted their own interests and those of beneficiary groups at the expense of objectivity and efficiency.

Rationalizing Projects for Political Purposes

A number of factors contributed to the tendency of government agencies to conduct biased benefit-cost analyses. Renshaw (1957, 4) suggests,

> Inasmuch as the benefits which accrue from public investment are more localized than the tax base which supports expenditure, the return from a particular project need not be as great as could be obtained by investing the same funds elsewhere in the economy in order to make a public project appear justified from a purely local point of view. On the basis of logic alone, one would anticipate that local groups would bring pressure to bear on Congress and the agencies involved in water resource development to construct local projects which would not be in the best interest of a nation as a whole.

The incentive structure in any bureaucratic system also tends to promote asymmetric feasibility analyses. In the traditional paradigm of welfare economics, optimization in the public realm implies maximizing the relevant social welfare function (Boadway and Bruce 1984, 16) which, of course, implies complete, accurate, and impartial evaluation of benefits and costs. But public choice theory suggests that political agents, like everyone else, are interested primarily in their own well-being rather than some remote and ethereal goal such as social welfare (Tullock 1965). In this case, self-perpetuation of the bureau becomes an underlying motive. In a bureaucracy, the achievement of broad social goals is not the measure of success; rather, it is bureau size and budget (Niskanen 1971; Gwartney and Wagner 1988, 14). In some cases, the clandestine goal of an agency is to exceed their allotted budget without completing their assigned tasks, thus proving to higher echelons in government that a larger staff and a bigger budget are "needed." And, consistent with the theory of the market for political favors, elected officials achieve their personal political goals by catering to their constituents in various ways in order to maximize their chances for re-election.

Clearly, one way to diminish intrinsic subjectivity in economic evaluation is to specify and require rigorous analytical guidelines. After benefit-cost analysis became a requirement, both reclamation opponents and governmental agencies, such as the National Resources Planning Board and the Water Resources Council, sought to establish consistent protocol for project evaluation (Holmes 1972, 19). However, ambiguity plagued the development of analytical methods for several reasons:

1. it was never clearly defined who had the authority to establish guidelines,
2. policy makers have displayed limited understanding of economic principles, and
3. policies were given in the form of suggestions rather than requirements.

Moreover, any *ex ante* analysis is inherently uncertain and relies on normative judgments about the future. Even if relatively stringent evaluation guidelines were established, it would still be possible for self-interested parties to bias results in their favor since, in this largely hypothetical world of *ex ante* estimation, factual contradiction is impossible to find.

As indicated earlier, consistent underestimation of costs and overestimation of benefits dates back to the earliest projects of the Reclamation era. In *A History of the Public Lands Policies*, Hibbard (1965, 444) describes the situation in 1914, after the first reclamation projects had been completed and the settlers were to reimburse the government for construction costs:

During this time [1902–1914], some eleven thousand families, perhaps fifty to sixty thousand people, were settled on reclamation projects. It will be remembered that payments for the water rights for this land were to be made in a maximum of ten (annual) installments. Estimates had been made showing the probable cost of such rights to be fifteen, twenty, or forty dollars per acre. The facts showed them to cost twice these amounts. It had been supposed that crops would be grown within the first year or two, but the years stretched out beyond all expectation before the returns became important. It had been prophesied that the demand for farm produce would keep pace with the supply, the mining camps, lumber mills, and similar industries growing as rapidly as agriculture. In reality, the settlers on various governmental reclamation tracts found no market for much of the crop actually produced—alfalfa hay, for example, going begging for buyers at various times at one dollar to three dollars per ton.

It seems reasonable to attribute at least part of the error in estimating costs and benefits in early project evaluations to inexperience[13] and to the prevailing sentiments of the age; optimism and faith in scientific planning. Since it was believed that the government was benignly promoting the public interest, its actions did not warrant close scrutiny implied by rigorous benefit-cost analysis. However, the advent of public choice theory and analysis provides less "innocent" explanations for these excessively biased predictions. "Vote-seeking politicians have an incentive to design programs and financing methods . . . [for which] benefits are clearly recognizable and the costs are partially concealed and difficult for voters to identify" (Gwartney and Wagner 1988, 18).

Moreover, other structural and political characteristics of the reclamation movement may have contributed to biased evaluation. Recall the earlier discussion that before the Reclamation Act was signed there was an understanding that at least one project would be constructed in each of the arid states, a politically expedient mechanism for consolidating western support for the bill. Note that the understanding did not limit project construction only to those that were economically feasible. Since the Reclamation Service[14] was under this mandate to authorize projects, perhaps the urgency encouraged overly optimistic evaluations.

To make matters worse, many project plans were altered or expanded after approval, yet no re-evaluation was required. Once a project passed muster, the service was allowed to change the size or location of the project without having to conduct another analysis (Haveman 1972, 96). Hence many costly improvisations could be introduced without any accountability in a benefit-cost analysis.

Finally, the Reclamation Service may have resorted to deliberate under-representation of costs in order to gain support from the local landowners who would be the principal beneficiaries of the federal projects. Certainly, the more attractive the service could make the projects appear, the more enthusiastically landowners would accept their proposals and promote them politically.[15]

Renshaw (1957, 15–16, 97–101) provides data from 34 Bureau of Reclamation projects, supporting the contention that the bureau consistently underestimated real construction costs of its early projects (Table 4.1). Thirty of 34 projects cost more than anticipated initially, and 14 cost more than three times their original estimates.

Further analysis of Renshaw's data supports the notion that the bureau deliberately misrepresented costs in order to attract political support from local land owners. The 34 observations can be divided into two major groups—17 early projects for which construction began between 1903 and 1912, and 17 later projects initiated between 1927 and 1946. There is a critical institutional distinction between the two classes of projects. The early projects were approved under the assumption that the project beneficiaries would repay the full construction costs within a relatively short period. On average, actual construction costs for the 17 early projects exceeded estimated costs by 352 percent. By the time the later 17 projects were approved, the repayment obligation had been significantly eroded by the ability-to-pay rule,[16] greatly weakening the need for local landowners to be wary of infeasible projects, and hence decreasing the incentive for the bureau to underrepresent costs. For this latter group of projects, actual costs exceed estimates by only 76 percent, significantly less than for the earlier projects.

Table 4.1

The Relation of Realized Costs to Expected Costs

Bureau of Reclamation Project	Excess Realized Cost Allocation to Expected Cost Allocation (%)
Yuma	114
All American Canal	241
Newlands	1125
Carlsbad	415
Tucumcari	68
Austin	91
Humboldt	−64
Truckee Storage	12
Baker	38
Ogden River	13
Weber River	−31
Mancos	148
Rathdrum Prairie (Post Falls)	30
Buford Trenton	14
Balmorhea	−19
Gila	218
Salt River	550
Grand Valley	109
Minidoka	28
Boise	118
Rio Grande	515
Deschutes	−30
Klamath	288
Owyhee	58
Strawberry Valley	206
Yakima	414
Bitter Root	89
Belle Fourche	145
Milk River	586
Sun River	367
Lower Yellowstone	88
North Platte	890
Shoshone	235
Umatilla	212

Source: Renshaw (1957, 99).

Generalized least squares regression was utilized to account for the degree to which actual costs exceeded estimated costs. The explanatory (independent) variables were year and project size (measured by irrigated acreage). The "year" variable was used to determine whether the earlier projects showed a greater tendency to underestimate costs than the later projects.[17] Indeed, the time variable was significant at the 99 percent level. The "size" variable was used to see whether the underestimation of costs was related to the size of the project. The regression coefficient was positive as expected, but not statistically significant, suggesting that the degree of underestimation is not strongly related to project size.[18]

Overestimation of project benefits may be just as pervasive as underestimation of costs, but the problem is more complex and difficult to quantify. In both *ex ante* and *ex post* analysis, measurement of benefits is much less straightforward than measurement of costs. Several specific abuses of benefit evaluation that have resulted in overestimation are worth mentioning.

It is common practice in the Bureau of Reclamation to record and publish statistics on the total gross cash value of crops grown on project lands. Irrigation advocates, and even bureau officials, have implied that these gross totals should be counted as project benefits (Golzé 1961, Larson 1955). This approach over-represents the net benefits of irrigation since costs are not deducted from gross revenues. Ascribing all agricultural revenues as benefits to irrigation presupposes that the resources used in production on project farms, including land, labor, and capital, have no alternative uses, a heroic assumption indeed. Only the profits (revenues from the sales of products minus opportunity costs of the inputs) attributable to irrigation on project lands should be counted as benefits.

In some situations, even the incremental profit overstates the true benefit to society. For example, if agricultural products are subsidized through a price-support program, the increase in supply resulting from the project will merely increase the size of the surplus. In this case, the benefit of increased production depends on what the government does with the surplus—disaster relief abroad generates intangible benefits to the nation—but the social value of increased production could easily be quite small. Indeed, opponents of federal reclamation have seriously questioned the validity of constructing water projects to increase agricultural output and simultaneously funding subsidies to reduce output.

Regional secondary benefits[19] have also been included in Bureau of Reclamation benefit-cost analyses in order to produce more favorable ratios (Holmes 1977, 33). But the logic behind their inclusion is flawed. Inasmuch as the purpose of feasibility analysis is to protect the interests of the entire country by ensuring that projects enhance national wealth, it is vital that benefit-cost analysis be conducted from a national perspective. Secondary benefits that accrue to the region of the project are often simply transfers from other regions and, therefore, do not add to the wealth of the nation as a whole.

If it can be demonstrated that regional economic benefits associated with a given project are greater than for alternative projects, then the difference might be counted as a project benefit (Renshaw 1957, 125). This prospect seems unlikely, however, except in unusual circumstances. Unusually high unemployment of land, labor, or capital in the region might warrant this type of consideration. Secondary economic effects were considered important (Holmes 1977, 33) as part of the "New Deal" solution to economic stagnation, for example, and some water projects were built during the Great Depression, not only by the traditional agencies, but also by the Civilian Conservation Corps (Baldridge 1971). But in the absence of widespread unemployment and excess capacity, regional economic effects should be ignored in benefit-cost analysis (see also Wahl 1989, 42–3).

Another shortcoming related to benefit estimation involves misapplication of the time element associated with water projects. The excerpt from Hibbard (1965, 444) above, suggests that planners had a poor concept of how much time would be required until project benefits would begin to be captured. The failure of the Reclamation Act to require interest repayment had the effect of stringing out project construction and delaying the timing of benefits. McQueen (1989, 16) reports one former Bureau of Reclamation commissioner as saying "if you wait long enough, every project will generate a positive return" (LeBaron 1985, 4). And some Bureau of Reclamation reports speak of "benefits outweighing costs" with absolutely no reference to discounting benefit and cost streams or accounting for changes in aggregate price levels (Larson 1955).

Yet another practice which weakened the efficacy of benefit-cost evaluation as contributing to efficient resource allocation is the lumping together of the components of a multiple-purpose project. In many cases, irrigation projects that, taken alone, would have been economically infeasible, were combined with hydroelectric power and flood control components to make them feasible. In these situations, it would have been economically efficient, from the national perspective, for the government to abandon the irrigation component altogether, and only provide the feasible components of the project. However, the Bureau of Reclamation may not be authorized to build power plants alone:

> The primary object of this chapter [43 USCA Ch. 12] is the reclamation of arid lands through irrigation, and production of power for pumping in connection with irrigation is an important incident to the main object, but disposition of surplus power not required for pumping or other uses of irrigation for commercial uses is authorized only as an incidental phase of reclamation and not as a primary or independent act in itself. (USCA 43, sec. 371, 380)

The practice of lumping together the various components of a project for repayment purposes permitted the bureau to construct projects for which the main purpose was to generate hydroelectric power by disguising them as irrigation works. There is little question but that this strategy increased the political viability of reclamation projects.

From Renshaw's data there may be a temptation to infer that the problem of poor benefit-cost analysis was primarily a characteristic of earlier reclamation works, and that over time, the bureau learned to evaluate projects more accurately. After all, the criterion that benefits must exceed costs for any project was not even formally adopted until the 1930s, and many of the methods employed for measuring benefits from reclamation were not developed until the late 1940s and early 1950s. A series of *ex post* studies by the Bureau of Reclamation, summarized in Haveman (1972), indeed demonstrate that the tendency for the bureau to underestimate cost of projects, *ex ante*, was markedly reduced between 1902 and 1960.

On the other hand, there are theoretical reasons for believing that feasibility estimation might have become even less accurate over time. Assume that the Bureau of Reclamation and western irrigation interests agree that it is in both parties' interest for the government to build as many water projects as possible, so long as the project benefits outweigh that portion of the costs borne by the beneficiaries. Given institutionally imposed budget constraints, it is not possible for the bureau to develop all potential reservoir sites immediately. It is logical to assume, then, that the most feasible or advantageous sites will be developed first. Technically complicated, expensive projects with low returns would be left for later. Thus, as time passes, the tendency will be for the bureau to construct projects with lower and lower real net returns. Many of these inferior projects would have negative returns from the national perspective, but would still generate positive returns from the point of view of the project beneficiaries.

The bureau is obliged to conduct benefit-cost analyses for all new proposals and must demonstrate that benefits exceed costs for the projects. However, there are no stringent rules governing the methodology used to measure costs or benefits. By manipulating benefit-cost analysis in one way or another, virtually any project can appear feasible under a benefit-cost ratio criterion. Over time, the bureau has had an incentive to make worse and worse projects look feasible, suggesting that the feasibility analysis used to justify the projects is becoming progressively more biased.

Financing the Reclamation Program

Another Progressive element in the reclamation law was the plan for financing irrigation works. The act created a revolving fund, fed by sales of public lands which was to finance the entire program:

> All moneys received from the sale and disposal of public lands in [the sixteen arid states] . . . shall be, and the same are hereby reserved, set aside, and appropriated as a special fund in the Treasury to be known as the "reclamation fund," to be used in the examination and survey for and the construction and

maintenance of irrigation works for the storage, diversion, and development of waters for the reclamation of arid and semiarid lands in the said States . . . and for the payment of all other expenditures provided in this Act. (USCA 43, sec. 391)

The fund was created to absolve the nation's taxpayers from any responsibility for providing resources for western reclamation. Not only would this method of financing make the legislation more acceptable politically, but it was generally assumed to be more equitable than paying for the program from the general treasury. In addition to the contribution from sales of public lands, the reclamation fund would be replenished perpetually by repayment of project costs by the beneficiaries, and the entire program would operate as Representative Mondell had suggested, "without the cost of a penny to any American citizen" (U.S. Congress 1901, 61). The West would pay for its own reclamation.

Whatever the real prospects for meeting the financing goals envisaged by the sponsors of reclamation, the view that funds ought to be generated from the sales of public lands reveals a curious regional perspective of who really owned the public lands. Obviously there was some sentiment that the public domain belonged to the West and thus using moneys from its sale would not redistribute resources between regions of the nation. In the main, however, the proceeds from public land sales went into the national treasury.[20] From the perspective of national taxpayers, therefore, it would appear to make little difference whether the money used to finance reclamation projects originated from the sales of public lands (that would have gone to the treasury) or were drawn directly from the treasury, especially if the level of public lands sales and the number of new irrigation projects were independent.

Nevertheless, the prevailing belief at the time of the Reclamation Act was that financing the program through an earmarked, revolving fund was ethically superior, and that it would reduce the trans-regional redistribution associated with the act. Moreover, the fund would limit the redistributive potential of the reclamation program by placing an effective cap on the number of projects that could be built.

In practice, however, this Progressive stipulation was quickly violated. As soon as the act was passed, the Reclamation Service embarked on a panoply of projects with little thought to the adequacy of the reclamation fund. Very early it became clear that the service would not be able to finish the projects it had started without help from the general treasury. An act of March 3, 1905, allowed the proceeds from "sales of material utilized for temporary work and structures" and "all other condemned property" purchased in connection with the 1902 act to be channelled into the reclamation fund. On June 25, 1910, an act was passed that authorized the secretary of the treasury to transfer up to $20 million to the reclamation fund, to be borrowed from the public through tax-free, five-year bonds. And in 1917, all moneys "received in connection with operation under the reclamation law, except repayments on construction and operation and maintenance charges," were credited to the project's appropriation, and became available for expenditure. More legislation in 1919, 1921, 1924, 1927, 1930, 1931, and 1938, also contributed to the broadening of the reclamation fund to include other sources of revenue. As our theory predicts, the Progressive concept of a revolving fund to finance an efficient reclamation program fell victim to bureaucratic and special interest legislation.

This paper has described the history of federal reclamation since 1902 as a continual abandonment of the Progressive aspects of the Reclamation Act in favor of pressure groups, and has informally attempted to explain this movement in the context of a market for political favors. The clear implication is that the existence of a market for political favors provides a strong reason to question the ability of any legislation to promote the public interest by empowering the government to intervene in the private sector.

Justifications for Federal Involvement in Water Development

Proponents of the Reclamation Act argued that federal involvement in water development was necessary for several reasons. They believed it was constitution-ally justified under the commerce clause,[21] that the redistributive purposes of the legislation were secondary,[22] and that the act was just as legitimate as the 1899 Rivers and Harbors Act (U.S. Congress 1901, 90; Hibbard 1965, 441; Wahl 1989, 20; Alexander 1971, 288). Believing the scale of efficient irrigation development had become too large for private efforts to undertake successfully, proponents called for federal support. In his first message to Congress in 1901, President Roosevelt stated that:

> Great storage works are necessary to equalize the flow of streams and to save the flood waters. Their construction has been conclusively shown to be an undertaking too vast for private effort. Nor can it be best accomplished by the individual States acting alone. Far-reaching interstate problems are involved; and the resources of single States would often be inadequate. It is properly a national function, at least in some of its features. . . . The government should construct and maintain these reservoirs, as it does other public works . . . (Congressional Record 1902, 86)

It is not at all obvious, however, that Roosevelt was correct in the suggestion that water storage works were simply "too vast" for private enterprise. Even in the early twentieth century, capital markets were extensive, even international in scope. Foreign capital, especially British, was very important in railroad building and livestock ranching in the West. Therefore, if profitability could have been clearly demonstrated with acceptable risk, it is far from clear that private capital would not have been available for water development. The private sector in the United States had demonstrated ability to undertake water development as evidenced by the fact that from 1900 to 1910, over 90 percent of the 6.5 million acre increase in irrigated acreage was furnished by private enterprise (Anderson 1983, 31). Therefore, the allegation that the private sector was incapable of responding to profitable investment in irrigation development because projects were "too vast" clearly seems premature.

Coupled with the capital market-failure argument was the Progressives' "gospel of efficiency" (Hays 1980). According to this gospel, the reason private firms failed to provide storage reservoirs was pervasive ignorance and lack of technical expertise. Seeming to fortify this position was the fact that a series of private commercial dams had failed in the late nineteenth century, allegedly from inadequate engineering (Davison 1979, 189–90). By contrast, the Progressives argued that governmental agencies could do a better job of finding and training geologists, hydrographers, and engineers, and of initiating and managing the complicated water development projects with complete safety.

This argument too is unconvincing. Certainly, federal water agencies have utilized some of the world's foremost hydrological engineers in their projects, but these experts were available to private developers as well. Moreover, recent theoretical developments produced primarily by the "Chicago" and "public choice" schools of economics have cast strong doubt that the government can develop and manage natural resources more efficiently, or even more safely, than can the private sector of the economy (Baden and Stroup 1981).

Another argument for federal reclamation was that private industry was too shortsighted. When the Reclamation Act was debated in the Congress, Representative Mondell of Wyoming suggested that "conditions of population" contributed to the unwillingness of private enterprise to build the needed reservoirs (U.S. Congress 1901, 13). Apparently, Mondell believed that the private sector would not take account of the fact that the population would eventually be large enough to justify large storage reservoirs.

However, it is difficult to find either theoretical or empirical justification for the claim that government decisions are, in fact, more future-oriented than decisions made in the private sector. Given the nature of political decisions, and the propensity of politicians to focus on the next election, Mondell's argument is better understood as an effort to achieve his short-term election goals. If anything, government is more likely to be myopic and shortsighted due to election biases.

Perhaps the most legitimate justification for federal reclamation was that private irrigation companies were unable to capture all of the benefits from their projects (U.S. Congress 1901, 76). This may have been the case if the private costs of enforcing payment on water contracts were relatively high, and given the police power to regulate and the power to tax, government's contract enforcement costs may have been relatively lower. Moreover, private firms may have been unable to capture other intangible benefits associated with water development which arise from the values and ethics of society.[23] Many Americans believed the Jeffersonian view that agriculture produces productive, responsible, and moral citizens

(Paarlberg 1989, 1157–64). Hence, if water development promoted these worthy goals, the private sector would have underproduced the public good for which it received no compensation. To the extent that subsidies would increase the amount of reclamation to some theoretical optimum, governmental promotion of water development would be justified.

Historical evidence from the period suggests that a prominent reason for the failure of private companies to build major water storage works was not market failure of the kinds envisaged but anti-monopolistic provisions in the law that made it virtually impossible for these companies to obtain public lands which were required for efficient development. The ethic against land monopoly had been firmly implanted during the American Revolution and became an important component of public lands legislation (Golzé 1961, 63–4). When early proponents of reclamation suggested that project scale was "too large" for private industry, it was implicitly assumed that private development would lead to monopolization of land.

In the late nineteenth century, concern over land and water monopoly had become pandemic, partly due to the influence of Major Powell himself (Davison 1979, 38–9). Under existing laws, only individual homesteaders could file for lands, and they could under no circumstance sell these lands to private reservoir companies (U.S. Congress 1901, 13). Therefore, mutual irrigation companies that might have developed storage reservoirs were prevented from doing so by anti-monopoly sentiment. Also, it was believed that the inherent scale of projects was too great for cooperative organizations like mutual companies and, therefore, only large corporations could even consider such development.[24]

Referring to the Reclamation Act, Senator Newlands stated:

The purpose was to present a comprehensive plan . . . which would preserve this vast domain for home builders, and save it from concentrated monopolistic holding. We all wanted to preserve that domain in small tracts for actual settlers and home builders. We all wanted to prevent monopoly and concentration of ownership. (Congressional Record 1901, 6673–74)

Public sentiment against monopoly in land holdings should not be too surprising given the emphasis of Roosevelt–Progressive movement on trust busting and monopoly bashing. But today it seems somewhat strange that there was not more attention given then to the critical role that private property plays in providing incentives for investment in economically feasible projects and in generating the saving that constitutes the pool of investable funds in the private sector.

Conclusion

A theory of the market for political favors has been advanced. This theory predicts that the imperatives sought by the Progressives (namely, conservation and efficient management of water resources) would ultimately give way to redistributive policies favored by regional interests. This prediction is clearly supported by the following historical facts:

1. The original policy of building at least one project in every state in the early period of the Reclamation Act ensured a wide distribution of the benefits of reclamation and consolidated the political support needed to get the act passed.

2. Overestimation of benefits and underestimation of costs have militated against the choice of only economically feasible projects and have increased subsidies to irrigators.

3. Exemption of irrigation from paying interest charges on construction costs has encouraged excessive capital investment in irrigation facilities, stretched out the period of project construction, and lengthened repayment periods, all of which have contributed to the building of inefficient projects.

4. The suspension of repayment obligations during the construction period has excessively extended the completion of projects and increased the extent of the subsidies to irrigators.

5. The implementation of the ability-to-pay rule for fixing water repayment charges has weakened the requirement to build only efficient projects and has increased the subsidies to irrigation.

6. The abandonment of the reclamation fund as the source of funding for reclamation development, and its replacement by appropriations from the general treasury, local government bonding, and applications of power and grazing revenues to support irrigation have facilitated income transfers from taxpayers to irrigators through inefficient federal water projects.

7. The practice of constructing benefit-cost tests for entire multiple-use projects, and not for individual components of such projects as well, has facilitated the building of components that cannot pass a benefit-cost test, and thus has produced inefficient projects and increased the irrigation subsidy.

In addition, it has been demonstrated that many of the arguments advanced in favor of federal reclamation were inadequate to justify the large-scale governmental provision of water development in the western United States. These lessons from the political economy of the American West should make us skeptical of modern Progressive programs.

Notes

1. Some of the material used in this model of the market for political favors is taken from Gardner (1994).
2. Some valuable by-products of holding political office may last long after leaving office if a capital stock of accumulated knowledge and contacts remains available. Many, perhaps most, politicians who wish to work after retiring from political office remain in Washington and elsewhere in jobs that capitalize on contacts and expertise gained while in office.
3. Other commodities of value transferred to the suppliers generally considered to be part of lobbying include: personal perquisites (traveling junkets, living and recreational facilities, food and drink, preferences of various kinds for family members, friends, political supporters, etc.); payments for appearances which have economic as well as political value to the demanders; and it is not unknown for demanders to make illegal payments (bribes) to politicians.
4. It must be clear that the effect of the actions or inactions of the politicians resulting from a transaction is expected, *ex ante*, to leave the demanding group better off. Of course, whether the demanders are actually better off, *ex post*, is another matter, since actions in political markets, like those in all markets, often produce unanticipated effects.
5. In addition, subsidies will cause misallocation of resources or "deadweight" efficiency losses which fall on the economy as a whole (Gardner 1987, 291). These deadweight losses may also produce political repercussions to the extent that they are known to the general public and are associated with a specific politician or political party.
6. The Republican platform stated, "In further pursuance of the constant policy of the Republican party to provide free homes on the public domain, we recommend adequate national legislation to reclaim the arid lands of the United States, reserving control of the distribution of water for irrigation to the respective States and Territories" and the Democrat platform, "We favor an intelligent system of improving the arid lands of the West, storing the waters for purposes of irrigation, and the holding of such lands for actual settlers" Congressional Record (1902, 6763). For the Silver Republican platform, see U.S. Congress (1901, 8). For more historical context, see Hibbard (1965, 440) and Lee (1980, 14).
7. William E. Smyth, chairman of the Irrigation Congress executive committee, and manager and editor of the periodical *The Irrigation Age*, succeeded Powell as the de facto "leader" of the reclamation movement in 1893. Then Smyth began to espouse avidly his vision of a new empire in the West, made up of colonies dependent upon irrigation, and attempted to establish such a colony at "New Plymouth." As early as 1895, however, it had become clear that Smyth's views were not those of the mainstream irrigation enthusiasts. In that year, Smyth lost his position in the Irrigation Congress and lost control of his magazine. See Davison (1979, 230–1).

8. Concerning the purpose of government action, the statement "the greatest good for the greatest number over the longest time period" has been attributed to Gifford Pinchot.

9. 57th Congress, 1st session, 392.

10. Rucker and Fishback (1983, 53) estimate that the initial subsidy to irrigators that resulted from the failure to charge interest was about 15 percent of costs, assuming a 3 percent discount rate. However, this assumes no risk and a ten-year payback period. If a 40-year repayment period is assumed, which was granted eventually, and a 10 percent discount rate is assumed to reflect risk, then the interest subsidy rises to a whopping 91 percent of costs.

11. Wahl (1989, 28) states that the bureau's administrative interpretation not to charge interest was based on the fact that the act did not specifically mention interest charges and on the implicit approval of Congress, which did not object to bureau practice over the years. However, evidence in congressional hearings (1901) makes it clear that Newell and the other framers of the legislation deliberately excluded interest charges from the act with the expectation that doing so would encourage development on lands that would not otherwise be utilized (Golzé 1961).

12. By the 1950s, "feasibility" was understood to include three components: engineering feasibility, which considered the potential water supply, geologic conditions of the dam site, availability of construction materials, and local soil conditions; economic feasibility, equivalent to a benefit-cost ratio exceeding unity; and financial feasibility, which was understood to be "the test of a proposed project to determine whether its reimbursable costs can be returned by the project beneficiaries" (Golzé 1961, 126–9).

13. Davison (1979, 24) believes that early estimates failed because early reclamation leaders failed "to seek out and utilize all the information and data which had been gathered by generations of private and corporate irrigators," and thus failed to anticipate many of the problems associated with water development. Also see Gates (1968, 657).

14. The Reclamation Service has had several name changes and has been known as the Bureau of Water and Power and is now the Bureau of Reclamation.

15. However, at the same time, the requirement of full repayment of costs by beneficiaries as initially imposed would restrain the agency from becoming too reckless in estimating or changing costs because putting the beneficiaries under financial stress would not engender their loyalty over the long pull.

16. In response to complaints from farmers that they could not meet their contractual obligations, Congress repeatedly extended the repayment schedule. As a result of the "Fact-Finders Act" of 1924, and subsequent legislation in 1926 and 1939, repayment contracts came to be negotiated on the basis of the land owners' "ability to pay" rather than on the total cost of the project. Essentially, ability to pay for water represents the revenues obtained from the crops minus all the non-land costs of producing them. The effect of using ability to pay to determine repayment schedules has been to greatly reduce the proportion of total separable

costs repaid by irrigators.

17. Alternatively, a dummy variable could be used to distinguish between early and late "regimes."

18. Heteroscedasticity in the data is immediately apparent: the variance of the second group of figures is considerably lower than for the first. The Goldfield-Quandt statistic for the data, ordering by year, is 17.96, where an F value of 6.03 is statistically significant at probability .01. This decrease in variance might be explained by the fact that benefit-cost analysis did not become a formal requirement until the 1930s; therefore, not only did analytical techniques become gradually more refined, but they became more uniform and more strictly enforced over time.

19. Any cost or benefit "induced by" or "stemming from" the direct costs or benefits of a project is considered to be "secondary." Increased profits in local nonagricultural industries such as construction supply companies and food processing plants are examples of secondary benefits. These benefits generally accrue in the geographic region surrounding the project.

20. The exception being the five percent of the proceeds of such sales dedicated to "educational and other purposes."

21. The Supreme Court decision in *Gibbons v. Ogden* (1824) justified federal regulation of interstate waterways and their tributaries under the commerce clause. Feldman (1991, 66–7) discusses the court's reasoning behind this interpretation. It was also argued that the Newlands bill was constitutional "inasmuch as it involved the general welfare" (Robbins 1976, 331).

22. On the other hand, Holmes (1972, 33) suggests that "the primary social objectives of the reclamation program were the secondary benefits of irrigation projects—regional economic development in the arid West and stabilization of agricultural economies subject to drought in the Missouri Basin."

23. Even though the market-failure jargon, including externalities and collective goods, had not been invented at the time, politicians and promoters of reclamation often referred to values outside the market like community development, preparing lands for homesteading, and building of infrastructure to support private development (U.S. Congress 1901).

24. It was believed that cooperative ventures could not be organized on such a large scale. For irrigation projects, the costs of controlling the free-rider problem and of settling disputes quickly increases as the size of the cooperative venture grows beyond a single community.

References

Alexander, Thomas G. 1971. An investment in progress: Utah's first federal reclamation project, the Strawberry Valley Project. *Utah Historical Quarterly* 39 (Summer).

Alston, Lee J., and Pablo T. Spiller. 1992. A congressional theory of Indian property rights: The Cherokee Outlet. In *Property rights and Indian economies*, edited by Terry L. Anderson. Lanham, MD: Rowman & Littlefield Publishers, Inc., 85–107.

Anderson, Terry L. 1983. *Water crisis: Ending the policy drought*. Baltimore: Johns Hopkins University Press.

Baden, John, and Richard L. Stroup, eds. 1981. *Bureaucracy vs. environment: The environmental costs of bureaucratic governance*. Ann Arbor: University of Michigan Press.

Baldridge, Kenneth W. 1971. Reclamation work of the Civilian Conservation Corps 1933–1942. *Utah Historical Quarterly* 39 (Summer).

Becker, Gary S. 1983. A theory of competition among pressure groups for political influence. *Quarterly Journal of Economics* 98: 371–401.

Boadway, Robin, and Neil Bruce. 1984. *Welfare economics*. Cambridge: Basil Blackwell, Inc.

Congressional Record. 1901. Vol. 34.

Congressional Record. 1902. Vol. 35.

Davison, Stanley Roland. [1952] 1979. *The leadership of the reclamation movement*. Reprint. New York: Arno Press.

Feldman, David Lewis. 1991. *Water resources management: In search of an environmental ethic*. Baltimore: Johns Hopkins University Press.

Gardner, B. Delworth. 1994. *Plowing ground in Washington*. San Francisco: Pacific Research Institute for Public Policy.

Gardner, Bruce L. 1987. Causes of U.S. farm commodity programs. *Journal of Political Economy* 95(2): 290–310.

Gates, Paul W. 1968. *History of public land law development*. Washington, DC: U.S. Public Land Law Review Commission.

Golzé, Alfred R. [1952] 1961. Reclamation in the United States. Reprint. Caldwell: Caxton Printers.

Gwartney, James D., and Richard E. Wagner. 1988. Public choice and the conduct of representative government. In *Public choice and constitutional economics*, edited by James D. Gwartney and Richard E. Wagner. Greenwich, CT: JAI Press.

Gwartney, James D., and Richard L. Stroup. 1992. *Economics: Public and private choice*, 6th ed. San Diego: Harcourt Brace Jovanovich.

Haveman, Robert H. 1972. *The economic performance of public investments: An ex-post evaluation of water resources investments*. Baltimore: Johns Hopkins University Press.

Hays, Samuel P. [1959] 1980. *Conservation and the gospel of efficiency: The Progressive conservation movement 1890–1920*. Reprint. New York: Athenium.

Hibbard, Benjamin Horace. [1924] 1965. *A history of the public lands policies*. Reprint. Madison: University of Wisconsin Press.

Holmes, Beatrice Holt. 1972. *A history of federal water resources programs, 1800–1960.* U.S. Department of Agriculture, misc. publication no. 1233. Washington, DC: U.S. Government Printing Office.

———. 1977. *A history of federal water resources programs, 1961–1976.* U.S. Department of Agriculture, misc. publication no. 1379. Washington, DC: U.S. Government Printing Office.

Larson, E. O. 1955. *Reclamation accomplishments: The Strawberry Valley Project.* Salt Lake City: U.S. Department of the Interior, Bureau of Reclamation, Region 4.

LeBaron, Allen. 1985. Measuring local and group benefits from subsidized (public) investment. Economic research study paper no. 85-33, Department of Economics, Utah State University, Logan (December).

Lee, Lawrence B. 1980. *Reclaiming the American West: An historiography and guide.* Santa Barbara: American Bibliographical Center-Clio Press.

McQueen, Stephen D. C. 1989. An estimation of primary benefits realized on three Bureau of Reclamation projects. Ph.D. dissertation, Utah State University.

Merrill, David, Donald L. Snyder, and Jay Andersen. 1982. *An historical mitigation study of the Strawberry Valley Project, Utah.* Provo: U.S. Department of the Interior, Bureau of Reclamation.

National Irrigation Congress. 1893. *Official proceedings of the International Irrigation Congress.* Los Angeles.

Niskanen, William A. 1971. *Bureaucracy and representative government.* New York: Aldine-Atherton.

Olson, Mancur. 1965. *The logic of collective action.* Cambridge: Harvard University Press.

Paarlberg, Robert L. 1989. The political economy of American agricultural policy: Three approaches. *American Journal of Agricultural Economics* 71(5): 1157–64.

Peltzman, Sam. 1976. Toward a more general theory of regulation. *Journal of Law and Economics* 19: 211–41.

Powell, John Wesley. [1879] 1983. *Report on the arid lands of the United States: With a more detailed account of the lands of Utah.* Cambridge: Harvard Common Press.

Reisner, Marc P. 1986. *Cadillac desert: The American West and its disappearing water.* New York: Viking Penguin.

Renshaw, Edward F. 1957. *Toward responsible government: An economic appraisal of federal investment in water resource programs.* Chicago: Idyia Press.

Robbins, Roy M. 1976. *Our landed heritage: The public domain 1776–1976.* Lincoln: University of Nebraska Press.

Rucker, Randal R., and Price V. Fishback. 1983. The federal reclamation program: An analysis of rent-seeking behavior. In *Water rights: Scarce resource allocation, bureaucracy, and the environment,* edited by Terry L. Anderson. San Francisco: Pacific Institute for Public Policy Research, 45–82.

Tullock, Gordon. 1965. *The politics of bureaucracy.* Washington, DC: Public Affairs Press.

U.S. Congress. House. 1901. Hearings before the House Subcommittee on Public Lands. Washington, DC.

Wahl, Richard W. 1989. *Markets for federal water: Subsidies, property rights, and the Bureau of Reclamation.* Washington, DC: Resources for the Future.

5

The Progressive Ideal and the Columbia Basin Project

Randy T. Simmons

The Columbia Basin Project (CBP) is a federally planned and designed attempt to provide affordable, family farms in a "desert wasteland," to provide irrigation water sufficient to transform the wasteland into productive cropland, to organize orderly settlement, and to lay all the groundwork necessary to create a productive, prosperous society in a relatively poor, unproductive region. The CBP succeeded in these goals but at such a high price that the gains to those who have benefited are less than the costs to taxpayers and electricity rate payers.

The story of the Columbia Basin Project is one of interaction between ideology and the pursuit of private interest. Because of its timing and essentially frontier location, the Columbia Basin Project provided an opportunity to act out Progressive ideology on a large scale. Progressivism is the ideology that animated most of U.S. politics from Theodore Roosevelt to Lyndon Johnson and is the belief that government can manipulate the economy to improve economic efficiency, individuals, and society. The CBP may be the single best example of Progressivism in action. It is also an example of the central tenets of modern political economy as there are rent-seeking interests, vote-maximizing politicians, and budget-maximizing bureaucrats. The pursuit of these private interests was both obscured and encouraged by Progressivism.

The purpose of this paper is to consider the Columbia Basin Project as embodying the Progressive vision, analyze consequences, and draw conclusions about Progressivism as political economy.

The Progressive Vision and the Pacific Northwest

The Pacific Northwest was the last portion of the continental United States to be settled during the period of "manifest destiny." Settlement expanded to the Pacific Ocean and water, forest, and mining resources were developed, often without direction or coordination by the federal government. Progressives spoke out against the "shortsightedness" of economic development without the direction of government. They wanted to institute a new political economy that would replace what they regarded as the unplanned, messy, wasteful, private use of resources and environment with political planning, organization, expert administration, science, and efficiency. The purpose was to establish a national community linked together for the public good. Their vision became a foundation of the public agenda in time to greatly influence the development and future of the Pacific Northwest.

The Progressives' primary goal was to organize society in ever more productive ways (Nelson 1991, 191). Thus, the Forest Reserves, for example, were to be managed "for the greatest good of the greatest number in the long run" (Pinchot 1947, 261). To achieve such goals, industry *and* government needed to be run according to scientific principles. Engineers were seen as "a new industrial intelligentsia, standing between capital and labor, and peculiarly fitted to resolve the nation's social conflicts" (Haber 1964, 46–7). In 1887, Woodrow Wilson wrote that in previous times, "the functions of government were simple, because life was simple." But times had changed and "the functions of government are every day becoming more complex and difficult" (Wilson 1941, 483–85). Politics, according to Wilson, was to provide general policy direction, but government was to be run by trained scientists.

Wilson's confidence in engineers and science was reflected by the conservation movement—a movement directed almost wholly by the Progressive faith in science. Historian Samuel Hays (1959, 41–2) explains:

> Conservation, above all, was a scientific movement, and its role in history arises from the implications of science and technology in modern society. Conservation leaders sprang from such fields as hydrology, forestry, agrostology, geology, and anthropology. Vigorously active in professional circles in the national capital, these leaders brought the ideals and practices of their crafts into federal resource policy. Loyalty to these professional ideals, not close association with the grass-roots public, set the tone of the Theodore Roosevelt conservation movement. Its essence was rational planning to promote efficient development and use of all natural resources. The idea of

efficiency drew these federal scientists from one resources task to another, from specific programs to comprehensive concepts. It molded the policies that they proposed, their administrative techniques, and their relations with Congress and the public. It is from the vantage point of applied science, rather than of democratic protest, that one must understand the historic role of the conservation movement.

Thus, the Progressive agenda contained the following components:

1. trust in engineers as the new industrial intelligentsia;
2. belief that markets were unplanned, unfair, and wasteful; and
3. faith that rational planning by scientific managers could organize society in more productive ways.

Each of these components is an integral part of the Columbia Basin Project.

Progressive Water Development

The Progressive definition of efficiency is an engineering definition rather than an economic definition. The concern is with how to make resources available to people, not necessarily with the value of those resources or the costs of delivery. This engineering mentality was a driving force in water development in the West including the Columbia Basin.

What Hays identified as "efficient development and use of all natural resources" was a special concern for settlers in the arid West. Water development was especially important to early settlers in the Columbia Basin and, like settlers in the rest of the West, they attempted several small-scale irrigation projects. A succession of irrigation companies, however, failed because of the high cost of pumping water and building ditches. The only successful irrigation efforts were around Moses Lake, where 3,000 acres were being irrigated from the lake or deep wells by 1943.

But there were still acres of unirrigated land and more people who wanted to come to the Pacific Northwest. The limit to further expansion of irrigation was not the quantity of water, but the seasonal flow patterns—the natural occurrence of precipitation badly out of phase with the growing season. Spring runoff was lost when crop demands were low, but flows decreased during the summer just when crop demands increased. The answer was to store winter and spring flows with dams and reservoirs, often at exponentially increasing construction and maintenance costs.

In the rest of the West, reservoir sites were established on small streams with no unusual engineering problems and where the work could be done with teams and scrapers during the off season. The increased costs were handled by the traditional, cooperative labor and low capital approach that had successfully diverted the run of the river for irrigation. But in the Columbia Basin geology presented difficult problems and costs were prohibitive for most irrigators. Thus, politicians, industry leaders, and settlers saw large tracts of potentially productive land lie dormant while large amounts of water flowed unutilized down the Columbia River. It was a problem to be solved by planners, engineers, and politicians.

The engineers and planners were found in the Reclamation Service, in a new agency created by Theodore Roosevelt's administration. Soon after becoming president, Theodore Roosevelt said, "The western half of the United States would sustain a population greater than that of our whole country today if the waters that now run to waste were saved and used for irrigation" (quoted in Reisner 1986, 119). He supported and orchestrated a bill that became the Newlands Reclamation Act of 1902. That act created the Reclamation Service, later to become the Bureau of Reclamation, and gave birth to the accounting and payback systems that allowed the bureau's dam projects to pass benefit-cost tests.

It was Franklin Roosevelt, however, who used the Bureau of Reclamation to promote the development of the Pacific Northwest. Early in his first term he announced "in definite and certain terms, that the next great . . . development to be undertaken by the Federal Government must be that on the Columbia River" (quoted in Reisner 1986, 159). The result was the Columbia Basin Project.

Engineering the Columbia Basin Project

The key physical structure of the CBP is the Grand Coulee Dam. Just over fifty years old, it is the largest concrete structure in the world and is the subject of folk songs, financial institution advertisements, and Bureau of Reclamation propaganda. It doubled the country's hydroelectric capacity when it was completed. By providing electricity to powerful irrigation pumps, it lifts almost 10 percent of the Columbia River's flow over the rim of the canyon wall 280 feet above the dam and irrigates over half a million acres of desert. The Bureau of Reclamation refers to the project and the dam as "two monuments of man's ingenuity and engineering ability which are part of an overall plan to harness the power of a great river and reclaim a desert wasteland" (U.S. Department of the Interior 1983, 11).

Grand Coulee Dam is on the main stem of the Columbia River about 90 miles west of Spokane, Washington. The extensive irrigation works extend southward on the Columbia Plateau 125 miles to the vicinity of Pasco, Washington, where the Snake and Columbia Rivers join. Today, the project provides full irrigation service to over 500,000 acres of farm land comprising approximately 2,171 farms. Water facilities serve nearly 15,500 people for irrigation and other uses and power generation totals 22,764,876,000 kilowatt hours per year.

As early as 1919, two large-scale plans had been proposed by residents of the region. One was to dam the Columbia River, and the other was to build a 130-

mile, gravity-waterway consisting of canals, natural waterways, and siphons from Pend Oreille Lake in Idaho (U.S. Department of the Interior 1978, 5). The Columbia Basin Commission, created by the Washington State Legislature in 1919, appropriated $100,000 to study both proposals and ultimately supported the gravity-waterway. The commission authorized a later study by Major General George W. Goethals of Panama Canal fame. He also favored the gravity method as being "cheaper and simpler to build." His report was contradicted by an Army Corps of Engineers' study funded under the 1926 Rivers and Harbors Bill. This study, completed in 1931, discounted the gravity method as "not economically feasible because of excessive costs," but favored the Grand Coulee Dam and pumping project as "economically feasible and engineeringly sound" (U.S. Department of the Interior 1978, 6–7).

President Franklin Roosevelt chose the dam and pumping project and included the Grand Coulee Dam as part of the new Public Works Administration Program in 1933 and designated $63 million for its construction, the largest amount thereto-fore allocated for a single project. The $63 million funding was provided by the Public Works Administration, under section 202 of the National Recovery Act of July 27, 1933. Marc Reisner speculates that Congress would never have allocated money for such a project but "Congress had undermined its own intention by giving FDR blanket authority, under the Public Works Administration and the National Industrial Recovery Act, to select and fund 'emergency' projects that would assist the relief effort" (Reisner 1986, 163).

In order to adequately serve irrigation purposes, the top of the dam had to be 350 feet above the level of the Columbia River. Roosevelt's initial approval and funding, however, called for a lower dam, meaning that the original purpose of irrigation would not be provided; the lower dam could only be used to produce electricity. The dam's foundation, however, was built for the higher dam and almost a year after Roosevelt's initial proposal, the secretary of the interior issued a change order that called for the construction of the higher structure. The higher dam, without canals, pumps, and holding reservoirs, cost $270 million[1] (Reisner 1986, 163).

Developing the CBP was a two-phase process. The first phase was to build the dam and produce electricity. This phase began in 1933 with the first construction of the dam's base and electrical generation began on March 22, 1941 (U.S. Department of the Interior 1983, 8–9). The second phase was to plan for the people who would use the soon-to-be-available irrigation water.

Planning for the People

As the dam neared completion, President Roosevelt sent the following memo to Harold Ickes showing how completely he accepted the Progressive assumptions about planning and markets:

In view of the fact that the Grand Coulee Dam will be finished early in 1941, I believe it is time for us to plan for its use.

This use divides itself into two parts:

a. Surplus power over and above power needs for pumping water into the Columbia Basin. This subject should be referred to the National Power Policy Committee. It affects, of course, the tie-in with Benefice and with existing power consumer cooperatives, rural lines, etc., and it has a bearing on a possible third dam in the Columbia River, half way between Grand Coulee and Bonneville.

b. The development of the Columbia Basin itself. I feel very strongly on this subject. I understand that it is believed by Reclamation Bureau that when water is provided, 80,000 families can be put on the land. If this estimate is correct, it will mean approximately 20,000 other families who will be engaged in services such as gasoline stations, small stores, transportation, local government operations, etc., etc. I hope the Government can lay down a definite policy that all lands will be open only to relief families or families which for many different reasons have abandoned their homes and fled to the coastal region or are now 'adrift' in various parts of the country. In other words, I want to give first chance to the 'Grapes of Wrath' families of the nation.

I realize that a percentage of the families are shiftless and an even larger percentage of them are ignorant of farm and home economics that without help they would make a failure of this new land.

The work of the rural rehabilitation and WPA colonization projects during the past seven years has demonstrated nevertheless that given supervision and instruction for a few years this condition of ignorance can, in most cases, be overcome. This entails in any planning a fairly large overhead covering supervision and instruction during the first few years. It envisages also a percentage of families who, no matter how much they are supervised and instructed, will fail to make good. Such families would, of course, have to be replaced by others who would make good.

All in all this is a tremendous subject and I call your attention to the definite possibility of planning the Columbia Basin for certain local industries to supplement agriculture—decentralized industries which will fill purely local needs and not export their production beyond the Columbia Basin.

It is obvious from the history of Oregon and Washington apple growing, for example, that there has probably been too much apple production in that area. There is, using the same illustration, a growing improvement in apple production in the Appalachian section with the result that proportionately fewer Pacific Coast apples are sold in local eastern markets than formerly. The eastern and southern growers have at last begun to learn how to grade, pick, and store their apples.

In the same way there is a tendency in the Far West to grow too many onions and similar specialized crops, thus creating too many dependencies on eastern markets and too little diversification of crops.

The Columbia Basin project requires, therefore, a comprehensive agricultural and industrial economic survey. The Basin can eventually support 500,000 of our citizens, and I should like to have it so planned that opportunity for settlement will be given primarily to those families which are today in need.

Finally, the whole Basin should be planned with the thought of making the Basin economically self-supporting as far as possible. There is no reason, for instance, why the Basin should not make the equivalent of its whole shoe supply because hides are available close to the site. Certain woolen goods can be manufactured and it might be possible to work out small glass and crockery factories. (Nixon 1957, 405–7)

It is clear that the purpose of the project was to do much more than just build a magnificent engineering project. It was to fit people into the engineering. Although the following description of the hopes of Bureau of Reclamation planners relates to the projects in general, it is a fitting description of the CBP planning and Progressivism:

Environmental engineering was just the first step. Then must come a process of fitting rural people to the apparatus: selecting settlers on the basis of capital, skill, and teachability; showing them how to farm in the new, intensive, regimented way; reorganizing them into a competent local managerial agency; furnishing them aid and direction at every point. Men and women simply had to be made capable of living up to the engineering. (Worster 1985, 180)

The planning process, called the Columbia Basin Joint Investigations, started in 1939 and was completed in 1942. Three hundred people representing forty agencies (federal, state, local, and private) took part in the investigations. These investigations were organized around twenty-eight problem areas, which were divided into sixteen divisions (Table 5.1). Notice that the problem areas include more than building irrigation structures. The purpose of the joint investigations was to develop a master plan that established rules and regulations for carrying out the goals established by the Congress and planners. Marion Clawson (1987, 148), who later became the first Director of the Bureau of Land Management and was the Department of Agriculture's coordinator with the Bureau of Reclamation on the Joint Investigations summarized the comprehensive nature of the plans: " . . . these studies were far and away the most complete, the most accurate, and the most dependable plans that had ever been made for a new irrigation project."

Following the report of the Joint Investigations, Congress passed the Columbia Basin Project Act (CBPA) and President Roosevelt approved it on March 10, 1943. The two major purposes of the act were to prevent "speculation in lands of the Columbia Basin Project" and "to provide substitute and additional authority related to the settlement and development of the project."[2] In addition, the Congress included in the act a means to "secure their previous investments" (U.S. Department of the Interior 1949, 26).

Table 5.1

Columbia Basin Joint Investigations Planning Topics

Division Number	Division Title	Problem Number	Problem Title
I	Basic surveys	–	Basic surveys
II	Types of farm economy	1	Farm experience
		2	Types of farming
		3	Insuring proper land use
III	Water requirements	4 & 5	Water requirements
IV	Size of farm units	6 & 8	Optimum farm size
		7	Special land units
V	Layout and equipment of farms	9	Farm improvement
		10	Patterns of rural settlement
VI	Allocation of costs & repayments	11	Allocation of cost
		12	Equitable payments
		13	Allocation of repayments
		14	Financial aid to settlers
VII	Control of project lands	15	Private owned lands
		16	State, county, and railroad lands
VIII	Rate of development	17	Development rate of project land
IX	Villages	18	Optimum number of new villages
X	Roads & transportation facilities	19	Road network
		20	Railroad facilities
		21	Columbia River as commercial route
XI	Underground waters	22	Underground waters
XII	Rural & village electrification	23	Rural & village electrification
XIII	Manufacturers	24	Manufacturers
XIV	Recreation resources & needs	25	Recreation resources & needs
		26	Use of Roosevelt Reservoir
XV	Rural community centers	27	Location of schools, etc.
XVI	Government organization public works programming & financing	28	Government organization public works programming & financing

Source: U.S. Department of the Interior (1941).

Politically Planned Development

The development of the project lands was guided largely by the Progressive concerns about real estate markets. The planners specifically wanted to replace the existing large blocks of privately owned land with small one-family, "self-supporting farms," make land available at "fair" prices, avoid windfall gains for anyone in the area, and prevent speculation. They sought to accomplish these goals through land transfer policies, repayment contracts, recordable contracts, and acreage limitations.

Land Transfer Policy

When the CBPA was passed, about 90 percent of the project land was privately owned, with the remaining 10 percent owned by state, county, or federal governments (U.S. Department of the Interior 1946, 6). Given the low population base (fewer than 10,000 people), some private landowners owned very large tracts of land. They became the target of the bureau's policy to transfer private and public lands to large numbers of new settlers. The bureau's means of persuading large, private landowners to sell their lands was the bureau's initial control over the allocation of the new water rights and its land classification and appraisal system.

Lands were classified as irrigable or non-irrigable. The 1,029,000 acres of estimated irrigable land were then divided into three different classes. Class 1 land was considered the best for irrigation purposes. Class 2 was average value land considered more costly to farm. Finally, those lands with low productive capacity, high cost, and low marginal value were designated as Class 3 lands.

Once classified, project lands had to be appraised *without considering the added value of future irrigation development*, i.e., at the land's dry-farm value. A board of appraisers evaluated the lands according to the adaptability to farming. The chief purpose of the land appraisal was to help insure that settlers could obtain land in the project at "fair" price, which meant pre-irrigation prices. The bill's architects were opposed to the original owners of the land gaining *any* windfall from the project. Instead, they wanted the value added to the land by the CBP to be received by the person who developed the land and paid the construction charges that were levied. The appraised values of project land ranged from less than $5 per acre for raw desert land to more than $30 per acre for some of the better land previously used for dry-farming (U.S. Department of the Interior 1946, 9).

Repayment Contracts

Before any of the irrigation features of the project could be constructed, not including the immediate structures of the Grand Coulee Dam or its pumping facilities and equalizing reservoirs, state irrigation districts and the federal government had to agree to repayment contracts for project construction costs.

According to the CBPA, the secretary of the interior was to decide how much of the construction costs had to be repaid by irrigation charges. Enforcement of the repayment contracts was to conform to requirements under all other federal reclamation laws.

Three irrigation districts were formed under laws of the state of Washington, with local governing bodies for distributing CBP water. The farmers were to make their construction cost payments to the irrigation districts, which in turn were to pay the federal government according to the requirements of the previously negotiated repayment contracts. Payments were based on the project farmers' "ability to pay." An average repayment of $85 per acre was originally established in the repayment contracts signed on October 9, 1945. Payments were to be made over a 40-year period at an average of $2.12 per acre per year (U.S. Department of the Interior 1978, 44). In addition, farmers were expected to pay annual operation and maintenance charges, including irrigation pumping costs amounting to about $5 per acre per year (Marts 1961, 5).

Recordable Contracts

To provide for the new settlement of the project area, the CBPA authorized the secretary of the interior to purchase "excess land" at the government appraised dry-land value, divide it into family-sized farm units, and resell it to settlers. Excess land was defined by the CBPA as, "lands within the project in excess of one farm unit held by any one landowner."[3] A farm unit could be any combination of Class 1, 2, or 3 land, as long as each unit was considered sufficient to provide an adequate living for the individual settler or family. The act further authorized the government to lease lands pending their sale under the project plan, establish town sites, and dedicate portions for public use. Until the federal government could purchase these lands for reselling and leasing to prospective settlers, purchases were made by the new settlers from private owners.

The recordable contract was the government's main method of monitoring sales and transfers of project lands. To receive irrigation water, an owner, new or old, had to register a recordable contract with the government by filing the contract in the official county records. The contract was a pledge by the individual to (1) purchase, sell, or exchange land at the appraised values; (2) dispose of any excess lands at the government appraised value; (3) give the secretary of the interior an irrevocable power of attorney to sell on behalf of the owner any excess lands at appraised values with the option for the government to buy the excess lands from said owner (unless the owner waived this requirement in writing); and (4) stipulate heirs and successors to the property.

In addition, either the purchaser or the seller had to file an affidavit with the county auditor describing the terms of the sale of land covered by a recordable contract. If the affidavit was not filed, the water rights of the land could be revoked by the secretary of the interior within two years after the deed was registered in the county records. Furthermore, a landowner who had signed a recordable contract agreed to sell his land at the government appraised dry-land value plus the newly appraised value of additional improvements, at least within the first five years of water being delivered to the land. After the five-year period, land covered by a recordable contract could be sold at market prices.

Acreage Limitations

The CBPA provided for subdividing project lands into farm units capable of supporting a living for an average-sized family, as long as the unit did not exceed 160 acres. The act did not define an "average-sized" family but did stipulate that project water could not be delivered to more than one farm unit per landowner. The one exception to this rule was that any project lands held by the owner before May 27, 1937 the date of the first anti-speculation act for the project) could receive water for more than one unit as long as the total acreage did not exceed 160 irrigable acres. The authority to subdivide the project lands rested with the secretary of the interior who was to weigh the individual factors of soil, topography, location, and other unlisted criteria, in deciding the size of a particular unit.

No landowner was to receive water on any unit totaling more than 160 irrigable acres. The owner in such a case had ten years in which to dispose of the land over the 160-acre limit *at the government appraised dry-land value*. Landowners could authorize the Department of the Interior to dispose of the land.

The Results

A central objective of the Columbia Basin Project was to provide the farming opportunities for Americans who might previously or otherwise not have farming opportunities (Weinkauf 1974). The planners attempted to design farms that would provide "acceptable economic opportunity for the maximum number of settlers" (Clawson 1987, 146). They expected a stable, growing regional economy would develop around the agricultural communities of small family farms.

The problem for the planners was that they had to look backward, not forward. The joint investigations did an excellent job of planning for the 1930s, but the planning was done during the 1940s. Consider the implications of planning the development of a region during an era of rapidly changing social, economic, and technological conditions. Weinkauf (1974, 76) illustrates the planners' responses:

> Horses were used as the most common source of power by most farmers on irrigated land, although there were a number of farmers using tractor power for some operations. After considerable debate among investigators, it was decided that in view of the scarcity of reliable information relating to tractor performance and operation, the analysis of labor, equipment, and capital

requirements for farms in the Columbia Basin would be based upon horse-drawn equipment.

Forecasting the types of farm economy for the Basin also, of course, entailed consideration of social, economic, and technological factors. For the purpose of their projections it was assumed that there would be 'no marked changes in technological development on the farm and no marked changes in the social structure.'

A price level and price structure was assumed comparable to the average for the period between 1921 and 1940.

The planners could do nothing else because no one at the time envisioned the remarkable changes taking place in American agriculture. Marion Clawson (1987, 148–50) explained, "Our planning was sound for the world we anticipated; but the world was different by the time water actually flowed onto the land." He concluded:

I do not wish to convey the impression that our studies were wholly useless. Several parts of them were operative in the actual settlement but, by and large, they were simply outdated by developments outside the Basin and unforeseen by us at the time the planning was under way.

The constraints government planning puts on technological change are illustrated by irrigation technology. When the CBP first started, a farm unit was restricted to no more than 80 acres and the excess land had to be sold. In 1957 farm units were increased to 160 acres and later increased again to 960 acres. The highest quality land was developed when acreage limitations were small with the lower quality land being developed under the increased acreage limitations. When center pivot irrigation systems were introduced to deliver water more efficiently, most of the premium lands were all tied up in farm units too small to take advantage of the new technology. The result is the best technology is used on the poorest land.

Settlers in the CBP were not poor "Grapes of Wrath" people. Most entered the project with an average net worth of $14,000.[4] Four out of five settlers were farming irrigated farms before settling in the CBP (Straus 1958, 9). College education levels among the settlers were considerably higher than for the nation or for the state of Washington. Ninety-nine percent had either been raised on a farm or had other, previous farming experience. The median value of assets was $17,800 at the time of settlement (Straus and Parrish 1956, 21–40). They were also familiar with the specific local conditions. One-third of the settlers were from the immediate area and most of the rest were from the surrounding states. Almost 40 percent of the settlers had relatives who were farming in the Columbia Basin (Straus and Parrish 1956, 3–4).

The successful applicants needed to be both patient and well financed. The application process was very lengthy and putting up with the many governmental changes took a great deal of dedication, patience, and mostly money or other income to sustain them during the waiting period. In one case it took over a year-and-a-half to select 17 out of 200 applicants for farms (U.S. Department of the Interior, 1959).

It should not be surprising that the CBP did not attract the poorer, landless people described by Franklin Roosevelt and by the bureau's original objectives. In the bureau's quest for a successful program, they selected those settlers most likely to succeed. These people had the required capital, could acquire more assets, and possessed the managerial skill to farm successfully.

Monetary Costs

In 1945 the total construction costs of the CBP were estimated at $487 million dollars. Although 70 percent ($342 million) of this cost was for irrigation facilities, the irrigators were required to pay for only 18 percent of the cost! This included the previously mentioned $2 per acre per year facility charge and $5 per acre per year operation and pumping charge. Moreover, the federal government financed the farmers' debt at zero percent interest. Power production was to repay the remaining 82 percent or $398,565,000 of the project cost (Marts 1961, 5).

By 1959, the total estimated costs of construction had risen to $773 million with the total increase to be paid by power revenues (Marts 1961, 8). This meant that the irrigation portion of the project costs increased while the irrigators' repayment share decreased to only 15 percent of total costs. Thus, electricity users were to repay more than three and one-half times the cost of producing the power.

Taxpayers also subsidized farmers through low interest or zero interest loans carried over a long period (Marts 1961, 5). A 1955 study estimated that irrigation investments will not be repaid until 2023. By then, the interest foregone by the treasury, at a very conservatively estimated 2.5 percent interest rate on the outstanding balance, will amount to over $600 million (Marken 1955). The combined power and interest subsidy results in a total income transfer to farmers of approximately $1.1 billion (Marts 1961, 11). Fifty-five percent of this is from the interest subsidies and 45 percent from higher electricity rates. Although an unknown but surely modest benefit accrues elsewhere in the region and the nation as indirect benefits, most of the benefits accrue directly to the 2,171 local farms.

Additional expenditures since 1959 increased the costs of construction and irrigation facilities by 1977 to $1.2 billion (U.S. Department of the Interior 1978, 42) and additional investments in the third power generating facility and in the pump generating plant were made in 1983. Even without correcting any of the cost estimates for inflation, the approximate total cost of the project is now more than $2.5 billion. This places the cost for each of 2,171 farms at over $1 million and the cost per irrigated acre at $4,550 (U.S. Department of the Interior 1983, 11).

Costs of Getting Around the Rules

The economic theory of rent-seeking predicts that enormous amounts of human energy and creativity would be expended trying to capture this subsidy. This was done by increasing the size of farms. A 1956 Bureau of Reclamation survey reported that nearly half the settlers thought their farm unit was too small to sustain the operation. Another study found that the most economically successful farmers were those who were able to farm more than one farming unit. Those ranked in the highest scoring sixth were farming an average of 2.8 units per farmer (Straus 1958, 35–6).

With the help of lawyers, accountants, family, and friends, farmers used nominees, strawmen, trusts, corporate layering, output contracts, and equitable interests to get around the acreage limitations. Titles often changed hands without the irrigation districts being notified. One method used by CBP farmers was to transfer title to friends, employees, or relatives who then transferred the land back to the original owner. The original owner, however, did not have the deed recorded. This allowed farmers to exceed acreage limitations without the Bureau of Reclamation's knowledge while retaining a protected interest in the land. Acreage limitations also were circumvented by lease-back provisions under which the original owner was given a lifelong lease on the property in exchange for listing his nonfarming children as the owners. Limited partnerships also allowed farmers to control a majority share in land and still qualify for project water.

Another means of obtaining larger units was through development leases. Under this system, the renter developed the land or constructed buildings or both. In exchange for the development, the renter got low or no rent payments for short periods, usually three to five years. In this situation, both landlord and tenant benefited through rents and larger farm size without violating acreage limitations.

People also found ways around the governmental limit on the price of excess land. A farmer required to sell his excess land for dry land prices might agree to the sale only if the buyer also bought another asset. There are, for example, unsubstantiated stories of $200 horses being sold for $70,000. No law was broken, and the market value of the land was realized through a greatly overpriced horse.

Clearly people go to great lengths to get around the rules and they do it for a variety of reasons. The following personal correspondence in 1985 from the Columbia Basin Project Manager made the following observations about their reasons:

> Most do not fully understand the regulations or their purpose and some do not want to. The majority of the people respect the laws and comply quite willingly. However, some people, usually the most aggressive who may benefit the most, tend to resist, delay, challenge, and avoid full compliance. They are frequently successful and effectively are less regulated than those who cooperate.

In our society and under our form of government, there are many who do not see this type of regulation as an appropriate role of government. We see this as the underlying reason that enforcement is difficult and incomplete.

His statement continues to reflect the Progressive view that individuals reacting to personal preferences, opportunities, and new technologies are outside "the plan" and are, somehow, acting against the society. He fails to recognize that when government tries to "give away" assets, rent-seeking inevitably results.

Conclusion

The successes of the CBP are many and visible. The dam and water delivery system are engineering triumphs. Crops grown because of the irrigation water make the desert bloom. The towns and network of roads are orderly and convenient. Families or family corporations operate many of the farms. The Progressive vision of a settled, stable, productive region is nearly complete.

The costs of the CBP are also many but they are less visible than the successes. The farmers succeed only because most of the costs of storing and delivering to their farms are paid by taxpayers or electricity ratepayers. Moreover, inefficiencies result because energy to drive the pumps is more highly valued for other uses and the irrigation water is more valuable left in the river to pass through turbines and produce additional electricity downstream. Farmers must apply subterfuge and even break the law to obtain these subsidies. Thus, the Joint Investigations—the most comprehensive, best staffed, most organized government planning effort in the United States—planned a political success but an economic failure.

Government cannot do what the Progressives asked of it for several reasons. First, planning requires intensive efforts by teams of experts who are expected to make policies for an unknown future. Much of the information in the plan is time and site specific and loses its value quickly as technology or preferences change. As illustrated with the CBP, the planning takes years, and the future is held hostage to the planners of the past: today's farmers are constrained by plans developed in 1940, based on horse-drawn agriculture and Depression-era prices.

Second, the managers of government agencies charged with carrying out the plans receive no direct rewards for establishing regulations or policies that promote economic efficiency. Yet they are soundly and loudly criticized if their efforts to change a plan offend an existing interest group. Arduous, often bitter debates precede any large scale innovation and even most marginal innovations. Despite decades of arguing, for example, farmers in the CBP still cannot legally exceed the 960-acre limit although larger farms make economic sense. The problem is that farms in excess of 960 acres do not make political sense.

Third, government allocation of resources discourages economic efficiency as organized groups seek favors and bureaucrats and politicians respond by granting the favors while also imposing their own values on the project. Politicians, business groups, farmers, and land speculators all lobbied Congress to create the largest public works project of the era even though the irrigation costs exceeded the benefits. They got the CBP, but they also got Progressive rules restricting speculation and farm sizes.

Finally, political plans are difficult, troublesome, and rigid. Getting around that rigidity requires otherwise law-abiding people to falsify and obfuscate—hardly an advertisement for the Progressive vision of a national community linked together for the public good.

The rent-seeking activities inherent in the CBP are compounded in every federal irrigation project throughout the West. No wonder Mark Twain concluded, "Whisky is for drinkin', water is for fightin'."

Notes

1. Multiply $270 million by twelve to convert to 1994 dollars.
2. *Columbia Basin Project Act, 57 Stat. 14*, March 10, 1943.
3. *Columbia Basin Project Act, 57 Stat. 16*, March 10, 1943.
4. Nationally the median average income in 1953 was $4,100; for American farm operators it was $13,500 (U.S. Bureau of the Census 1955).

References

Clawson, Marion. 1987. *From sagebrush to sage*. Washington, DC: Ana Publications.
Haber, Samuel. 1964. *Efficiency and uplift: Scientific management in the Progressive Era, 1890–1920*. Chicago: University of Chicago Press.
Hays, Samuel P. 1959. *Conservation and the gospel of efficiency*. Cambridge: Harvard University Press.
Marken, R. E. 1955. The Columbia Basin Project. University of Washington. Photocopy.
Marts, Marion Ernest. 1961. Regional vs. local level: Objectives and social accounting of the Columbia Basin Project. Ph.D. dissertation, University of Washington, Seattle.
Nelson, Robert H. 1991. *Reaching for heaven on Earth: The theological meaning of economics*. Savage, MD: Rowman & Littlefield Publishers, Inc.
Nixon, Edgar Burkhardt, ed. 1957. *Franklin D. Roosevelt and conservation*. Hyde Park, NY: General Services Administration.
Pinchot, Gifford. 1947. *Breaking new ground*. New York: Harcourt, Brace.
Reisner, Marc P. 1986. *Cadillac desert: The American West and its disappearing water*. New York: Viking Penguin.

Straus, Murray Arnold. 1958. Matching farms and families in the Columbia Basin Project. Institute of Agricultural Sciences Bulletin 588. Washington Agriculture Experiment Station, State College of Washington, Pullman.

Straus, Murray Arnold, and Barnard D. Parrish. 1956. The Columbia Basin settler: A study of social and economic resources in new land settlement. Institute of Agricultural Sciences Bulletin 566. Washington Agriculture Experiment Station, State College of Washington, Pullman.

U.S. Bureau of the Census. 1955. Statistical Abstract of the United States: 1955. Washington, DC.

U.S. Department of the Interior. Bureau of Reclamation. 1941. Columbia Basin joint investigations, character and scope. Washington, DC: U.S. Government Printing Office.

————. 1946. *Settlement of the Columbia Basin Reclamation Project.* Washington, DC: U.S. Government Printing Office.

————. 1949. *Columbia Basin Project.* Washington, DC: U.S. Government Printing Office.

————. 1959. *Settler Selection Program, annual report.* Washington, DC: U.S. Government Printing Office.

————. 1978. *The story of the Columbia Basin Project.* Denver: U.S. Government Printing Office.

————. Pacific Northwest Region. 1983. *Columbia Basin Project.* Washington, DC: U.S. Government Printing Office.

Weinkauf, Ronald K. 1974. The Columbia Basin Project, Washington: Concept and reality, Lessons for public policy. Thesis, Oregon State University, Corvallis.

Wilson, Woodrow. [1887] 1941. The study of administration. Reprint. *Political Science Quarterly* 61:481–506.

Worster, Donald. 1985. *Rivers of empire: Water, aridity, and the growth of the American West.* New York: Pantheon Books.

6

Rents From Amenity Resources: A Case Study of Yellowstone National Park

Terry L. Anderson and Peter J. Hill

The American West is known throughout the world for its spectacular national parks. The glaciers of Mt. Rainier National Park, the colors and enormity of the Grand Canyon, the geysers of Yellowstone National Park, and the giant peaks of Glacier National Park are but a few of the scenic resources set aside by the federal government.

Conventional wisdom suggests that these scenic resources would have been destroyed by development had farsighted conservationists not managed to have the lands set aside in the public domain. Ise (1979, 1) captures this common perception:

> we have this system of national parks, monuments, and other areas not as a result of public demand but because a few farsighted, unselfish, and idealistic men and women foresaw the national need and got the areas established and protected in one way or another, fighting public inertia and selfish commercial interests at every step.

Similarly, Brubaker (1983, 103) contends that

> Securing the interests of future generations (beyond one or two) is a social and not a private concern. Ordinarily it is beyond the ability of a private owner to

do much about genetic or ecological preserves, for example. . . . If there is a
social interest in these matters, it can only be protected by public intervention;
private individuals lack the power or incentive to do it.

Political economy, however, leads us to question whether altruism and public
interest were the only forces behind the establishment of national parks. Incentives
and information are crucial components of any decision process, and the institutional environment influences both of these. This approach raises numerous issues.
Who first recognized the scenic values now included in the national park system?
Who benefited from the preservation, as opposed to the development, of the scenic
areas? Did the existing institutional arrangements mitigate against their preservation? Would alternative institutional structures have produced different amounts
and qualities of amenity values?

To answer these questions, we present a history of the formation and operation
of Yellowstone National Park. As the first national park, Yellowstone offers
insights into the process and pitfalls of preservation. It illustrates that the amenity
rents were recognized early in the exploration of the West but that capturing those
rents required innovative institutional change. Rent measures the difference
between the value of a resource in one use and the value in its next best alternative. In the case of Yellowstone, we can think of the value in amenity uses
compared to the value for agriculture, mining, or geothermal energy. Of course
the values are generated by the subjective evaluations of individuals, and, in most
situations, will be well represented by market prices. However, if there are
substantial externalities or free-rider problems, market forces will not necessarily
reflect all rents.

Our analysis is based on the proposition that the choice of property rights
arrangements depends on the perceptions of rents by entrepreneurs and the costs
of capturing those rents. Because rents represent a return above opportunity cost,
individuals will devote effort to capturing them. How this effort is channeled,
however, will depend on the institutional framework in which this pursuit takes
place. If there is open access to the resource, the rents will be dissipated through
overuse. On the other hand, if access can be restricted, rents will be captured,
rather than dissipated, by the individual or group who controls the access. Though
strictly private property rights offer one way of capturing rents, alternative
institutional arrangements may evolve if the costs of defining and enforcing private
ownership claims are too high.

Within this framework, we examine several questions regarding the history of
Yellowstone National Park. Who first perceived the value of the area as a scenic
resource? Was it necessary for these individuals to use government ownership of
the resources to prevent their spoilation? Was the park an open-access resource?
If so, did rent dissipation occur? What were the transaction costs that prevented
private ownership? Were there alternatives to fee-simple land rights that approximated private rights? How effectively did they function?

Recognizing the Rents From Yellowstone

The history of Yellowstone suggests that it was not necessarily "unselfish, and idealistic men and women . . . fighting public inertia and selfish commercial interests at every step" who recognized and preserved the amenity values of the region. Indians had long used Yellowstone for summer hunting and were very familiar with the thermal features. John Colter, a member of the Lewis and Clark expedition, left the returning explorers in August of 1806 and returned to the Rockies. In the fall of 1807, he became the first white man to explore the upper Yellowstone basin. Other trappers followed, and the unique features of the area became a part of western folklore. Early in the 1860s gold fever brought more explorers to the region, and finally, formal expeditions to map and explore the area were mounted in 1869, 1870, and 1871.

Each of these groups added to the perception that the area had special value as a scenic resource. Extant letters by trappers writing to friends in the 1820s described the thermal features in some detail. In 1827, an article appeared in the *Philadelphia Gazette and Advertiser* describing the geysers (Bartlett 1974, 224–5). Warren Angus Ferris, an employee of the American Fur Company, traveled to the region in 1834 because, in visiting with other trappers, he found "the accounts they gave, were so very astonishing, that I determined to examine them myself, before recording their description, though I had the united testimony of more than twenty men on the subject" (Bartlett 1974, 103).

All of this added to the region's reputation as a source of wild and scenic wonders, and finally, in 1869 a visit to the area by three Helena, Montana residents led to the publication of a detailed description of the area in *Western Monthly Magazine*. This was followed in the fall of 1870 by a larger expedition of nineteen men led by Henry D. Washburn, surveyor general of Montana, and accompanied by a military escort from the Second Calvary, stationed at Fort Ellis outside of Bozeman, Montana. The main impetus for the trip came from Nathaniel P. Langford, politician and sometime territorial official. In July of that year he visited with Jay Cooke, financier of the Northern Pacific Railroad, at his estate in Philadelphia. Cooke, because of his financial interests in the Northern Pacific Railroad, asked Langford to promote exploration of the upper reaches of the Yellowstone Valley, probably to publicize future travel opportunities on the railroad.[1]

The next year an even larger expedition was mounted, led this time by Dr. Ferdinand Vandiveer Hayden, head of the U.S. Geological and Geographical Survey in the territories. This group spent a month in the Yellowstone region and provided an accurate set of maps of the area and its features and also collected numerous geological and biological specimens.

Thus from John Colter's first exploration of the area in 1806, people were astounded and amazed by the scenic wonders of the Grand Canyon of the Yellowstone, the peacefulness of the Lamar Valley, and the uniqueness of the thermal features like Old Faithful. It did not require a special group of "altruists" with a far more public spirited vision than the ordinary citizen to perceive that the area had special amenity value. Certainly the potential rents that were available from putting the region to use as a scenic vista were not perceived uniformly by all who traveled in the area. But it did not require people with fundamentally unselfish motives to think of the upper Yellowstone as valuable for other than timber, mining, or grazing.

Indeed it was the opportunity to capture some of the superior rents from amenity uses that caused individuals to think creatively about potential ways to capitalize on the amenity values. The first individuals to attempt to establish property rights in the area were two men who, in 1870, cut poles to fence off the geyser basins and charge admission. In 1871, two others preempted 320 acres that included Mammoth Hot Springs with the intent of establishing mineral baths. Others who perceived and attempted to capture rents from the area were C. J. Baronett, who built and maintained a toll bridge (at first just for pack strings) across the Yellowstone River just above its junction with the Lamar River in 1871, and Yankee Jim, who built a toll road through the narrow stretches of the Yellowstone Canyon just below the northern entrance to the park.

These efforts were very minor, however, compared to those of the Northern Pacific Railroad, the organization that could capture a substantial portion of Yellowstone's rents. Originally chartered in 1862 and slated to cross the middle of the country, the Northern Pacific lost the central transcontinental race to the Union Pacific Railroad. The next most plausible alternative for the Northern Pacific was further north, and in 1867 a preliminary survey was completed for a route from Lake Superior to Puget Sound. This route took the railroad up the Yellowstone River and over the Bozeman Pass, thus placing it only 60 miles north of Mammoth Hot Springs, the northernmost significant feature of the park area. In 1869 the directors of the Northern Pacific sought additional financing from Jay Cooke and Company, and the resulting contract gave Cooke operating control of the railroad.

The owners of the railroad recognized very early that the unique features of the area would be a strong attraction to tourists and that the Northern Pacific would be in a strong position to serve those tourists as the only major transportation carrier in the area. The only question for the railroad was how to ensure that the rents from the amenities would not be captured or even dissipated by small developers like those fencing the geyser basins and developing the hot springs.

Given the land laws of the time, it would have been very costly for the railroad to establish private ownership of an area the size of Yellowstone. Beginning with the Homestead Act in 1862, land laws made it expensive to put together large blocks of land. The original act restricted initial ownership to 160 acres and was built around the concept of traditional agricultural production. Even though the maximum allotment expanded to 320 and eventually to 640 acres, settlers were still required to engage in agricultural activities in order to establish ownership.[2]

Thus the railroad was faced with two unattractive paths for establishing private ownership. First, it could have hired individuals to homestead the land on behalf of the railroad and then to sell the land to the Northern Pacific. This approach undoubtedly would have brought charges of fraud, and the transaction costs would have been extremely high.[3] Second, the Northern Pacific could have waited for the land to be claimed under homesteading, logging, and mining laws and then purchased the land once it was in private ownership. Two risks would have been encountered with this method. In addition to paying for the land, the railroad would have confronted the holdout problem with the person who controlled the most valuable locations such as Old Faithful or Mammoth Hot Springs. Furthermore, in order to establish a legitimate claim under the various laws, the land had to be farmed, logged, or mined, all of which would have been counter to the values the railroad wanted to preserve.

For the railroad with a virtual monopoly on transportation to the region, there was an alternative; namely, preserve the region intact as public domain for use as a scenic resource. Of course, this required a degree of entrepreneurial perception by railroad owners. First, they had to look ahead to the time when the American public would have the income and leisure time to enjoy the amenities of Yellowstone. Second, they had to understand that fragmented ownership would dissipate some of the amenity values through externalities and hence had to support unified control of Yellowstone that might approximate private ownership.

The following correspondence from Jay Cooke to his aide in Montana, W. Milner Roberts, following a congressional report recommending establishment of a national park suggests that Cooke was aware of these issues.

It is proposed by Mr. Hayden in his report to Congress that the Geyser region around Yellowstone Lake shall be set apart by government as park, similar to that of the Great Trees & other reservations in California. Would this conflict with our land grant, or interfere with us in any way? Please give me your views on this subject. It is important to do something speedily, or squatters and claimants will go in there, and we can probably deal much better with the government in any improvements we may desire to make for the benefit of our pleasure travel than with individuals. (quoted in Bartlett 1974, 207–8)

Roberts responded by telegram three weeks later: "Your October thirtieth and November sixth rec'd. Geysers outside our grant advise Congressional delegation be in East probably before middle December" (quoted in Bartlett 1974, 208).

The railroad not only perceived the benefits from establishing the region as a national park; it was also instrumental in securing congressional action.[4] Aubrey L. Haines, a leading Yellowstone National Park historian, claims "agents of the Northern Pacific initiated the project to reserve the Yellowstone region as a park" (Haines 1977, 1:165).[5] The 1870 expedition was probably a direct result of Nathaniel Langford's visit with Jay Cooke at his Philadelphia estate on July 4 and 5, 1870. Although it was not certain at the time that there would be substantial scenic value to the area, Cooke evidently had heard enough to give him a vision for potential tourist travel in the region. Langford was under contract to Cooke to give a series of lectures following the expedition, most of which he did not complete because of illness. However, immediately after the completion of the expedition, he did work hard at putting 35,000 words of notes into a manuscript suitable for publication, and he gave several lectures on the East coast in which he unfailingly highlighted the wonders of the area and the fact that the Northern Pacific Railroad would provide transportation to the region (Runte 1990, 16).

The Northern Pacific was also involved in the expedition led by Ferdinand V. Hayden. The Northern Pacific provided financial support for noted landscape artist, Thomas Moran, to accompany the expedition. The railroad believed his paintings would be helpful in publicizing the area.

When it actually came time for Hayden to deliver his report to Congress, the Northern Pacific became even more involved. Runte (1979, 45) notes that

> on October 27, 1871, Professor Hayden himself received an official request from an agent of the Northern Pacific project to lobby on behalf of the park proposal. "Let Congress pass a bill reserving the Great Geyser Basin as a public park forever. . . . If you approve this, would such a recommendation be appropriate in your official report?" Cooke and his associates realized, of course, that if Yellowstone became a park, their railroad would be the sole beneficiary of the tourist traffic.

The railroad very early recognized the potential rents from the use of the park area as a tourist resource, and it believed the transaction costs of establishing private rights to those rents would be very high. Therefore it chose a lower cost method of achieving the same end, the creation of a national park with the Northern Pacific's monopoly control of access still giving it the opportunity to capture most of those rents.

With the lobbying power of the railroad behind it, the legislation to create the park was passed easily. It was introduced on December 18, 1871, in both the House and Senate, passed both bodies without any speeches against it, and was signed into law by President Grant on March 1, 1872. The passage was undoubtedly made easier because Langford and Hayden were both present to lobby for the bill and because photographs of the area by William Henry Jackson and paintings by Moran were made available by the Northern Pacific to influential senators and congressmen (Bartlett 1974, 208).

Three Property Rights Eras of Yellowstone National Park

The establishment of Yellowstone as a national park ushered in a century of changing philosophies regarding management. Our focus here is on whether the various phases of management encouraged rent dissipation or rent maximization. During the early period of open access, rents were dissipated as few controls were placed on entry into and use of the park. As the railroad gained control of entry through its transportation monopoly, it captured many of the amenity rents from Yellowstone. However, when the park was opened to automobiles in 1915, open access and overuse again dominated.

1872–1883: Yellowstone as an Open-Access Resource

With the creation of Yellowstone National Park and the Northern Pacific Railroad ready to begin service to the area, the stage should have been set for the railroad to influence management in ways that would allow it to capture the rents. However, the financial panic of 1873 put the Northern Pacific into bankruptcy and delayed completion of its transcontinental route by a decade. The fact that the railroad was not delivering passengers to the area and was having difficulty organizing its own financial affairs meant there was no private party interested in or capable of controlling access or preventing overuse.

This also meant there was no lobbying effort pushing Congress to establish rules for use of the park or to provide funding for administration. It was not until six years after the creation of the park that the first appropriations were made for park operation, and then only $10,000 was appropriated to cover the superintendent's salary, road and trail construction, and enforcement efforts to control poaching and vandalism. The first park superintendent, Nathaniel P. Langford, who served from 1872 until 1877, only entered the park twice during his term.

Without any active presence by the railroad or the federal government, the park was treated very much as an open-access resource, with all the associated problems. People tended to overuse the region and to exploit the resources with little thought for the future. William Strong (quoted in Haines 1977, 1:207–8), a visitor to the park in 1875 reported that

In 1870 when Lieutenant Doane first entered the Yellowstone Basin, it was without doubt a country unsurpassed on this continent for big game. Large herds of elk, mountain sheep, the black and white-tail deer, and the grizzly, cinnamon and black bears were numerous. The Yellowstone Valley was swarming with antelope, and the mountain lion was frequently killed. During the first five years the large game has been slaughtered here by professional hunters by thousands, and for their hides alone. When the snow falls and the fierce winter storms begin in November and December, the elk, deer and sheep leave the summits of the snowy ranges and come in great bands to the foot-hills and valleys, where they are shot down shamefully by these merciless human vultures. An elk skin is worth from six to eight dollars, and it is said that when the snow is deep, and a herd gets confused, one hunter will frequently kill from twenty-five to fifty of these noble animals in a single day.

Over four thousand were killed last winter by professional hunters in the Mammoth Springs Basin alone. Their carcasses and branching antlers can be seen on every hillside and in every valley. Mountain sheep and deer have been hunted and killed in the same manner for their hides. The terrible slaughter which has been going on since the fall of 1871 has thinned out the great bands of big game, until it is a rare thing now to see an elk, deer, or mountain sheep along the regular trail from Ellis to the Yellowstone Lake. . . . But few years will elapse before every elk, mountain-sheep, and deer will have been killed, or driven from the mountains and valleys of the National Park. . . . It is an outrage and a crying shame that this indiscriminate slaughter of the large game of our country should be permitted. The act of Congress setting aside the National Park expressly instructs the secretary of the interior to provide against the wanton destruction of the game and fish found within the limits of the park, and against their capture or destruction for merchandise or profit. No attempt has yet been made, however, to enforce the act in the park, and unless some active measures are soon taken looking to the protection of the game there will be none left to protect.

An official expedition led by Captain William Ludlow (quoted in Hampton 1971, 40–1) in 1875 reported similar despoliation of the physical features.

The ornamental work about the crater and pools had been broken and defaced in the most prominent places by visitors. . . . The visitors prowled about with shovel and ax, chopping and hacking and prying up great pieces of the most ornamental work they could find; women and men alike joined in the most barbarous pastime.

And Philetus W. Norris (quoted in Haines 1977, 1:55), later to become a park superintendent, estimated that the slaughter of 1875 took over 7,000 animals based on "the unquestioned fact that over 2,000 hides of the huge Rocky Mountain elk, nearly as many each of the big horn, deer and antelope, and scores if not hundreds of moose and bison were taken out in the spring of 1875."

The annual visitors to the park during this period were probably 1000 or less[6] so the overexploitation was not due to an excess of people as in more recent years. Rather it occurred because there was no monitoring of park use. A party with a claim on future rents would have prevented such actions, since both the slaughter of game animals and defacing of the natural wonders decreased the rents. However, there was no such claimant and rent dissipation occurred.

1883–1915: The Private Property Era

By 1879 the Northern Pacific had its financial affairs in order and resumed laying track west from Mandan, North Dakota. In 1883 it finished its route to the

West Coast and added a spur from Livingston to Cinnabar, a few miles from the park entrance. This gave the railroad a virtual monopoly on transportation to Yellowstone, although the monopoly was not as complete as it would have been if the following plans had been approved by the Congress.

Six prominent capitalists of St. Paul & Minneapolis, including Senator Windom, J. B. Gillfillen, of Minneapolis, E. H. Bly, of Bismark, and Mr. Hobart, of the Northern Pacific, have agreed with the Northern Pacific to build a railroad, standard gauge, from the point on the Northern Pacific nearest the park, to the geysers and Yellowstone Park; or, to speak more definitely, forty miles of road outside of the government park reservation and forty miles within it, the cost to be $420,000 per mile, and allowing for contingencies, nearly $2,000,000. Sixty thousand dollars are to be put up by the six as an earnest of good faith, and the Northern Pacific will then furnish the money to build and equip the road, taking a mortgage as security. The six men will build a large hotel, being assured by the Government of a monopoly therein. A large influx of summer visitors is expected annually. (quoted in Haines 1977, 1:259)

Pressure in Congress prevented the railroad from securing the right to build within the park, so its terminus was the park entrance.[7]

There were some alternatives to the Northern Pacific, but none were sufficient to negate its substantial transportation monopoly that enabled it to capture a share of rents generated from the amenity value of Yellowstone. Residents of Montana, Wyoming, and Idaho could make their way to the park without using the railroad, but others would have found it prohibitively time consuming and expensive to come by steamboat, wagon, or horse.

Some competition also came from the Union Pacific which offered service to Corrine, Utah, a 480-mile stagecoach ride to the park. By the 1880s one could take the narrow gauge Utah Northern to Beaver Canyon, Idaho (the present site of Monida, Idaho) and again use stagecoach service to reach the park. However, train service to the west entrance only came in 1907, when the Union Pacific completed a spur to West Yellowstone.[8]

With the Northern Pacific in position to capture the rents, the management of Yellowstone Park approximated what would be expected with private ownership. Because the fares the railroad could charge depended on the quality of the visit, it had a strong incentive to prevent overcrowding which could create a congestion externality and to prevent destruction of geyser cones and slaughter of wildlife. Dust on the roads was the most obvious congestion externality which the railroad controlled by carefully scheduling stagecoach departures from its terminus. The Northern Pacific also devoted its own resources to policing use of the park, especially trying to control poaching and vandalism.

As a powerful lobby in Congress, the Northern Pacific helped secure funding and additional legislation to more clearly specify enforcement powers. In 1883,

Congress increased the park's annual appropriations from $15,000 to $40,000, including compensation for ten assistants who would reside continuously in the park.

With the improved access to Yellowstone came three major expeditions in 1883 that publicized the amenity values. President Chester Arthur, accompanied by several other important political figures, spent several weeks in the park. The expedition was so extensive that 150 pack mules were required to carry the necessary supplies, including china, crystal, sterling, and linens (Haines 1977, 1:280). The second excursion was promoted by Rufus Hatch, president of the Yellowstone Park Improvement Company, an enterprise organized to provide tourist facilities in Yellowstone. Hatch provided seventy-five dignitaries from the U.S. and Europe an expense paid tour of the park with the hope of promoting tourist activity. Finally, Henry Villard, president of the Northern Pacific Railroad, provided a thirty day excursion "at no personal expense" to 300 business leaders and journalists to celebrate the beginning of railroad service to Yellowstone (Haines 1977, 1:287). All of this activity, of course, added to the public's knowledge about the scenic value of the region and to the Northern Pacific's opportunities to profit from the tourist trade.

The railroad received substantial assistance in managing and monitoring the park when the United States Army was posted there in 1886. There had been proposals to use the army to patrol Yellowstone and prevent poaching and vandalism in the 1870s and early 1880s, but it was not until 1883 that legislation authorized the secretary of interior to request the secretary of war to assign troops to the park. That request was made, and on August 17, 1886, the first troops arrived. A permanent fort was established at Mammoth Hot Springs, and the army actively patrolled the park and enforced regulations for thirty-two years. Army engineers designed roads and other improvements, and soldiers also battled fires. However, with the advent of World War I, the army found it was needed elsewhere and formally exited in 1917.

Thus the period from 1883 to 1915 can best be described as a period of active management of Yellowstone, with the Northern Pacific Railroad controlling enough of the access to prevent overcrowding. It was also able to secure adequate government assistance to prevent tourists from overuse in other ways. The fact that it captured rents generated from amenities gave it an incentive to act as if it owned Yellowstone.

1915–1993: Return to Open Access

August 1, 1915, the day automobiles were admitted into the park, marked a major turning point in Yellowstone's history. The pressure to admit autos into Yellowstone had been building for several years, especially since they had been allowed into Mount Rainier National Park in 1908, into Crater Lake in 1911, into Glacier in 1912, and into Yosemite and Sequoia in 1913 (Bartlett 1985, 84). With the opening of Yellowstone to automobile traffic, the Northern Pacific lost its ability to restrict the number of park visitors, thus eroding its monopoly power.[9] Yellowstone National Park returned to its pre-railroad status of an open-access resource in the absence of governmental restrictions on use.

The attitude towards park visitors under the new regime is captured well by Stephen Mather, the first director of the National Park Service in 1916: "We've got to do what we can to see that nobody stays away because he can't afford it." If this led to overcrowding and litter, Mather contended that "We can pick up the tin cans. It's a cheap way to make better citizens" (quoted in Haines 1977, 2:347–8).

The National Park Service policy of unrestricted visitation inevitably led to overuse especially in light of rising incomes and lower transportation costs for the American population. Ise (1979, 7) argues that

> the greatest danger to the parks is not commercial exploitation, but deterioration of the parks from overuse by the swarming hordes of vacationists. We need not indulge in prediction here, for a serious condition is upon us now, today, and it is likely to grow worse. Old Faithful area is a town, laid out in blocks of nearly identical cabins, with a mile or more of parked cars and drivers of other cars seeking parking places, and hundreds of people hurrying over to see Old Faithful in eruption . . .

In 1972 another commentator wrote, "Potential visitors apparently consider Yellowstone already so overcrowded that the park experience has lost its true meaning, the re-creation mentioned by Thoreau more than a century ago" (Huser 1972, 17). And two decades later researchers were explicit in arguing that "with a record breaking 2.8 million visitors in 1990, the park had exceeded it's human 'carrying capacity'" (Coates 1991, 3).

To test whether the coming of the automobile marked a return to the open access regime, we can compare the trend in visitation prior to and following admission of automobiles. Comparing pre- and post-1915 visitations, we can reject with 99.9 percent confidence the possibility that the two samples come from the same population.[10] In other words, when the railroad had monopoly power, it could and did restrict park visits in an effort to maximize rents.

Of course, the National Park Service, created one year after admission of automobiles, might have replaced the railroad in this capacity, but it had little incentive to maximize rents or revenues. The legislation establishing Yellowstone which required the park to be self-supporting would have given the National Park Service an incentive to worry about revenues and costs. But Congress revised the law in 1918 requiring that all fee revenues collected go to the U.S. Treasury general fund (White 1992, 2). Under such an arrangement, the National Park Service was more interested in maximizing visitors in order to maintain political clout and to maximize its budget than in maximizing the rental value of amenities.

Rather than using higher entrance fees to restrict entry and reduce the congestion externality, Yellowstone officials have used overcrowding as a justification for increased congressional funding. As described by Chase (1986, 203–4),

> Mission 66 was designed to prime the pump of federal dollars by packaging Park Service demands in a way that would capture public imagination and impress on Congress how many millions of voters such appropriations would serve. . . . Yellowstone was to be the showcase of Mission 66. . . . Plans called for $70 million of construction, mostly for roads and bridges. They also called for nearly doubling the capacity for overnight accommodations.

Of course, expansion of the facilities and roads simply lowered the cost of access to Yellowstone and thus increased the number of visitors. Overuse continued with the number of visitors increasing rapidly. In 1980 the National Park Service completed a major study, *State of the Parks 1980: Report to the Congress*, that reported numerous cases of congestion and exploitation of resources. Again, rather than increasing entrance fees, the National Park Service requested more funding from Congress to improve facilities and make access easier.

Over the years, there have been instances when park entrance fees have increased, providing a data base to estimate visitor response. If the demand for Yellowstone is inelastic, revenues would increase with rising fees. Regressing annual visitations on entrance fees and other independent variables, such as population density in surrounding states and travel costs between 1929 and 1990, Walker (1993) estimates the elasticity of demand for Yellowstone at −0.205. In other words, a 10 percent increase in fees would decrease visitation by 2.05 percent and increase total receipts. Thus the park could have reduced the congestion externality *and* increased revenue by raising the entrance fee.

Conclusion

The history of Yellowstone National Park is not unlike many other major western national parks. Railroads and national parks proved to be a "pragmatic alliance" (Runte, 1974). Indeed prior to the formation of Yellowstone as the first of the national parks, the Southern Pacific Railroad lobbied for the establishment of Yosemite, Sequoia, and General Grant reserves. The Great Northern Railroad aggressively supported the establishment of Glacier National Park in 1910, and "between 1911 and 1915 Hill [the Great Northern's major owner] supervised the construction of three huge lodges and a dozen Swiss-style alpine chalets in the Montana park" (Runte 1974, 15). To the south, the Santa Fe Railroad argued for the establishment of Grand Canyon National Park and built its El Tovar hotel on the South Rim in 1904.

Establishment of national parks did not require "a few farsighted, unselfish, and idealistic men and women" who "foresaw the national need and got the areas established and protected in one way or another, fighting public inertia and selfish commercial interests at every step" (Ise 1979, 1). Rather they depended on a few farsighted entrepreneurs who could capture the amenity rents the scenic wonders had to offer. It was the desire to capture these rents that led to Yellowstone's creation. Surely the Northern Pacific would have preferred fee-simple ownership of the park, but the transaction costs of establishing private ownership were prohibitively high. As soon as the Northern Pacific obtained and as long as it maintained some monopoly control of entry into Yellowstone, problems associated with open access were avoided. During the period from 1883 to 1915, the Northern Pacific was in position to capture enough of the rents from Yellowstone's unique resources that overcrowding was avoided. After the automobile entered in 1915, the park reverted to an open-access resource. Lacking an ability to capture the rents, the National Park Service has had little incentive to limit overcrowding and indeed, as a budget-maximizing bureaucracy, has an incentive to encourage congestion externalities.

Notes

1. Little is known about the actual conversation or agreement between Cooke and Langford, but the expedition was organized immediately after Langford's return to Helena, and as we discuss later, Langford was under some sort of contract to Cooke for a publicity tour after the completion of the exploration to give lectures throughout the East on the wonders of the region.
2. For a discussion of the costs of establishing property rights under the early land laws, see Anderson and Hill (1990).
3. For a discussion of how this technique was used by timber companies, see Libecap and Johnson (1979).
4. The origin of the idea for the park is shrouded in controversy, with several people claiming credit for the original concept. One story has the concept coming from a campfire conversation during the 1870 expedition. That is suspect, however, because there is no record of such an idea from the first published news stories by expedition members. Only thirty-five years later when editing his diaries does Langford detail such a conversation. Montana's Territorial Delegate, William Clagett, who introduced the bill creating the park in Congress, also said he first originated the idea, as did Ferdinand Hayden. General Phillip H. Sheridan and photographer William Henry Jackson also claimed credit for the idea of creating the first national park.
5. Another park historian concurs: "The evidence, though fragmentary, is sufficient to credit the inspiration for the creation of the Yellowstone National Park to officials of the Northern Pacific Railroad" (Bartlett 1974, 208).
6. See Table II in Haines (1977, 2:478).

7. Because of a land dispute, the spur line originally terminated at Cinnabar, three miles downstream from the park entrance. In 1902 the Park Line of the Northern Pacific was extended to Gardiner (Bartlett 1985, 234).

8. The Northern Pacific lost some of its monopoly power when the Burlington came to Cody, Wyoming in 1901, but that still left the potential tourist 53 miles from the east entrance and farther yet from the prominent features for which Yellowstone is famous.

9. As discussed earlier, the Northern Pacific had lost some of its rents with the coming of the Burlington to Cody in 1901 and the Union Pacific to West Yellowstone in 1907. However, the three railroads still had an interest in limiting access, and there is evidence that they actively colluded in setting fares for transportation within the park and cooperated in park management decisions.

10. The F-statistic is 138.044 and the likelihood ratio is 135.478.

References

Anderson, Terry L., and Peter J. Hill. 1990. The race for property rights. *Journal of Law and Economics* 33 (April): 177–97. Reprinted this volume.

Bartlett, Richard A. 1974. *Nature's Yellowstone.* Tucson: University of Arizona Press.

———. 1985. *Yellowstone: A wilderness besieged.* Tucson: University of Arizona Press.

Brubaker, Sterling. 1983. Land use concepts. In *Governmental interventions, social needs, and the management of U.S. forests,* edited by Roger A. Sedjo. Washington, DC: Resources for the Future, 95–114.

Chase, Alston. 1986. *Playing God in Yellowstone: The destruction of America's first national park.* San Diego, CA: Harcourt Brace Jovanovich.

Coates, James. 1991. Creature comforts taking toll on park wilderness. *Chicago Tribune,* April 22.

Haines, Aubrey L. 1977. *The Yellowstone story: A history of our first national park.* 2 vols. Boulder: Yellowstone Library and Museum Associate with Colorado Associated University Press.

Hampton, H. Duane. 1971. *How the U.S. Calvary saved our national parks.* Bloomington: Indiana University Press.

Huser, Verne. 1972. Yellowstone National Park, use, overuse, and misuse. *National Parks and Conservation Magazine: The Environmental Journal* 46(3): 8–17.

Ise, John. [1961] 1979. *Our national park policy.* Reprint. New York: Arno Press.

Libecap, Gary D., and Ronald N. Johnson. 1979. Property rights, nineteenth-century federal timber policy and the conservation movement. *Journal of Economic History* 39(1): 129–42.

Runte, Alfred. 1974. Pragmatic alliance: Western railroads and the national parks. *National Parks and Conservation Magazine: The Environmental Journal* 48

(April): 14–21.

———. 1979. *National parks: The American experience.* Lincoln: University of Nebraska Press.

———. 1990. *Trains of discovery.* Niwot, CO: Roberts Rinehart, Inc.

Walker, Sheryl Robin. 1993. Pricing our national parks: The motivations behind, and the problems associated with, current price policies. Master's thesis, Department of Economics, University of Georgia, Athens.

White, Chris. 1992. Legislative history of outdoor recreation fees. *Recnotes.* U.S. Army Corps of Engineers, Waterways Experiment Station, Vicksburg, Mississippi, vol. R-92-3 (August).

7

Foreseeing Confiscation by the Sovereign: Lessons From the American West

David D. Haddock[†]

O, it is excellent
To have a giant's strength; but it is tyrannous
To use it like a giant.
—William Shakespeare, *Measure for Measure*

Sovereignty means that a political entity has the ability to make unilateral decisions, a power which is necessary if government is to overcome free-rider problems. Sovereign powers, however, have the disadvantage of making it possible for the sovereign political entities to renege on agreements with other parties, leaving those other parties with no ability to appeal to an independent arbiter. For example, if a citizen of another country enters into a contract with a foreign government, the sovereign government could renege on the agreement, and the

[†] Michele Thorne provided such extensive research and comments on earlier drafts that she could have become a coauthor, an invitation she declined due to other commitments. Thoughtful criticism came from Peter J. Hill, Fred McChesney, Robert McCormick, Thomas Merrill, Ian Ayres, Charlotte Crane, Thráinn Eggertsson, David Friedman, D. Bruce Johnsen, and from numerous workshops and seminars.

foreign citizen might have no recourse. Indeed, in the absence of constitutional limits, even citizens of the sovereign nation might find themselves in the same position. The exercise of sovereign powers in this way diminishes gains from trade as potential associates shy away from agreements (Barzel 1991 and 1992; Grandy 1989; Haddock and Hall 1983). The degree to which gains from trade are diminished by the sovereign's ability to change the contract unilaterally will depend on the contractual options available to both parties and on the range of mechanisms that can potentially reduce the likelihood that the sovereign will exercise its power.

To set the stage for understanding how sovereignty can drive a wedge into the gains from trade, first consider the relationship between parties to a contract that does not include a sovereign. Suppose that citizen A promises to undertake some task for B in return for B's promise to remunerate A. If A doubts B's promise to pay, B has at least the following three responses:

1. "Reneging will reduce my valuable reputation, so you can trust me."
2. "If you won't contract with me, I will vertically integrate and undertake the role that I have urged on you myself."
3. "I will sign a contract that will be enforced by the sovereign."

These responses are not perfect substitutes. Risking reputation will not be a very credible bond if B has not previously invested in creating a good reputation. That will be difficult, for example, if B is a new participant in the market. Moreover, the association contemplated by A and B must be one in which B's misbehavior would be apparent to A and all other future associates. Otherwise, B's reputation, whatever its value in the abstract, will not be at risk (Klein and Leffler 1981; Williamson 1983). Threatening to vertically integrate is only credible if B possesses the ability to undertake the task with efficiency similar to A's. Thus, in some instances contractual assurance supported by the sovereign's coercive power will offer the most attractive bond, and both A and B would be disadvantaged if appropriate contract law was unavailable.

On the other hand, consider contracting between citizen A and sovereign nation X. Suppose that A agrees to make an investment in return for X's promise not to change the tax and regulatory regime. If A disbelieves sovereign nation X's promise, there is little possibility for relying on a third-party enforcer. To whom will A appeal to coerce the unwilling sovereign to retain the promised regulations or taxes?

This raises a paradox: *Ceteris paribus*, the greater the sovereign's ability to impel submission by citizens, the less the ability of a third-party arbiter to compel performance by the sovereign, and so the less the sovereign's ability to induce voluntary cooperation. This paradox turns the sovereign's power into the sovereign's handicap. As will be seen, overcoming the sovereign's paradox is especially difficult for economically small sovereigns, immature sovereigns, and sovereigns with short life expectancies.[1] By ceding some sovereignty to another sovereign that is more likely to adhere to promises, however, the paradox can be mitigated.

The sovereign's paradox has some important applications to the American West. Most importantly, the model implies that American Indian reservations' small economic size, their legal immaturity, the uncertainty about the future of their status as sovereigns, and a chronic possibility of free-riding on other tribes' reputation especially weakens any tribal government's ability to overcome the sovereign's paradox. That, in turn, creates a serious disadvantage to both the tribal governments and tribal citizens, but is only a minor irritant for nontribal associates who have many options for avoiding tribal law by selecting nontribal associates. Reservation governments and residents, on the other hand, find it much more difficult to avoid tribal laws and courts.

The sovereign's paradox has been exacerbated for Indian tribes by a series of recent Supreme Court decisions. These decisions have expanded the power of the tribes to exercise their sovereignty vis-à-vis private investors and hence to extract quasi-rents from those who invest on the reservation. Some would argue that the Court has merely been pursuing the laudatory goal of furthering an Indian desire for self-determination. Be that as it may, the decisions have also enlarged the potential for tribes to engage in post-contractual opportunism which reduces gains from trade on reservations and further tarnishes tribal reputations as sovereigns that can be trusted.

The model also explains two legal patterns widely observable on America's western frontier. First, it explains why many frontier territories implicitly adopted older states' codes and legal precedent wholesale upon admission to the Union; in so doing, they mitigated their unavoidable status of legal immaturity. Second, the model explains why economically small states (mostly in the West) have especially strong incentives to subscribe to multi-state legal codes. By sharing common rules, states are better able to share precedents established in other members of the set, and thus better guarantee performance.[2]

The Sovereign's Stake in Contract Enforcement

Understandings that require time to reach fruition are fraught with dangers of opportunism (Klein, Crawford, and Alchian 1978; MacNeil 1978; Williamson 1988). Conditions can change unexpectedly during a relationship, with one party eventually regretting the commitment. Or, if sequential investments are required, the party with the more delayed obligations may eventually benefit by reneging. In either event, one party will want out of a relationship prematurely, even though the termination may impose substantial injury on the other party. If the law can and will obstruct opportunism, both parties benefit, *ex ante*, from the enhanced ability to form mutually beneficial agreements.

Admittedly several extralegal "self-enforcement" mechanisms diminish contractual opportunism without resort to coercion (Telser 1980), but, because these mechanisms are not perfect substitutes for one another, legally imposed and enforced sanctions may be necessary. For example, in the case of end-period contracts when parties do not expect to be repeat players, self-enforcement based on reputation is unlikely to be sufficient to prevent opportunism. As an illustration, most nineteenth century railroads could be relied upon to make good faith efforts to repay borrowings because they intended to be repeat players in the capital markets and did not want to sully their reputations. But once the railroad industry began to decline, unfettered shareholder interest would have dictated an excessive dividend flow. At that point, repayment of the outstanding debt became much more reliant on corporation and bankruptcy law. Thus, even though other (imperfect) mechanisms may exist, contractual enforcement by a sovereign government can be advantageous.

It is ordinarily in a sovereign's interest to encourage mutually beneficial agreements between subjects because such agreements enhance the sovereign's tax base. But interest and willingness of the sovereign to enforce agreements may be reduced if a subject, whose assets are readily taxable by the sovereign, wishes to renege on an agreement with an outsider whose returns are regularly withdrawn from the realm. Or, more directly, the sovereign itself may wish to renege, leaving the other party with no recourse to third-party arbitration. Hence there is a tension between the sovereign's *ex ante* desire to expand mutually advantageous trades and its *ex post* incentive to act opportunistically.

The threat of sovereign opportunism reduces the willingness of outsiders and subjects alike to deal with the sovereign government and to depend on it for contractual enforcement. Some potential gains from trade will be lost unless the sovereign can make credible commitments to bind its own hands. Although self-enforcing agreements based on reputation and repeat dealing do provide some limits on the sovereign, the *law* constrains the sovereign only if the sovereign will tolerate arbiters' decisions that are adverse to itself (Landes and Posner 1975); hence the sovereign's paradox. But the extent to which the sovereign succumbs to opportunistic temptations will vary in predictable ways with sovereigns' observable attributes.

Legal Learning Costs and Sovereign Opportunism

> Ultimately all ownership rights are based on the abilities of individuals, or groups of individuals, to forcefully maintain exclusivity. . . . If some individual, relatively proficient in the use of force, received less of the wealth . . . than he could have gained through the use of forceful persuasion, he will disregard the outcome and take his share. . . . [All] allocative systems require agreement; all except force. It is this characteristic which sets it apart from other rationing systems. (Umbeck 1981, 39–40)

A farsighted sovereign would covet its share of the returns from voluntary agreements and consequently try to provide legal predictability, including assurance that decisions by third-party arbiters will obstruct opportunism and will be respected even if unfavorable to the sovereign. Such assurance, however, is costly for the sovereign to establish and maintain and costly for private parties to ascertain.

On the other side of the transaction, it is costly for the private party to ascertain the degree of protection against sovereign opportunism that any legal system has previously afforded similarly placed individuals. Such legal learning costs are the private costs of gauging legal protection afforded the sovereign's associates under the myriad circumstances that may ultimately jeopardize a contractual outcome.

These legal learning costs have both a fixed and a marginal component. The fixed component arises from scale economies inherent in the fact that mastering how a legal system applies to one agreement carries over to different agreements in the same system. *Ceteris paribus*, an individual who has learned one system will have an incentive to enter into agreements governed by that system in preference to other systems. Marginal legal learning costs arise because each new agreement will have some differences that require additional investment in the law's applications and because different legal systems have different amounts of precedent. Contractual choice will depend on differences in these marginal costs.

Both the fixed and the marginal legal learning costs pose more difficulty for economically smaller, immature sovereigns with poor prospects for continuing their reign. Because parties are more likely to have already incurred the legal learning costs for a larger economic system, a larger system will offer greater scale economies. If the sovereign is expected to be long-lived, it makes more sense for parties to invest in learning about that legal system. Moreover, a mature sovereign is more likely to offer greater useful precedent record. Even if the mature and immature sovereign have the same propensity to act opportunistically, there will be fewer contracts in the smaller, immature jurisdictions because both fixed cost per contract and marginal costs will be higher. The problem is exacerbated to the extent that the sovereign must incur costs to establish a predictable and unbiased legal system. Indeed the small, immature sovereign may not incur these costs, finding it more profitable to act opportunistically.

This argument suggests that capital investment will vary systematically with various characteristics of the legal system that relate to sovereign opportunism. First, the average useful design life of invested capital will be positively correlated with the sovereign's longevity and life expectancy. If the sovereign is expected to be around in the future, it is more likely that long-term capital investments will be made. Second, the average useful design life of invested capital will be positively correlated with the sovereign's economic size because parties will be more familiar with larger jurisdictions and because more precedent-setting cases will have been litigated in larger jurisdictions. Third, the locational specificity of capital will be positively correlated with the legal system's precedent; investors will be less willing to place long-lived, immobile assets at risk where legal treatment is unpredictable. And finally, capital investments will be more secure if legal learning costs are lower and precedent greater. These two, in turn, will exist if judges have long tenure and little prospect for promotion to higher judicial positions. In such cases, the judges themselves will have less incentive to act in a way that opportunistically addresses the short-term interests of the sovereign.

Institutional Controls on Sovereign's Opportunism

The economically small, immature, or insecure sovereign faces two problems in establishing precedential legal capital. First, lacking voluminous precedent, such a sovereign will have difficulty informing private parties of its law's operational nature. Second, if the sovereign can overcome the first problem, the sovereign still will face difficulties assuring private parties that the legal system will be impartial and unbiased for all parties including the sovereign.

How such problems can be overcome is evident in the manner in which colonies, such as those that became the United States, Canada, Australia, and Brazil, became sovereign countries. Because these colonies were at that time economically small and legally immature, their newly minted legal systems were untested and lacked precedent. To mitigate such disadvantages, the new sovereigns copied massively from older sovereigns' constitutions and statutes. Indeed, that widely maligned institution of colonialism reduced legal learning costs in newly colonized areas.

Similar progressions can be seen in the transition of territories in the western U.S. to statehood.[3] Territories were legally subservient to the federal government. Moreover, territorial residents were given little political voice at the national level and many were not permitted to select their own territorial governments or laws. Whatever disadvantages these restrictions posed for territorial residents, they did endow the territories with some precedential capital.

Once territories attained statehood, in contrast, they became endowed with the substantial sovereignty that is granted states by the Constitution. Though sovereignty allowed states to establish their individual legal systems, it also expanded the scope for governmental opportunism within the former territory's boundaries. To minimize the potential for opportunism, new state governments often copied their legal institutions from older, well-established states. The older sovereigns that were selected as models were not, as might be suspected, neighboring states with similar endowments, but were nearly always economically important, precedent-laden states further east. Although such an adoption would not completely reduce legal uncertainty, it did pressure the judiciary to follow the model state's precedent when difficult questions of first impression arose.[4]

Of course, if there is significant variance in economic constraints, states will have a demand for legal institutions that mesh with the differential constraints. But specialized law increases legal learning costs, especially for economically small sovereigns; therefore larger economic units are more likely to undertake specialized legal changes. For smaller sovereigns, it will make sense to act jointly to homogenize parts of their law through uniform codes. Examples in the United States include a Uniform Commercial Code, a Model Business Corporation Act, a Uniform Probate Code, and a Uniform Sale of Goods Law. States are not compelled to adopt these codes, and in fact, economically important states often do not. Consider the Model Business Corporation Act (MBCA). States doing a large volume in corporate chartering deviate substantially from the MBCA. Therefore, Delaware can afford to specialize its code in ways that are appropriate for the set of firms likely to charter there, even though this will increase legal learning costs. The codes of states that are relatively unimportant chartering sites, however, cannot afford these costs and adhere to the MBCA. Such evidence is consistent with the hypothesis that states actively try to lower legal learning costs, even if it means adopting standardized law rather than a specialized law cobbled more precisely to the economic environment within the state.

Another way that sovereigns assure impartial and unbiased legal dealings is to cede some sovereignty to another, better-known sovereign. Such sovereign cessions are observable in the histories of those British colonies that, unlike the United States, became independent with relatively little acrimony. Upon attaining independence, former British colonies typically signed "reception treaties" with the United Kingdom. Among other things, those treaties permitted judgments rendered in the new nations' court systems to be appealed to the British Privy Council. Though it entailed a reduction of sovereignty, the private right of appeal to the Privy Council was valuable to the new nations because it added credibly to contractual arrangements within their borders.

Indeed, even the United States carefully conserved the common law tradition inherited from the mother country and adopted clauses in the Constitution that enabled individual states to benefit from the lower legal learning costs associated with dealing with the federal government. For example, through the Supremacy Clause federal legislation preempts inconsistent state law, providing that preemption does not infringe on constitutionally protected powers reserved to the states.[5] Similarly, present rules governing "diversity" permit a litigant under state law to "remove" a case to the federal courts if the contending parties are from different jurisdictions. The diversity rules assure an out-of-state contracting partner that state courts will be unable to bias adjudication toward an in-state party.

The Sovereignty of Indian Reservation Governments

An exception to the above examples that illustrates how sovereign opportunism can be reduced by binding the sovereign to larger, more mature, and more secure sovereigns is the relationship between American Indian tribes and federal and state governments. Through a series of cases discussed below, the United States Supreme Court has failed to retain the potential for a beneficial partial transfer of sovereignty from dependent Indian tribes to other sovereigns.

Though the 295 fully recognized Indian reservations (*World Almanac* 1992, 394) have small populations and small economies compared to the 50 states, they have legal sovereignty that resembles the states. County and municipal ordinances exist at the will of state government; only the federal government can claim supremacy over tribal governments. In brief, anyone who deals widely with reservation Indians confronts an exceptional number of distinct statutory codes, tribal constitutions, and bodies of common law. Disputes must be adjudicated in tribal courts where budgets are small, judges are typically untrained in the law,[6] decisions are not formally recorded to encourage reliance on precedent, and politics heavily influence decisions (Cooter and Fikentscher 1993; Getches and Wilkinson 1986, 389–91).

> There are a number of scattering forces that push Indian law away from any center. Taken together, these splintering influences have the potential of creating a body of law almost [devoid of legal] precedent, of reducing each dispute to the particular complex of circumstances at issue—the tribe, its treaty or enabling statute, the races of the parties, the tract-book location of the land where the case arose, the narrow tribal or state power involved . . . (Wilkinson 1987, 3–4)

The above theory suggests that such an environment would encourage attempts to cede some sovereignty to another entity, but legal decisions regarding American Indians actually increase reservation government sovereignty.[7] The Supreme Court's 1959 holding in *Williams v. Lee*[8] established that disputes between a reservation citizen and a non-Indian, arising from interactions occurring on the reservation, must be taken to tribal courts, not to the courts of the state within which the interaction occurred. Subsequent Supreme Court decisions have shown substantial deference to tribal courts.[9]

Merrion v. Jicarilla Apache Tribe

This increase in tribal sovereignty has been particularly evident in cases involving mineral exploration following *Merrion v. Jicarilla Apache Tribe*. In 1953 northern New Mexico's Jicarilla Apache Tribe concluded a lease with Phillips Petroleum to search for oil and natural gas under parts of the reservation. The lease was a common one, similar in most important respects to those used by off-reservation farmers and ranchers (Haddock and Hall 1983). Regardless of the outcome of the search, the tribe was to receive a specified, fixed sum in exchange for granting an exclusive 10-year exploration right. If oil or gas were discovered, the lease extended automatically for as long as commercial production continued, and the tribe was to receive twelve and one-half percent of the minerals produced.

In one important respect the tribe's lease with Phillips was atypical; it stated that Phillips would abide by all subsequent regulations pertaining to the reservation, *except that no such regulation would effect a change in the royalty or annual rental rate* unless both parties agreed in writing to such a change. The contractual stipulation was intended to protect Phillips against potential opportunism that would result if the tribe could alter the royalty obligation. Similar leases with other exploration companies also included this clause.

After oil and gas were discovered and production initiated, the Jicarilla Tribe imposed a severance tax on oil and gas removed from the reservation. The tax increased tribal receipts from the stipulated one-eighth of recovery to nearly one-fifth. The lessees sued, believing that the tribe lacked power to impose the severance tax. The case ultimately reached the United States Supreme Court[10] which upheld the tax, remarking that the tribe must have taxing power to finance tribal government services. The Court did not explain why the mutually agreed royalties could not finance tribal government services.

To understand the potential deleterious impact of this decision, focus on the nature of the investments with which reservation governments often seek external aid. The search for oil or natural gas is an expensive, high-risk enterprise. It requires extensive seismographic exploration to map deep geological features, followed by exploratory drilling into promising rock domes and traps that might (but probably do not) hold commercially usable mineral reservoirs. Test wells often pierce several miles of rock, at a cost of millions of dollars. But only about one-tenth of exploratory bores strike producible minerals. If a field is developed, additional production wells typically are required for efficient extraction. Then the field must be tied into the wider economy somehow, as through rail spurs or pipeline construction that can cost a million dollars *per mile* (DeFrange 1990). In brief, a staggering investment is sunk before a penny is recovered. Moreover, the bulk of that investment is geographically immobile; investing companies cannot credibly threaten to move bore holes, completed pipelines, or location-specific knowledge. Thus, companies are especially vulnerable to opportunism and therefore undertake exploration contracts that are extraordinarily detailed.

Given these large specific investments, Indians are likely to be the losers from the *Jicarilla* decision. First, even if there was no decrease of exploratory effort, investors entering new relationships would adjust upwards the contractually stipulated returns they would require before commencing investment, on the expectation that some earnings ultimately will be taxed away. *Ceteris paribus*, we would expect exploration companies to reduce the fixed-fee noncontingent offers made to tribes because the companies' expected returns will be lower on reservations than off reservations. But the increased potential for tribal opportunism also would divert investment funds from on-reservation projects to off-reservation ones. Even the Jicarilla Apache Tribe itself recognized the potential for this negative impact. In an amicus brief filed in *Cotton Petroleum Corp. v. New Mexico*,[11] the tribe contended that a severance tax increase by the state of New Mexico imposed after substantial investment had been sunk by Cotton Petroleum Corp. would deter future on-reservation investment.

Constitutional Limits on Tribal Sovereigns

The Jicarilla Apache Tribe surprised the lessees with an unanticipated tax that raised the possibility of additional opportunistic behavior and lowered the likelihood of investment on reservations. Because the Supreme Court refused to act as a third-party check on tribal sovereignty, we must now consider whether constitutions provide an alternative *ex post* mechanism to guard against opportunism.

The Jicarilla Apache Tribe had adopted a constitution pursuant to the Indian Reorganization Act of 1934.[12] That constitution foresaw the imposition of certain taxes, but required that they be reviewed by the secretary of the interior. Such a review affords individuals with reservation interests some protection against unreasonable treatment by the tribe because the secretary's constituency includes other tribes who gain nothing from the particular opportunism and potentially lose credibility. But even if the secretary offers some protection, tribal constitutions *may* not stipulate such oversight. Even then, however, at least prior interpretations of the constitution would provide some advance warning of possible tribal actions, though the relatively high legal learning costs will discourage many potential associates.

But the Indian Reorganization Act did not require tribal governments to be organized under a constitution, thus reducing the efficacy of this constraint on opportunism. The impact of tribal government unconstrained by a constitution is illustrated in the case of *Southland Royalty Co. v. Navajo Tribe of Indians*.[13] The Navajo have no constitution. Yet the Tenth Circuit Court of Appeals decided that the Supreme Court's reasoning in *Jicarilla Apache* was not founded on the existence of a constitution, nor on any requirement that taxes be approved by the secretary of the interior. The circuit's position was consistent with the Department of Interior's own view that

> The Department's power to approve ordinances of Indian tribes must, in our view, be authorized either by an act of Congress, or by a tribal constitution or legislative act. . . . Enactment of tribal ordinances without Secretarial approval, except where that approval is required by statute, a tribal constitution, or a tribal ordinance, is an exercise of "inherent powers of a limited sovereignty which has never been extinguished."[14]

The circuit court's position was indirectly affirmed by the Supreme Court in the factually similar *Kerr-McGee Corp. v. Navajo Tribe.*[15]

In *Jicarilla Apache*, the Court stated that it sought to advance tribal financial independence. But the tribe's financial independence depends on both tax revenues and royalty revenues. If *Jicarilla Apache* means reservation governments possess an inalienable threat to increase taxes, but that threat reduces royalty revenues by more than the potential tax, the decision may have *decreased* tribal financial independence. Given that the tribe raised the tax knowing that it might decrease future royalty payments, we can only assume that it believed the tradeoff was worth it. The tribal government had voluntarily chosen to impose the tax, and thus to assume the threatening status.[16] The same need not be true, however, for Indians on other reservations, who, due to the Jicarilla success in court, may now be viewed with skepticism when making promises regarding taxes and royalties.

Contracting Out of Opportunism

If there is not an unbiased third-party enforcer and if constitutional limits do not protect against opportunism by sovereign tribes, is it possible for tribes to bind themselves through private contracting? Is there a way for a farsighted sovereign to use the courts to guarantee that it will not subsequently and unilaterally alter its take from private assets through unexpected taxes, regulations, or changes in infrastructure? To insure against a potential associate's fear of opportunistic tax-law innovation, tribal governments might include very explicit clauses in contracts to bar tribal taxation of the associate's quasi-rents.

Such contracts might offer a viable mechanism to prevent opportunism, but there is no case involving reservation governments that is directly on point. Cases involving states offer a glimpse of how this might work.[17] The contract clause of the United States Constitution prohibits state impairment of contractual obligations, but a state may justify incidental impairment by showing a significant and legitimate interest behind the regulation. Where the state regulation incidentally impairs contracts between private parties, the judiciary will defer to the state legislature's judgment, but when "the state is a contracting party, the legislative judgment is subject to stricter scrutiny than when the legislation affects only private contracts."[18] The scrutiny is especially strict where such legislation has a retroactive effect.[19]

However, a state may not contract away or limit its legislature's prospective taxing power.[20] The rationale behind this limit is that it prevents incumbent politicians from selling the state's taxing authority for recompense that benefits the incumbents rather than the state.

Hence, the law regarding tribal taxation of associate's investment returns is murky. Any potential investor who so wishes can innovate contractual clauses attempting to guard against tribal opportunism and test the tribal powers in the absence of legal precedent. For instance, one could define the royalty to be net of tribal taxes so that it decreased dollar for dollar if the tribal tax increased.[21] Since the tribe could impose a tax greater than the stipulated net royalty, the lease would also have to provide for negative royalties to be paid by the tribe to the leaseholder. Investors innovating such novel contractual clauses would surely provide a public good in the form of precedent. The innovating party, of course, would bear the full costs of designing the clause, testing it in court, and possibly paying an adverse judgment. Such a situation resonates with suboptimal incentive.

Alternatively, a tribe might facilitate the vertical integration of exploratory efforts by alienating part of its reservation altogether. Unfortunately, statutes and Bureau of Indian Affairs policy discourage tribal alienation of territory at present and seem unlikely to change in the near future (McChesney 1990).[22] Moreover, such alienation would extinguish tribal sovereignty over all aspects of law, not just that covering contracts, taxes, and a few other appropriate areas. And, as indicated above, there is no reason to believe that tribal sovereignty over the potentially alienated territory is undesirable for many other types of law. A farsighted tribe would want a more limited sovereignty cession, even if the courts seem disinclined to facilitate such a thing. Alternatively the tribe could vertically integrate by undertaking mineral exploration on its own. Such vertical integration might save on costs associated with opportunism, but it surely would ignore the principle of comparative advantage.

Conclusion

All else equal, economically small and immature sovereignties comprise unpromising environments for long-term, immobile private investment. It is especially costly to learn what protection such a sovereign's legal system offers against the sovereign's opportunism. In the face of that cost, potential investors may simply assume the worst, and curtail investment.

In the case of Indian reservations, many parties will simply choose to avoid dealings with tribes altogether. Since commercial interactions with Indians comprise a very small part of the economy as a whole, however, the overall social rate of return on investment will hardly be altered. On the other hand, the rate of return on tribal assets could be reduced substantially, and the risk they face will increase.

But an expectation of biased law can be self-fulfilling. If the investments are to be curtailed in any event, why should the sovereign bear the extra costs associated with a sophisticated legal system?

This is neither an occasional nor a purely academic problem. Ramifications should be on the minds of those contemplating an independent Quebec, for example. The issue is palpable in Eastern Europe; Czechoslovakia's president proclaims a market less fettered than perhaps any other on earth, yet investment funds arrive not in a flood but in such a disappointing trickle that the nation disintegrates. The inheritors of the entire Eastern bloc find little legal capital in their patrimony. Due to their predecessors' fragmented and tenuous nature, there was little legal capital to begin with, and much of that has been discarded along with Marxist ideology. Despite vast potential, Africa's economy has slumbered since colonizing powers left. Other examples abound in Asia and Latin America. They all share one feature: profound uncertainty concerning what the law is and what it is to become. A well-conceived, well-polished, and well-understood body of law and legal process is intangible capital of enormous, if poorly appreciated, value to a sovereign.

There exist several techniques by which a sovereign can reduce the damage imparted by its small economic size, by its immaturity, and by the legal uncertainty that results. Some techniques such as modeling law on a better-known sovereign's or joining with other disabled sovereigns to adopt uniform codes arise from the sovereign's own actions.

But one important technique, ceding some sovereignty to another, requires the other's acquiescence. The smaller and more immature the sovereign, the more urgent that result. Yet ceding some sovereignty is impossible without the better-formed jurisdiction's cooperation. Recent United States' court decisions have not been helpful in that regard. The governmental sovereignty of American Indian reservations have been jealously defended, even enhanced, by the federal courts (Taylor 1987). If no credible judiciary will guarantee an Indian's word then who will? An inattentive, undiscriminating determination to retain and enhance every aspect of tribal sovereignty cannot improve the typical reservation Indian's economic prospects, although it may well improve the prospects of those tribal politicians who channel the benefits, and optimize over an abbreviated period.

It is certainly not the argument here that all, or even most, aspects of tribal sovereignty are inappropriate. That small, insular, culturally homogeneous populations would want to undertake unusually numerous joint activities is neither surprising nor regrettable. That reservation criminal and tort law may reflect ancient tribal understandings is unchallenged here. But if some aspects of sovereignty are valuable to a sovereign, others are not. Being able to tie one's own hands if one so chooses is a *very* valuable attribute, one that the courts are willing to afford to any non tribal citizen. However, it is an attribute that small, legally immature sovereigns have difficulty establishing unless a better positioned sovereign will lend a hand. Unfortunately, that lesson seems incomprehensible to the federal courts.

Is sovereignty to be sought for its own sake? Or is it to be sought only if it improves subjects' welfare? Implicitly the prevailing legal opinion would seem to opt for the former, urging increased tribal sovereignty in all its aspects at any cost. Where sovereign opportunism is a serious threat, the problem for ordinary reservation *residents* was not that the state had power that the tribal government wanted; the problem *is* that either one has that power. Less *can* be better than more. Social scientists explain all about logical fallacies; judges then commit them.

Notes

1. A reasonable proxy for economic size would be the real value of market transactions that occur within the sovereign's borders. For example, by such a measure,

Italy would loom twice as large as China, and thus an implication would be that Italy would have the more predictable and less biased legal system. The statement in the text, of course, assumes "all else equal." Two things specifically that are being assumed equal are the ability of subjects and their assets to exit a sovereign's realm, and the resources dissipated in rent-seeking activities. However, a realm's *geographical* size is positively correlated with its economic size and negatively correlated with the ability of subjects and assets to exit. Friedman (1977) provides the seminal discussion of this. Further, a realm's *stability* may be positively correlated with rent-seeking dissipation (Olson 1982). Thus, the present *ceteris paribus* statement is stronger than it might seem. Nevertheless, for the examples examined here, those correlations seem peripheral. In other instances, however, they will be of paramount importance. See Haddock (1993) for a more general analysis.

2. Some states are economically important in some particular regard for reasons that are poorly understood. Delaware, for example, is a prime example; trivial in area, population, and natural resources, yet the leading corporate chartering state. While Romano (1985) has initiated a tentative but insightful inquiry into that mystery; nobody knows how Delaware wrested that status from New Jersey, nor why Nevada (which has tried) has been unable to wrest it from Delaware, though politicians in other states crave that knowledge.

3. Some states are exceptional because they had other legal precedent. For example, California, Texas, and parts of New Mexico were taken from Mexico with operating legal systems largely intact. Similarly, Louisiana was a relatively advanced French possession well before becoming a state, a fact still evident in its French style law and procedure.

4. It is noteworthy that, rather than copying a model state's law, new states sometimes instituted unusual, specialized codes dealing with activities in which the state was economically important. Thus, Nevada's mining law contained innovations with respect to silver mining and the prior appropriation law of the West reflected a change from the riparian law of the east.

5. "This Constitution, and the Laws of the United States which shall be made in pursuance thereof . . . shall be the supreme Law of the Land." A federal law preempts state law when the state law "stands as an obstacle to the accomplishment and execution of the full purposes and objectives of Congress" (U.S. Constitution Article VI, clause 2).

6. For example, "the Navajo Tribal Courts . . . [consist of] a Supreme Court of the Navajo Nation, comprised of the Chief Justice and two Associate Justices, eight Navajo District Judges, . . . a Navajo Children's Court, and the Peacemaker Court. . . . [Many judges] have paralegal or law enforcement backgrounds. Currently one Trial Judge and one Supreme Court Justice are graduates of accredited law schools. All Judges are members of the Navajo Tribe" (Mason 1989, 3).

7. Several small tribes have indeed begun to form intertribal legal systems (Taylor 1987, 236). That is a promising trend, somewhat resembling state efforts to

decrease legal learning costs by jointly adopting uniform codes. At present, however, the most obvious result has been to foster a full-time judiciary. As yet the intertribal jurisdictions unify too little Indian law to substantially affect the legal learning costs on reservations.

8. *Williams v. Lee*, 358 U.S. 217 (1959).

9. *National Farmers Union Insurance Cos. v. Crow Tribe*, 471 U.S. 845 (1985) and *Iowa Mutual Insurance Co. v. LaPlante*, 480 U.S. 9 (1987).

10. *Merrion v. Jicarilla Apache Tribe*, 455 U.S. 130 (1982).

11. *Cotton Petroleum Corp. v. New Mexico*, 490 U.S. 163 (1989).

12. 25 USC §§ 461–79.

13. *Southland Royalty Co. v. Navajo Tribe of Indians*, 715 F.2d 486 (10th Cir. 1983).

14. Letter dated November 19, 1980, citing Cohen (1942, 122), and signed by the deputy assistant secretary–Indian Affairs (569 F.Supp. 801, 802 [1983]).

15. *Kerr-McGee Corp. v. Navajo Tribe*, 471 U.S 195 (1985).

16. However, a sovereign may guard its sovereignty even if the costs, which are distributed across its subjects over long periods, exceed the benefits, which may be concentrated in the sovereign's hands in the near term. Cognizant that political power is especially transitory, many sovereigns discount the future more heavily than do their subjects. Many costs will be visited upon a later period, and thus quite possibly on a different sovereign. Therefore, even if it was fully informed, the tribal government's voluntary decision to impose the severance tax, and thus to incite both the legal action leading to *Jicarilla Apache* and possible demoralization of potential tribal associates, would not necessarily imply that there was a net expected advantage to the tribal population as a whole over time.

17. That tribes will be treated like states is hardly a foregone conclusion, however. For example, the contract clause of the U.S. Constitution probably does not apply to Indian tribes and the clause literally applies only to states. The Court has generally construed the clause narrowly rather than broadly, and in particular it has refused to extend it to the federal government. See *Nat'l R.R. Passenger Corp. v. Atchison, T. & S. Fe Ry. Co.*, 470 U.S. 451 (1985).

18. *Nieves v. Hess Oil Virgin Islands Corp.*, 819 F.2d 1237 (3d Cir. 1987) at 1249. The contract clause does not bar modification of the state's own financial obligations (*United States Trust Co. of New York v. New Jersey*, 431 U.S. 1, reh'g denied 431 U.S. 975 [1971]), but courts show less deference where the state is self-interested (*Keystone Bituminous Coal Ass'n v. DeBenedictis* 581 F.Supp. 511 [D.Pa.1984]).

19. *Maryland State Teachers Ass'n v. Hughes*, 594 F.Supp. 1353 (D.Md. 1984) at 1360.

20. *Reserve Min. Co. v. State*, 310 N.W.2d 487 (1981), appeal after remand 334 N.W.2d 389 (Sup.Ct. Minn. 1983). There are some very old cases holding that state contracts exempting private entities from taxation are enforceable under the contract clause. See the discussion in *United States Trust Co. of New York v. New*

Jersey, 431 U.S. 1, reh'g denied 431 U.S. 975 (1971). Although the Court has never overruled those cases, tax exemptions are construed very narrowly.
21. Even if successful, that would not defend against more subtle expropriations via more indirect taxes such as those on firm employees living on the reservation or inputs procured locally. Nor would the clause protect against expropriations manifested through regulatory or infrastructural changes. All those things would have to be foreseen and protected against individually if courts are determined to ignore the contracting parties' underlying intentions whenever one is a sovereign.
22. Indeed, many individual Indians are forbidden to alienate their *private* rights to land even to other tribal members (Indian Reorganization Act of 1934). Tribal territory can be alienated, with or without the tribe's approval, if the federal government so directs (*Lone Wolf v. Hitchcock*, 187 U.S. 553, 1903). Present sentiment inside and outside the BIA, however, seems to be that tribal territory should be expanding, not contracting.

References

Barzel, Yoram. 1991. Property rights and the evolution of the state. Manuscript, Department of Economics, University of Washington, Seattle.
————. 1992. Confiscation by the ruler: The rise and fall of Jewish lending in the Middle Ages. *Journal of Law and Economics* 35: 1–13.
Cohen, Felix S. 1942. *Handbook of federal Indian law*. Washington, DC: U. S. Government Printing Office.
Cooter, Robert D., and Wolfgang Fikentscher. 1993. Is there Indian common law? Manuscript, School of Law, University of California, Berkeley.
DeFrange, Ann. 1990. Gas pipeline carries hope to Southeast. *Sunday Oklahoman* (October 21): 1.
Friedman, David D. 1977. A theory of the size and shape of nations. *Journal of Political Economy* 85: 59–77.
Getches, David H., and Charles F. Wilkinson. 1986. *Federal Indian law: Cases and materials*, 2nd ed. St. Paul, MN: West Publishing.
Grandy, Christopher. 1989. Can government be trusted to keep its part of a social contract? *Journal of Law, Economics, and Organization* 5: 249–69.
Haddock, David D. 1993. Classical liberal or despot? A model of sovereign behavior. Manuscript, Northwestern University Law School, Chicago.
Haddock, David D., and Thomas D. Hall. 1983. The impact of making rights inalienable. *Supreme Court Economic Review* 2: 1–41.
Klein, Benjamin, Robert G. Crawford, and Armen A. Alchian. 1978. Vertical integration, appropriable rents, and the competitive contracting process. *Journal of Law and Economics* 21: 297–326.
Klein, Benjamin, and Keith B. Leffler. 1981. The role of market forces in assuring contractual performance. *Journal of Political Economy* 89: 615–41.

Landes, William M., and Richard A. Posner. 1975. The independent judiciary in an interest-group perspective. *Journal of Law and Economics* 18: 875–901.

McChesney, Fred S. 1990. Government as definer of property rights: Indian lands, ethnic externalities, and bureaucratic budgets. *Journal of Legal Studies* 19: 297–335.

MacNeil, Ian R. 1978. Contracts: Adjustment of long-term economic relations under classical, neoclassical and relational contract law. *Northwestern University Law Review* 72: 854–906.

Mason, James Jay. 1989. Practice before tribal courts. In *Mineral development on Indian lands*. Denver: Rocky Mountain Mineral Law Foundation.

Olson, Mancur. 1982. *The rise and decline of nations*. New Haven: Yale University Press.

Romano, Roberta. 1985. Law as product: Some pieces of the incorporation puzzle. *Journal of Law, Economics, and Organization* 1: 225–83.

Taylor, Michael. 1987. Modern practice in the Indian courts. *University of Puget Sound Law Review* 10: 231–75.

Telser, Lester G. 1980. A theory of self-enforcing agreements. *Journal of Business* 53: 27–44.

Umbeck, John R. 1981. Might makes rights: A theory of the formation and initial distribution of property rights. *Economic Inquiry* 19(1): 38–59.

Wilkinson, Charles F. 1987. *American Indians, time, and the law*. New Haven: Yale University Press.

Williamson, Oliver E. 1983. Credible commitments: Using hostages to support exchange. *American Economic Review* 83: 519–40.

———. 1988. The logic of economic organization. *Journal of Law, Economics, and Organization* 4: 65–93.

World almanac and book of facts. 1992. New York: Pharos Books.

8

Public Policy and the Admission of the Western States

David W. Brady and Roger G. Noll

Between the Mexican War and World War I, the United States granted statehood to the vast and largely unpopulated territories of the West. These states had several unique climatic, social, topographic, and economic characteristics. Because of the climate and the natural resource base, compared to the rest of the country, less of the West was devoted to the Jeffersonian family farm, and more to ranching, mining, and trapping. Moreover, in most of the West, population density was lower than in the rest of the nation, and the inhabitants were of a different racial and ethnic mix, including significant numbers of Hispanics, Asians, and nomadic native Americans.

The purpose of this chapter is to explore the effect the admission of the Western states had on the policies of the federal government. Specifically, we examine the legislative history of the United States during the period that the Western states were granted admission to determine whether western representatives sought and achieved different policy objectives than representatives from the rest of the nation. In addressing this question, we base our work on three disparate strands of scholarly research. The first is the modern rational actor theory of political decisions, which models policies as emanating from the interactions of individuals motivated by the desire to satisfy their personal preferences, given personal and societal resource constraints. The second is research on the history of the West, particularly the work that focuses on the effect of westward expansion on the economic, political, and social development of the United States. We regard this work as useful for two reasons: it describes the character and background of the people who settled the Western territories, and it explains how they attempted to solve the special circumstances associated with settling the Western lands. Both are useful in developing hypotheses about the policy objectives that Western citizens and politicians might have pursued as rational actors. The third strand is research on modern Western state-building since the seventeenth century. This work addresses why modern nation-states came into existence, why success in terms of economic growth and political stability seems to require a liberal democratic state, and, in the case of the United States, how and why the federal government adopted pro-active state-building policies (ranging from homesteading and railroad land grants to the decisions to fight the Civil War and emancipate slaves).

These three areas of scholarly inquiry merge to form the basis of our central research questions: Why did rational political actors decide to admit the Western states to the Union at the time and in the order that they did, and what policy consequences flowed from these decisions? Of course, in the rational actor approach to politics, these two questions are linked, in that the admission decisions must have taken into account the policy consequences of admission. Indeed, the Missouri Compromise and the Kansas–Nebraska Act conclusively demonstrate that federal officials regarded admissions decisions as highly political and explicitly took into account the policy consequences.

Historical Background

The role of the West in shaping American political, economic, and social history has been a matter of considerable controversy among scholars throughout the twentieth century.[1] One common historical theme focuses on the mythic West of larger-than-life legendary characters.[2] An important element of most of this historical work is how the harsh life of the West tested the true character of its inhabitants, creating the vilest villains and the most admirable heroes. The mythic vision of the West reached its pinnacle in Frederick Jackson Turner's (1963) much celebrated and later much maligned frontier thesis. This thesis hypothesized that the ongoing conquest of new lands strengthened the American character by promoting self-reliance, a respect for the individual, and democratic government, all of which were said to be threatened by the ultimate closing of the western frontier around 1890. Beyond the controversial political hypotheses surrounding the Turner thesis, this literature focuses on the opportunities and constraints facing nineteenth century Western settlers, and so is useful in understanding the demands that these people were likely to place on government, and hence the policy objectives that their representatives were likely to pursue.

Since the mid-1980s, a new version of the history of the West has emerged: the "New Western History," which has taken on something of a moral crusade to demystify the traditional western hero. This work focuses on two negative aspects of western settlement. One is the violent displacement of Native Americans and Hispanics by white northern Europeans, and the generally harsh treatment of racial minorities and women.[3] The message of this scholarship is that western racism and sexism undermined the victory of Northern abolitionists in the Civil War. The other focus is on the excessive exploitation of western natural resources, allegedly driven by the vain attempt of capitalistic promoters and developers to attract more people to the West than could be supported by its resource base.[4] The conclusion advanced by this work is that western resource exploitation bred into American culture an anti-conservationist, anti-environmentalist set of values that still threatens the long-run economic viability of the region and the nation.

Although the work of all schools of western historians is controversial, our starting point is to take seriously the inferences that all historians have made about the basic values and personal circumstances—interpreted by us as purposes and constraints—of citizens and politicians from Western states. Our focus is on the period between the Civil War and World War I. The first nationally chartered railroads were built in the early 1860s, giving the western hinterland access to national and world markets. During this period, the federal government promoted western development through such policies as railroad land grants, homesteading, mining laws, federal land management for timber and grazing, and water reclamation. In addition, the post-bellum federal government pursued many other policies affecting the entire nation, such as policies concerning tariffs, national expansion beyond the contiguous states, and civil rights. Our aim is to identify how the admission of the Western states influenced these policies.

Regional Preferences and Western Exceptionalism

The argument that the settlement of the West and the admission of the Western states had an important effect on national policy requires that the policy preferences of Westerners differed from most of the rest of the nation and that Western preferences were influential in the federal government. The latter turns on the theory and the facts of Western representation in Washington, and is addressed in the next section. The former turns on how the nature of Western citizens and their opportunities and constraints may have produced goals and preferences over policies that differed from those of citizens elsewhere. To address this issue, we turn to western historians.

Wallace Stegner is perhaps the most renowned proponent of the view that the defining characteristic of the West is aridity. Stegner defines the West as the region where the absence of rainfall during the growing season makes intensive agriculture like that found in the Midwest impossible without extensive irrigation. Based on this concept, he defines the West as beginning somewhere between the 98th and 100th meridians, along a line that passes through the eastern portions of the states running from North Dakota south to Texas. According to Stegner's definition, the West includes Rapid City, Wichita, Dallas, and San Antonio, but not Sioux Fails, Omaha, and Houston.

We adopt Stegner's definition of the West because it provides a reasonable basis for formulating theoretical hypotheses about the policy preferences of western citizens. Both the old and new western histories focus on the climatic differences between the West and the rest of the nation, and their debate over the extent to which western development was excessively exploitative should not obscure the part of the story that is clearly correct. Somewhere near the eastern borders of the states running from the Dakotas to Texas, the resource base of economic life shifted dramatically. Successful agriculture depended on access to a year-round supply of river or lake water. Farming techniques and animal husbandry differed substantially, usually requiring less labor and generating less value per acre.

United States water and land policies were developed to deal with environmental circumstances prevalent in the East. Water was allocated according to a riparian rights system, where the obligation of the user was to leave the flow undiminished in quantity and quality for downstream users, and public land was assigned to homesteaders in 160-acre tracts. While these policies were adequate for areas with abundant water and land suited to intensive use in small parcels, they made no sense in the arid West. The quarter-section farm was inadequate for agriculture and was useless for ranching. And, aridity required a water allocation system that accommodated large-scale diversions from streams and lakes. Hence Western states adopted the appropriative rights system which quantified rights to divert water on the basis of "first in time, first in right" and made those rights transferable (see Anderson 1983).

The twin problems of land aggregation and water scarcity arose from the same source: an inappropriate prior definition of property rights in common and statutory law. Not surprisingly, western settlement inevitably gave rise to demands for corrective policy actions. It was the inappropriate combination of environmental constraints and institutions that led to pressures for public policy change. Settlers, seeking access to more low-valued land and better water supplies, focused on using but not owning public lands. Hence, the federal lands became a form of ranching commons, with resource management (including water) left to the government rather than in private hands (see Sanchez and Nugent, this volume). Likewise, as settlement quickly exhausted water supplies on private lands, political demands arose to increase water supplies from federal lands and waterways (see Mayhew and Gardner, this volume; Simmons, this volume).

In addition to physical differences between the East and the West that affected farming and ranching, the West also contained wild, rugged, and remote areas rich in mineral resources. Although mining was important elsewhere in the United States, western mining had two unique features (see Paul 1963). First, most mining areas were in mountainous terrain not served by early transportation routes and unsuited for support industries, such as agriculture or other supplies. Second, mining camps with thousands of residents would emerge in a matter of months, work a lode intensively for a few years, and then, when the lode played out, disappear into ghost towns. These two factors produced a constant demand for more railroad trackage.

The settlement of the West also created a competition for land with indigenous, largely nomadic populations. The new historians emphasize that Native American rights to land were simply ignored and that the newly asserted rights of settlers were backed by force. The old history places more emphasis on the inefficiency and economic backwardness of Native American society and the violence of Indians against whites. But both sides agree that western settlement created a conflict between indigenous populations and settlers. Not surprisingly, the often-violent confrontations between settlers and indigenous people led the former to ask for government protection, and hence induced a preference among Western-ers for a strong military presence.

Still another important feature of the West was a persistently tight labor market. Mining booms, cattle booms, and railroad booms all required labor to construct the infrastructure and subsequently to operate the mines, ranches, and transportation system. Because the western life was harsh and remote, and because substantial economic growth in the nineteenth century raised wages in the East, attracting labor to the West was not easy. Consequently, entrepreneurs of the West imported workers from other countries, such as Latin America and Asia. In many cases, these workers were recruited for the least desirable jobs, so were not regarded as a threat to high-wage cowboys, miners, and rail workers. Thus, as a political matter, Westerners had reason to prefer relatively lax immigration laws.

A purely economic theory of Western society and politics also has implications for Western attitudes about individual rights. Although the new western history emphasizes the denial of rights to ethnic minorities and women, the scarcity of labor implies that individual rights would be accorded more, not less, protection in the West than elsewhere. Just as labor scarcity led to high wages, the same competition for settlers would lead to greater guarantees of individual rights. Moreover, very low population density should have increased the value of one person to another, and hence generated a greater willingness to tolerate differ-ences.[5] And we would expect that the unbalanced sex ratio in the early West would lead to greater accommodations for women to attract them as settlers.

The economic status of the West also has ramifications for western attitudes about international relations. As already noted, Westerners favored open immigra-tion. The late nineteenth century also witnessed the transition of tariff policy from one that generated tax revenues to one that protected certain industries from foreign competition. Because western economic interests were highly focused on primary products from mining, ranching, and farming, which, we suspect, faced little foreign competition (except from newly emerging cattle and sheep ranches in Latin America, Australia, and New Zealand), Westerners might have feared retaliation against United States' protective tariffs more than foreign competition. Similarly, because western communities were dependent on other areas for almost all consumer goods and inputs to their industries, they should have been more interested in free trade than more self-sufficient communities with products facing foreign competition.

The other aspect of international relations deserving attention is military intervention outside the United States. During the late nineteenth and early twentieth centuries, the United States pursued an aggressive interventionist policy in Latin America and the Philippines. Attitudes of Westerners on this issue must have been subject to conflicting influences, both arising from the role of the military in protecting settlers from Indians. On the one hand, a more active role for the military in international theaters would have led to some reduction in military protection in the West, at least in the quality if not the quantity of troops stationed there. On the other hand, Westerners should have been supportive of the military because of its importance to them. On balance, then, pure regional self-interest should lead Westerners to support the military, but not to be aggressive interventionist.

Many of our inferences about western preferences, while based on the descriptive accounts of both old and new western historians, are at variance with their overarching theories. Both the mythic and the antihero Wests, with violent conflicts between settlers and indigenous people, between outlaw bands and quasi-legal law officers and vigilante committees, and between settler groups over scarce water and arable land (e.g., the Johnson County War, not to mention "Shane"), emphasize a certain nonrational commitment to a particular set of values and way of life. But we are dealing with instrumental preferences arising from more prosaic objectives, such as earning a living and otherwise leading a safe, happy life. The wars between Indians and settlers, nesters and ranchers, and to some degree outlaw bands and posses, reflected a fundamental failure of the political system to define and to enforce a viable system of property rights in the face of scarce resources and conflicting interests.

This synopsis of western development also suggests some key tests for the idea that Westerners had unusual policy preferences which they brought to bear on the federal government. In essence, the test is whether western preferences in policy making in Washington reflected the influences described here, and whether western politicians were influential in shaping legislation to suit these preferences.

The Institutional and Political Base of Western Influence

For western preferences to have affected policy, two conditions must have prevailed. The first, described above, is that Westerners generally differed from other representatives in their policy goals. The second is that within the context of national political institutions, western preferences were decisive. How and why this could be true is the subject of this section.

The beginning assumption of our model is that citizens and their representatives prefer alternative government policies depending on the net benefits to them which are derived from two sources. One source is the "public goods" associated with policies and measured in terms of railroad miles constructed, cavalry units in place, or immigrants allowed into the United States. The other is the distributive effect of federal policy, such as who gets the contract, who is appointed to patronage jobs, and which communities get a railroad hub. The institutional structure of Congress—its organization into parties and committees—is the mechanism by which winners and losers are determined on both sets of issues.[6]

Our underlying model is a simple median voter model. Without the addition of Western states, the median policy position in the Senate would be different from the median with Western states. If the Western states were predominantly one-party states, then the median would shift toward policies favored by that party. For ease of exposition we employ a simple idea; the Republican Party admitted Western states to the Union because at the time of their admittance the new states voted Republican. During most of the 1850–1910 period, the two political parties were about evenly divided. This is true even during the Civil War years. Abraham Lincoln dropped Hamlin (R-Maine) from the ticket in 1864 and added Andrew Johnson, a Union Democrat, to increase his probability of winning. And, it should be noted that he barely beat his Democratic opponent in the 1864 election. The Western states were largely pro-Republican because, with the formation of the party in 1854–1856, the Republicans adopted the Whig position of using the federal government to expand the West. Thus Republican platforms from 1856 forward favored western expansion. In power, Republicans passed legislation giving railroads right of way, giving land to homesteaders, and increasing military appropriations for the West. Given these policy positions, Westerners were more likely to be Republican than Democrat. Admitting Western states would assure continued Republican control of the U.S. Senate and enhance the party's chance of control in the House. And assuming that Western Republicans voted with other Republicans, the median voter would favor policies closer to the Republican Party's position. In short, the admission of Western states enhanced Republican control of institutions and policy.

Western states were largely unpopulated, and were admitted long before justified by their populations. Stewart and Weingast (1992) document how the Republicans improved their fortunes in elections for national office by admitting sparsely populated states. These effects were most pronounced in the Senate, where each state is given two votes regardless of its population. The states admitted between 1850 and 1910 (all Western states in the contiguous United States except Arizona and New Mexico) constituted 15 of the 46 states in 1910, or nearly one-third of the votes in the Senate, despite having only 17 percent of the nation's population. Of course, because the United States' constitutional system gives the House, the Senate, and the President each a veto over legislation, the Western senators were very likely to have significant influence not only in the

Senate, but on ultimate policy outcomes.

In reality, the admission of the Western states had a substantial effect on partisan control of the federal government. During the period 1860 through 1912, the Republicans were the dominant political party in the United States. From 1860 to 1876, the Republicans controlled the presidency and the Senate continuously, and the House for all but two years. The disputed presidential election of 1876, in which Hayes (R) edged out Tilden (D), brought the end of Reconstruction and a resurgence of Democrats in the north, largely in response to the corruption and ineptness of the Grant regime. Even in the West, the election of 1878 reduced the Republican share of senators, but only from 70 percent to 57 percent. In the 1880s, the Democratic candidate for president gained a plurality in two of three elections. Even in one of these, the Democrats lost because Cleveland (D) lost the electoral vote in 1888. Historians have referred to this period as the "Era of No Choice" because neither party managed to gain a firm control on all three branches of government. And, in particular, the Republicans gained a divided government on several occasions because they persisted in controlling the Senate throughout the 1880s. In 1890, the Republicans gained control of the federal government, keeping it until 1910 when they lost control of the House of Representatives. We now turn to the role of Western Republicanism during the Republican hegemony of 1860–1910.

The order of admission of Western states to the Union (Texas 1845; California 1850; Oregon 1859; Kansas 1861; Nevada 1864; Nebraska 1867; Colorado 1876; Montana, North Dakota, South Dakota, and Washington 1889; Idaho 1890; Utah 1896; and Oklahoma 1907) affected the Republican composition of the Senate as shown in Table 8.1. In the 1860–1864 period, Kansas and Nevada were admitted with both sending pairs of Republican senators. Only six years prior, no Republicans represented Western states. However, in 1864, six of eight Western senators were Republican, constituting 14 percent of the total number of Republicans. The addition of Nebraska in 1868 brought two more Republicans to the Senate. In 1868 all ten Western senators were Republican, and they made up 16 percent of their party's total. Republicans dominated United States government from 1860 to 1874, and the Western states contributed to that dominance by being overwhelmingly Republican.

The mid-1870s gave rise to a Democratic resurgence as Southern states were readmitted to the Union and the northern states turned against the corruption of the Grant regime. In 1876, for example, Republicans held a bare majority; without the West sending over 70 percent Republicans (over one-fourth of the total Republican majority), the Democrats would have controlled the Senate. The nascent Democratic Party led to Grover Cleveland's two presidential victories and to a spate of new Western state admissions in 1892. The six new Western states increased Western Senate representation to 26 seats. The new states predictably sent Republicans to the Senate thus ensuring that party's domination during the 1890s. In 1892 Western Republicans were 60.5 percent of the minority party in the Senate, and in 1898, when Republicans were in the majority, Western Republicans constituted 43.5 percent of the party's seats. Though Western Republicans declined in relative importance during the party's reign from 1896 to 1910, by the turn of the century, they still accounted for over 30 percent of the Senate Republicans. In prosperous political times for the party, Western Republicans were important, and in hard political times they were crucial, as attested to by their numbers in 1910 when Westerners comprised 47 percent of the bare Republican majority.

Table 8.1

Western Republicans in the U.S. Senate
1858 – 1910

Year	Republican Senators		Western Republicans as Percent of West		Western Contribution to Republican Senate
	Number	**Percent**	**Percent**	**Number**	**Percent**
1858	26	.406	0.0	0	.000
1864	42	.808	75.0	6	.142
1868	61	.847	100.0	10	.164
1876	39	.520	71.4	10	.256
1884	41	.547	64.3	9	.220
1892	38	.463	88.4	23	.605
1896	56	.659	60.7	17	.304
1900	56	.659	60.7	17	.304
1906	61	.667	71.4	20	.328
1910	49	.538	76.6	23	.469

Overall, the table shows that over the entire period, Western states were disproportionately Republican and that their admission was crucial for Republican Senate majorities. Kansas and Nevada were admitted during the crucial 1860–1864 period, but only Colorado and Nebraska during the next twenty years of Republican dominance. Especially during the period of Populist unrest and the realignment of 1894–1896, the newly admitted Western states contributed heavily to Republican dominance. In short, the pattern of Western state admittance to the Union is consistent with the theory that the West was a crucial element in Republican dominance over the 1860–1910 period.

We now turn to a discussion of the effects of Populism and Progressivism on the West between 1870 and 1920 and compare Western politics with those of the rest of the country. In the period 1860 through 1874, Western Republicans could be considered mainstream; however, by the late 1880s the West was a center of Populist reform. During the 1890s, the West sent 18 Populists to the Senate. The major issue driving Western Populism was the free coinage of silver at a 16-to-1 ratio with gold. Heretofore solid Republican senators, such as Teller of Colorado, were driven from the party and returned to the Senate as Populists or Populist–Democrats. But the rise of Western Populism was brief. The economic recovery in the second half of the 1890s, after the panic of 1893, cut into Populist support and reduced the number of third-party Western senators from six in the 57th Congress (1901–1902) to one in the 58th Congress.

The Progressive movement in the period 1900–1920 was not really a third-party movement. The Progressive leaders, such as LaFollette (Wisconsin) and Borah (Idaho) won elections as Republicans and caucused and received committee assignments through the Republican Party. Although Western elections during this period show continued Republican dominance, Western Republicanism was strongly influenced by the Progressives. Senators such as Borah, Johnson (California), and Norris (Nebraska) opposed the Republican stalwarts or "stand-patters" and were national figures by virtue of their policies favoring a larger role for government in the economy.

In the 1870s, the Western Senate delegation was somewhat more Republican than the non-Western North.[7] In the non-Western North, 59 percent of the senators were Republican, compared to 70 percent in the West. From 1880 to 1900, the West did not appear much different from the rest of the North. Both sent more Republicans to the Senate than Democrats at about a 3-to-1 ratio; however, the West sent about six times as many Populists and Populist–Democrats to the Senate as the non-Western North. After 1900, Republicans continued to dominate in both areas, but the nature of the Republicans differed. The West and Midwest were electing a number of Progressive Republicans, although the West had more third-party candidates. Although all of the North was also electing stalwart Republicans, the stalwart leaders, such as Aldrich (Rhode Island) and Allison (Iowa), were from the non-Western North.

Westerners played a key role in determining party control of the Senate. From 1871 to 1900, thirteen of the fifteen Senates were controlled by the Republicans. In eight of these Congresses, the Western states admitted after the Civil War—Idaho, Montana, the Dakotas, Utah, Washington, and Wyoming—provided the margin of Republican plurality. Had these states not been admitted, the Democrats would have controlled the Senate in ten of fifteen Congresses instead of two. From 1901 to 1906, the Western Republicans were unnecessary to Republican control because the Republican margin was so overwhelming.

The increase in the number of Western states and senators in the post-bellum era, combined with Republican dominance, created a problem for Western senators. During this era, the Senate was characterized by "Aldrichism"—a strongly hierarchical organization controlled by Aldrich, Allison, and Spooner (Wisconsin). These senators sat on crucial committees and dominated House-Senate conference committees by virtue of dual assignments. For example, Aldrich would chair Finance and be the second-ranking Republican on Appropriations, while Allison would chair the latter and rank second on the former. Senate rules at the time sent the two top-ranking majority-party members to conference committees, thus assuring that no bill would pass unless the stalwart view was satisfied. This system left loyal Western Republicans out of power positions. An example is Mondell (Wyoming), who held no important positions despite years of continuous service after the admission of Wyoming as a state.

At the beginning of the 59th Congress (1905–1906), Western Republicans, regarding themselves as underrepresented in power positions, petitioned the Republican majority leader for better committee assignments. This petition was readily granted because the policy positions of the petitioners did not differ from those of the stalwarts. Mondell and six other Western senators were granted new positions, and by the 60th Congress, stalwart Westerners held their proportionate share of leadership positions, including majority whip.

Meanwhile, Progressive Republicans continued to be shut out of important positions, regardless of their regional base. Then, just as the Progressives were gaining strength in the Republican Party, the Democrats won control of the House, the Senate, and the presidency. Consequently, from 1912 to 1918, the issue of the role of Progressives in Republican leadership was moot. In 1919, when the Republicans regained a slim majority in the Senate, the Progressives, led by Johnson (California), threatened Lodge, the Republican majority leader, with defecting to the Democrats if the rules and assignments were not changed. Lodge skillfully managed to isolate Johnson and Norris by branding them as radicals, but in the process he assigned several Progressives to important committees and changed the conference rules to exclude double appointments from conference rights.

During the first two decades of the twentieth century, Western senators played an important role in changing the Senate's rules and practices to accommodate growing Western representation and the increasing importance of the Progressive movement. In both cases, however, these changes did not reflect unique Western politics or point of view. Western Progressives did not gain power as Westerners so much as they acted as part of a new national liberal wing of the party which had to be accommodated if the party was to retain a working majority. Whereas Progressives were somewhat more common in the West, throughout the West both stalwarts and Progressives won elections. The fact that the Western stalwarts won power earlier than the Western Progressives simply reflected the national circumstances in the party. Moreover, both the post-Reconstruction politics and the reforms of the early twentieth century reflect the importance of the West to Republicans.

The decision to admit the Western states helped to produce an almost uninterrupted period of Republican dominance for a half-century after the Civil

War. At the same time, because of the importance of Progressive Republicans in the West, eventually the party changed to accommodate these members so as to regain its national dominance in the 1920s.

Senate Roll Call Votes

To ascertain the differences in policy preferences between the West and the rest of the country, we have analyzed a large sample of Senate roll call votes on several issues. We focus on the Senate because the representation system in the federal government makes the Senate the place where Westerners have most of their influence during the period under study. Because population figures much more heavily into House representation and the electoral college, Westerners account for a larger share of the votes for the Senate than for the House or the President. Because each of these three institutions has veto power over legislative proposals, the strong representation of the West in the Senate makes the position of Western senators on legislation especially important in determining national policy. Methodologically, we test whether the pattern of votes among Western senators, in general and after adjusting for party, differs from the pattern in the Senate as a whole. We test two null hypotheses: (1) the Western senators voted the same as the mean for the entire Senate, and (2) Western Republicans voted the same as all Republicans.

The votes included in the analysis were chosen as follows. All roll call votes in the Senate between 1870 and 1910 were scrutinized to determine the issue to which they pertained. Normally, the consideration of a bill leads to many roll calls, as the floor considers amendments, procedural motions, final passage, and subsequent motions to reconsider. For each bill in each issue category, we selected between one and three votes that appeared to be on key aspects of the legislation and that divided the Senate with the winning side of the vote receiving less than 80 percent of the votes cast.

To perform statistical tests of voting differences, we calculated the frequency of "yes" votes on selected matters before the Senate for all senators and for just Republicans. Under the assumption that this frequency is the probability of voting "yes" for the group of senators in question and that voting is binomially distributed, we calculated the estimated variance of this distribution among Westerners. If f is the frequency of yes votes and N is the number of Westerners voting, the standard deviation of the actual frequency as an estimate of the true probability is given by:

$$\text{s.d.} = [\, f\,(1 - f\,) \,/\, N \,]^{\frac{1}{2}}$$

The test consists of determining whether the voting frequency in the West is within two standard deviations of the voting frequency for the entire Senate. For a single vote, this test has low power. Consider a vote in which 60 percent of the senators vote affirmatively, and the total number of votes cast among Westerners is 16. Applying the above formula, two standard deviations equal 0.24. Thus, any fraction of affirmative votes between 0.84 and 0.36 would satisfy the null hypothesis.

To deal with this problem, we selected a large number of roll calls on each issue and pooled the votes over an entire decade. Thus, we test the hypothesis that, in a particular decade, Western senators in general voted differently than all senators and that Western Republicans voted differently than all Republicans. Typically, this pooling produces a total number of votes of two hundred or more, and brings the estimated standard deviation down to numbers in the range of 0.05. Thus, we can distinguish between groups of senators who differ by less than 0.1 in the fraction of affirmative votes recorded on a given category of issues.

The weakness of the procedure described above is that it combines heterogeneous votes, raising the possibility that voting differences cancel out across different aspects of the issues and mask markedly different shares on each particular vote.

Thus, our second procedure is to analyze the voting patterns for each vote to determine whether either of two important circumstances arose: (1) the Westerners voted in the opposite fashion as other regions (e.g., the Westerners mostly voted for a measure that senators from all other regions voted against); or (2) the Westerners were pivotal to the outcome—that is, had the Westerners not voted, the outcome of the vote would have been the opposite of the actual result.

The first test involves examining votes from each of the other three regions—the Midwest, the South, and the Northeast—to see whether all three regions cast votes that, on balance, opposed the votes of the West. Although a vote could be in both categories if Westerners voted overwhelmingly in one direction while all other regions voted by a small margin in the opposite way, in practice this outcome almost never occurs. Most votes in which Westerners were pivotal pitted Western and Midwestern senators against the East and South.

Lands Issues

The analysis of the votes pertaining to the management of federal lands, other than Indian reservations, has been the most thoroughly analyzed, and so we will present it in some detail to illustrate the method and the primary conclusions that can be drawn from it. Votes are included in the land management category if they dealt with homesteading and other issues related to the conversion of federal lands to private ownership, management of federal lands, forests and parks, federal land leases, the creation of territories and states, and conflicts between land grants for railroads and other lands policies (e.g., homesteading). Railroad rights of way and their associated land grants were classified separately, and were analyzed as part of railroad policy. Land votes are pertinent to the effects of Western admissions because they are central to the economic interests of Westerners.

Table 8.2

Total Senate Votes Cast on Land Issues
1871 – 1910

	Western States		All States	
Period	Republican	Total	Republican	Total
1871–1880	120	165	463	853
1881–1890	205	291	707	1365
1891–1900	206	321	449	986
1901–1910	144	196	393	586
1871–1910	675	973	2012	3790

Table 8.3

Distribution of Votes on Land Issues
1871 – 1910

		Yes Votes				Total Votes	
		West		Total			
Period	Group	#	%	#	%	West	Total
1871–1880	Rep.	55	.46	236	.51	120	463
	All	85	.52	499	.59	165	853
1881–1890	Rep.	138	.62	432	.61	179	205
	All	193	.58	768	.56	291	1365
1891–1900	Rep.	146	.71	314	.70	206	449
	All	191	.60	554	.54	321	986
1901–1910	Rep.*	77	.53	176	.45	144	393
	All	107	.55	291	.50	196	586

* Vote shares differ by more than two standard deviations (95 percent confidence level).

Table 8.2 summarizes these votes for four decades, from 1871 to 1910. Although only a bare majority of the votes cast were by Republicans, the West remained overwhelmingly Republican throughout the period. Thus, the voting patterns of the Western states are consistent with the view that Republicans succeeded in shoring up their dominant political position in the nineteenth century by admitting to the Union states that were more solidly Republican than the average for the rest of the nation.

Table 8.3 contains the basic data for the tests of the hypotheses regarding the voting behavior of Westerners on land-use issues. Neither the fraction of the total vote in the affirmative nor the distribution of the Republican vote differs significantly between the West and the rest of the nation except in the case of the Republican vote in the first decade of the twentieth century. During this period, Western Republicans voted midway between Democrats and Eastern or Midwestern Republicans. An examination of the issues involved during this period provides a ready explanation. Between 1901 and 1910, most of the votes were concerned with the statehood debate for Oklahoma, Indian Territory (now western Oklahoma), New Mexico, and Arizona. These statehood debates split the Republican Party in the West. Perhaps reflecting their common boundaries with Texas and hence a belief that they would be Democratic, the Democrats generally favored and the Republicans generally opposed the admission of New Mexico and Oklahoma. Western Republicans, while casting more negative than positive votes, were divided.

Table 8.4

Number of Key Land Votes by Westerners
1871 – 1910

Period	Total Votes Studied	West Pivotal	West Differs
1871–1880	17	2	0
1881–1890	42	4	2
1891–1900	21	4	1
1901–1910	13	1	1

Table 8.4 contains summary data on the number of votes in which Westerners were decisive or voted differently than the rest of the country. During the entire

forty-year period there were eleven instances in which Western senators were decisive on lands issues. These votes were as follows:

- 44th Congress: a procedural vote, failing due to Western opposition, to kill a bill that would resolve a claim dispute between railroads and homesteaders in favor of the latter (the bill then passed);

- 44th Congress: a procedural vote to table a bill about managing the national forests in California, Oregon, and Washington so that the Senate could resolve a dispute about filling a vacant Senate seat in Louisiana (the motion to table failed, with the Western votes decisive, but the vote was along strict party lines throughout the country);

- 47th Congress: three votes concerning states sharing in the proceeds from federal land sales, in which Western and Midwestern senators succeeded in getting some revenue sharing over the opposition of Eastern and Southern senators;

- 48th Congress: grandfathering the land claims of settlers in the Rio Grande Valley who were made citizens as a result of the Treaty of Guadalupe Hidalgo or whose families had lived on their claims for fifty years;

- 50th Congress: the admission of Dakota Territory to statehood as two states, rather than one, which also was along straight party lines;

- 52nd Congress: a bill to grant relief to settlers for fees and commissions for void claims on public lands, which was decided by a straight party split;

- 52nd Congress: two votes on managing the Arizona Territory debt, having the effect of letting Arizona pay its debt in currency rather than gold, in which Republicans in the East split with Republicans in the West and Midwest;

- 58th Congress: a vote to give New Mexico statehood without Arizona as part of the single state, which was opposed by Republicans but which passed the Senate due to a split among Western Republicans (New Mexico statehood was not enacted in this Congress).

Each of these votes is easily understood by either economic self-interest or expected political consequences. Western Republicans tended to favor the admission of more Western states, favorable land claim rules for their citizens, and measures that improved the financial status of Western state governments. In none of these cases did the Western vote go in the opposite direction from all other regions, either in total or along party lines. Usually Westerners were allied with

Midwesterners when the Republicans split, and in no case did a majority of Western Republicans defect to the Democrats. Even in the New Mexico vote, 11 of 18 Western Republicans voted against admission, but these 11 plus the Democrats were not sufficient for passage in the Senate.

The Western senators voted differently from all other regions only four times over the forty-year period. These cases were as follows:

- 48th Congress: a bill to quiet claims disputes in the Des Moines River Valley in Iowa, which was favored only by Westerners;

- 49th Congress: a bill to confer the status of Territory on the Indian lands of Western Oklahoma, which initially failed but subsequently passed;

- 52nd Congress: a vote that was declared invalid for want of a quorum concerning relief from fees and commissions on void claim entries for settlers as discussed above;

- 61st Congress: a measure to create a federal territorial land court to determine the rights of homesteaders affected by claims disputes.

None of these votes was particularly important. Even the last, which would have created a forum for perfecting property rights for claims on federal land that was favorable to homesteaders, was largely moot by 1910, when it was considered.

Conspicuous by their absence on these lists are all of the great public lands votes of the period. The Westerners were neither different nor pivotal on important votes regarding establishment of the national parks, the means for managing national forests, the land grant colleges, federal reclamation policy, and numerous other issues of the era. Likewise, most of the statehood admissions votes do not appear on either list.

Conclusion

We began this paper by asking two questions: Why were Western states admitted when they were, and what, if any, were the political consequences? The answer to the first question is that Western states were admitted during Republican presidencies, and they elected Republican senators, thus contributing to Republican dominance during the 1860–1910 period. In the 1860s, Kansas, Nevada, and Nebraska were admitted, and all elected Republican senators. Colorado was admitted in 1876 during the last Grant term, immediately after the Democrats' resurgence in the 1874 elections and, like those states admitted in the 1860s, elected a pair of Republican senators. The next thirteen years were characterized by divided government, and no new states were admitted. Then in 1889–1890 six new states—Idaho, Montana, North and South Dakota, Washington, and Wyoming—were admitted under President Harrison, and all sent a pair of Republican senators to Congress. Utah was admitted to statehood on January 4, 1896, under a heavily Republican Congress, and Utah followed the established pattern by sending a pair of Republicans to the Senate. Not until the admission of Oklahoma in 1907 were any Democratic states admitted to the Union, and only with the Democrats' victory in 1910 were Arizona and New Mexico admitted in 1912. The pattern is reasonably clear—Republican governments admitted Western states to the Union over the 1860–1910 period, and the new states promptly increased Republican strength in the Senate.

The policy consequences of the addition of Western states appears to be minimal. We investigated roll call voting on issues of concern to Western interests and found no significant differences in voting between Western Republicans and stalwarts. Western Republican senators voted like their non-Western counterparts. The rise of Progressive interests in the West paralleled their rise in the Midwest, and the proportions within regions were comparable. That is, for every Progressive like Borah there was a Francis Warren (R-Wyoming) and a Wesley Jones (R-Washington). In short, even though Western senators were disproportionately Republican, and at times were a sizeable portion of the Republican majority, they did not vote as a bloc within the Republican Party. Rather they appear to have followed the rules, voted with Republican leaders, and, by the early twentieth century, taken their place in the Republican hierarchy. It is possible that detailed examination of policy issues in certain areas could show that Westerners exerted subtle *ex ante* power to shift proposals toward their preferences, but such research is the subject of another paper. Our results of roll call votes show no major region-specific policy consequences flowing from the admission of Western states in the 1860–1910 period.

In regard to the broader point of how to approach the study of western history, our approach leads to different conclusions. The tradition of mythic western history overemphasizes the difference between the Western character and "American character." The demystifying counter to mythic history is equally guilty of understating and underinterpreting Western difference. Political economists focus on the linkages between economic interests and political institutions as the key to understanding government policy. Explaining public policy in this fashion takes the analysis away from grandiose themes and emphasizes rational political actors responding to constituent preferences within institutions. Rather than emphasizing great heroes, vile villains, and a distinct Western character as the moving forces behind western history, we see normal politicians, senators, and congressmen, working and voting for policies that allow them to be reelected. The admission of Western states to the Union was achieved largely because it enhanced the Republican Party's electoral hold on the U.S. Senate. Newly elected Republican senators worked and voted for policies that benefited their constituents. In sum, they voted for policies that increased western population and economic development.

The primary advantage of studying western history through the rational actor model is that it emphasizes causal relationships and observable explanatory variables rather than depending on ad hoc theories and events. As this paper illustrates, the history of western development will be moved forward by the straightforward study of rational politicians and constituents pursuing self-interest.

Notes

1. For a remarkably insightful survey of the differences between the old and new western histories, see McMurtry (1990).
2. Good examples are Smith (1950); Webb (1964); and Stegner (1964).
3. See, for example, Athearn (1986); Limerick (1987); and Riley (1988).
4. See, for example, Udall et al. (1990); and Worster (1982) and (1985).
5. An elaboration of this argument is made in DeVoto (1954) about the equalizing effect of the harsh western environmental groups entering the West, whether as army battalions, wagon trains, or exploratory expeditions.
6. For an explanation of how the structure of Congress is determined, and how it affects policy, see Cox and McCubbins (1993).
7. Because the South after Reconstruction was the bastion of Democratic strength, a comparison with it is not particularly relevant. The more useful comparison is with the non-Western North.

References

Anderson, Terry L. 1983. *Water crisis: Ending the policy drought.* Washington, DC: Cato Institute.

Athearn, Robert G. 1986. *Thy mythic West in twentieth century America.* Lawrence: University of Kansas Press.

Cox, Gary W., and Mathew D. McCubbins. 1993. *Legislative leviathan: Party government in the House.* Berkeley: University of California Press.

DeVoto, Bernard. 1954. *The course of empire.* Lincoln: University of Nebraska Press.

Limerick, Patricia Nelson. 1987. *The legacy of conquest: The unbroken past of the American West.* New York: W. W. Norton.

McMurtry, Larry. 1990. How the West was won or lost. *New Republic* (October 22): 32–8.

Paul, Rodman W. 1963. *Mining frontiers of the Far West, 1848–1880.* New York: Holt, Rinehart and Winston.

Riley, Glenda. 1988. *The female frontier: A comparative view of women on the prairie and the plains.* Lawrence: University of Kansas Press.

Smith, Henry Nash. 1950. *Virgin land: The American West as symbol and myth.*

Cambridge: Harvard University Press.

Stegner, Wallace. 1964. *Beyond the hundredth meridian*. Berkeley: University of California Press.

Stewart, Charles, III, and Barry R. Weingast. 1992. Stacking the Senate, changing the nation: Republican rotten boroughs, statehood politics, and American political development. *Studies in American Political Development* 6 (Fall): 223–71.

Turner, Frederick Jackson. 1963. *The significance of the frontier in American history*. New York: Ungar.

Udall, Stewart L., Patricia Nelson Limerick, Charles F. Wilkinson, John M. Volkman, and William Kittredge. 1990. *Beyond the mythic West*. Salt Lake City: Peregrine Smith Books in association with the Western Governor's Association.

Webb, Walter Prescott. 1964. *The great frontier*. Austin: University of Texas Press.

Worster, Donald. 1982. *Dust bowl: The southern plains in the 1930s*. New York: Oxford University Press.

———. 1985. *Rivers of empire: Water, aridity, and the growth of the American West*. New York: Pantheon Books.

Index

About the Political Economy Forum
and the Authors

The Political Economy Research Center (PERC) is a nonprofit think tank located in Bozeman, Montana. For over ten years, PERC has been a pioneer in recognizing the value of the market, individual initiative, and the importance of property rights and voluntary activity. This approach is known as the New Resource Economics or free market environmentalism. PERC associates have applied this approach to a variety of issues, including resource development, water marketing, chemical risk, private provision of environmental amenities, global warming, ozone depletion, and endangered species protection.

In 1989, PERC organized the first of an ongoing program called the Political Economy Forum aimed at applying the principles of political economy to important policy issues. The purpose of this forum was to bring together scholars in economics, political science, law, history, anthropology, and other related disciplines to discuss and refine academic papers which explore new applications of political economy to policy analysis.

The papers in this volume emanate from the Political Economy Forum held in June 1992. This forum focused on the political economy of the American West. In response to a plethora of articles and books by revisionist historians, the forum authors examined the political economy of Western institutions. A combination of voluntary associations and political choices shaped the institutional environment that governs resource use throughout the West today.

We at PERC believe that forums of this type can integrate "cutting edge" academic work with crucial policy issues of the day. It is becoming increasingly evident that the interface between government and the individuals in society is vital in determining the rate and direction of economic progress. We anticipate that future forums will provide equally stimulating ideas for other important policy issues.

Douglas W. Allen is associate professor of economics at Simon Fraser University. His research explaining the evolution and pattern of property rights in both private contracts and public institutions and agricultural contracts and the organization of farming has been published in the *Journal of Law and Economics*, the *Journal of Law, Economics, and Organization*, and the *RAND Journal of Economics*.

Terry L. Anderson is professor of economics at Montana State University and senior associate of the Political Economy Research Center. In addition to his books on water issues, he is coauthor with Donald R. Leal of *Free Market Environmentalism*. Dr. Anderson is editor of PERC's Political Economy Forum series, which includes, *Property Rights and Indian Economies* (1992), *The Political Economy of Customs and Culture* (1993), and *Taking the Environment Seriously* (1993), in addition to this volume. He has an active research, writing, and lecturing agenda focusing on natural resource and environmental policy, water marketing, and American Indian economic development.

David W. Brady is McCoy Professor of Political Science at the Graduate School of Business and the Department of Political Science at Stanford University. Professor Brady has written numerous books and articles, the most recent being *Critical Elections and Congressional Policy Making*, which won the Richard Fenno Prize of the American Political Science Association.

B. Delworth Gardner is a professor of economics at Brigham Young University, where his research focuses on the economics of water and the public lands. He is a fellow of the American Agricultural Economics Association and has been President of the Western Agricultural Economics Association. He has served on the faculties of Utah State University, Colorado State University, and the University of California at Davis. He was Director of the Giannini Foundation of Agricultural Economics at University of California at Berkeley from 1976–82 and Visiting Scholar at Resources for the Future in Washington, D.C., in 1965–66. Professor Gardner's forthcoming book, *Plowing Ground in Washington*, is a study of the political economy of American agriculture.

David D. Haddock is Stanford Clinton, Sr., Research Professor at Northwestern University School of Law. His research in law and economics ranges widely across many substantive areas of law, including those most relevant to the chapter in this volume—federal Indian law, contracts, corporations, and property. His present research includes an inquiry into the factors that nurture relatively classical liberal sovereigns in some environments, but lead to despotic sovereigns under other conditions. That research began with "The Impact of Making Rights Inalienable," coauthored with Thomas Hall, has continued through the writing of the present chapter, and is now being applied to predict the likely futures of the various nations emerging from under Soviet domination in Eastern Europe.

Peter J. Hill is professor of economics at Wheaton College, Wheaton, Illinois, and senior associate of the Political Economy Research Center. His research and articles, especially on the evolution of property rights in the American West, helped found the New Resource Economics. He is coauthor with Terry L. Anderson of *The Birth of a Transfer Society* and several published articles, "Property Rights as a Common Pool Resource" and "Privatizing the Commons." An economic historian, Professor Hill is presently researching the history of environmental theology. As an economic consultant, he has worked with the Bulgarian government in their attempts to privatize agricultural lands.

Stewart Mayhew is a doctoral student in finance at the University of California, Berkeley, Walter A. Haas School of Business. His diverse research interests have included cultural economics and copyright law, history of water policy, and free market economics. He is currently researching the microstructure of financial markets and the effects of margin requirements on trading patterns. He manages the Berkeley Options Database, a transactions-level record of activity on the Chicago Board Options Exchange.

Roger G. Noll is the Morris M. Doyle Professor in Public Policy, Department of Economics, Stanford University. He is the author or coauthor of seven books and over 100 scholarly essays on topics ranging from the economics of regulation and the politics of campaign strategies to the business of professional sports. His most recent book, *The Technology Pork Barrel*, examines the management and performance of federal projects to develop new commercial technologies for the private sector. Professor Noll is currently writing a book analyzing administrative and constitutional law using the modern economic approach to political theory.

Jeffrey B. Nugent is professor of economics at the University of Southern California. In 1986 he won the Raubenheimer Award for outstanding performance in teaching, research, and service within the College of Letters, Arts and Science. His field of specialization is development economics. Professor Nugent is author of *Economic Integration in Central America* and coauthor with Pan Yotopoulos of *Economics of Development: Empirical Investigations* and Mustapha Nabli of *New Institutional Economics and Development: Theory and Applications to Tunisia*. His geographic areas of specialization range from Latin America to Southern Europe, North Africa, the Middle East, South Asia, and East Asia.

Nicolas Sanchez is associate professor of economics at the College of the Holy Cross in Worcester, Massachusetts. He is currently working with Jeffrey Nugent on a series of papers that explore the impact of the environment and technological constraints on institutional arrangements. Their first joint article, on the Spanish Mesta, "The Efficiency of the Mesta: A Parable," appeared in *Explorations in Economic History*; their second paper, "Tribes, Chiefs and Transhumance: A

Comparative Institutional Analysis," appeared in *Economic Development and Cultural Change*. The chapter in this book is their third joint project, and a fourth paper is now complete. Professor Sanchez's work has appeared in *The Review of Economics and Statistics*, *Weltwirtschaftliches Archiv*, and other books and journals.

Randy T. Simmons is professor of political science and head of the department of political science at Utah State University, where he was recognized as Researcher of the Year by the College of Humanities, Arts, and Social Sciences in 1986 and 1991. After receiving his Ph.D. from the University of Oregon in 1980, he spent two years in Washington, D.C., as a policy analyst in the Office of Policy Analysis of the Department of the Interior. He specializes in applying the methods and assumptions of economics to policy questions, especially to environmental and natural resource policy. His current policy interest is in the design of policy to allow indigenous people to benefit from wildlife. Dr. Simmons is coauthor with William Mitchell of the forthcoming book, *Politics, Markets, and Welfare*.